GUARDIAN OF THE TREATY

IN THIS SERIES*

1. Daire Hogan and W.N. Osborough (eds), *Brehons, serjeants and attorneys: studies in the history of the Irish legal profession* (1990)
2. Colum Kenny, *King's Inns and the kingdom of Ireland: the Irish 'inn of court', 1541–1800* (1992)
3. Jon G. Crawford, *Anglicizing the government of Ireland: the Irish privy council and the expansion of Tudor rule, 1556–1578* (1993)
4. W.N. Osborough (ed.), *Explorations in law and history: Irish Legal History Society discourses, 1988–1994* (1995)
5. W.N. Osborough, *Law and the emergence of modern Dublin: a litigation topography for a capital city* (1996)
6. Colum Kenny, *Tristram Kennedy and the revival of Irish legal training, 1835–1885* (1996)
7. Brian Griffin, *The Bulkies: police and crime in Belfast, 1800–1865* (1997)
8. Éanna Hickey, *Irish law and lawyers in modern folk tradition* (1999)
9. A.R. Hart, *A history of the king's serjeants at law in Ireland: honour rather than advantage?* (2000)
10. D.S. Greer and N.M. Dawson (eds), *Mysteries and solutions in Irish legal history: Irish Legal History Society discourses and other papers, 1996–1999* (2000)
11. Colum Kenny, *King's Inns and the battle of the books, 1972: cultural controversy at a Dublin library* (2002)
12. Desmond Greer and James W. Nicolson, *The factory acts in Ireland, 1802–1914* (2003)
13. Mary Kotsonouris, *The winding-up of the Dáil courts, 1922–1925: an obvious duty* (2004)
14. Paul Brand, Kevin Costello and W.N. Osborough (eds), *Adventures of the law: proceedings of the 16th British Legal History Conference, Dublin 2003* (2005)
15. Jon G. Crawford, *A star chamber court in Ireland: the court of castle chamber, 1571–1641* (2005)
16. A.P. Quinn, *Wigs and guns: Irish barristers and the Great War* (2006)
17. N.M. Dawson (ed.), *Reflections on law and history: Irish Legal History Society discourses and other papers, 2000–2005* (2006)
18. James Kelly, *Poynings' Law and the making of law in Ireland, 1660–1800* (2007)
19. W.E. Vaughan, *Murder trials in Ireland, 1836–1914* (2009)
20. Kevin Costello, *The Court of Admiralty of Ireland, 1575–1893* (2010)
21. W.N. Osborough, *An island's law: a bibliographical guide to Ireland's legal past* (2013)
22. Felix M. Larkin and N.M. Dawson (eds), *Lawyers, the law and history: Irish Legal History Society discourses and other papers, 2005–2011* (2013)
23. Daire Hogan and Colum Kenny (eds), *Changes in practice and law: a selection of essays by members of the legal profession to mark twenty-five years of the Irish Legal History Society* (2013)
24. W.N. Osborough, *The Irish stage: a legal history* (2015)
25. Thomas Mohr, *Guardian of the Treaty: the Privy Council appeal and Irish sovereignty* (2016)

ALSO AVAILABLE

The Irish Legal History Society (1989)

*Volumes 1–7 are published by Irish Academic Press

Guardian of the Treaty

The Privy Council Appeal and Irish Sovereignty

THOMAS MOHR

FOUR COURTS PRESS

in association with

THE IRISH LEGAL HISTORY SOCIETY

Typeset in 10.5pt on 12.5pt EhrhardtMt by
Carrigboy Typesetting Services for
FOUR COURTS PRESS LTD
7 Malpas Street, Dublin 8, Ireland
www.fourcourtspress.ie
and in North America for
FOUR COURTS PRESS
c/o ISBS, 920 N.E. 58th Avenue, Suite 300, Portland, OR 97213.

A catalogue record for this title is available
from the British Library.

ISBN 978-1-84682-587-3

Printed in England,
by Antony Rowe Ltd, Chippenham, Wiltshire.

To Catriona Anne Mohr

Contents

Illustrations

Acknowledgments

A NUMBER OF SOURCES provided much-needed funds for my precarious first years of research. These were the Rodney Overend Memorial Trust, and the National University of Ireland Travelling Studentship Programme. I also received two years funding from the Irish Research Council while I was completing my doctorate. A generous scholarship from the Ireland Canada University Foundation, sponsored by Glen Dimplex, allowed me to examine archive material in Canada. This added a whole new dimension to this research that would otherwise have been limited to material available in Ireland and the United Kingdom.

I would like to thank all my friends and colleagues at the School of Law, University College Dublin, who provided practical help and advice, in particular Professor W.N. Osborough. Dr Deirdre McMahon deserves special gratitude for reviewing the text with great care and and providing many useful suggestions to improve the work. Marta Stokłosa provided her photographic skills which can be admired in several of the pictures included in this work. Thanks are also due to Sir Declan Morgan for assisting in getting permission to use other pictures reproduced here. I must also thank Robert Marshall, president of the Irish Legal History Society (2012–15), who did a great deal of work behind the scenes to allow this project to reach fruition. Finally, the School of Law at University College Dublin provided funding for many of the images used, while the College of Social Sciences and Law provided funding for the index.

I owe a great debt to the many librarians and archivists who assisted me throughout the last few years. In particular, the staff at the National Library of Ireland, the archives at University College Dublin and the National Archives of Ireland, the United Kingdom and Canada. I am also grateful for the patience of my family and friends during my frequent and lengthy monologues on the project. My parents Paul and Ann Mohr were the most frequent victims and deserve special thanks for this and for so many other reasons.

Acknowledgements

Note on terminology

IN ORDER TO AVOID unnecessary anachronisms I have chosen to adhere to the terminology that was actually used in the 1920s and 1930s in preference to that used in the early twenty-first century. This means using the terms 'Commonwealth' and 'Empire' interchangeably. The term 'British Commonwealth' was in use as a direct alternative to the term 'British Empire' since the late nineteenth century. The two terms were often mixed together to form the hybrid term 'Imperial Commonwealth'. The 1921 Anglo-Irish Treaty itself uses both terms without any differentiation.[1] After 1922, Irish statesmen had an understandable preference for the use of the term 'Commonwealth' over that of 'Empire'. There were academics in this period that attempted to promote a technical differentiation between these two terms. This involved the use of the term 'Commonwealth' to refer to the group of self-governing entities and 'Empire' to refer to the group of 'non-self-governing' entities. This differentiation did not receive universal acceptance in the inter-war years.[2] A legal analysis of this question carried out by the British government in 1930 suggested that the term 'British Empire' might be considered a geographical description while the term 'British Commonwealth of Nations' might be seen as a political description. This analysis did, however, recognize that the two terms were often used as direct alternatives.[3] The term 'Empire' was still being used interchangeably with 'Commonwealth', and holding its own in terms of popularity, on the eve of the Second World War.[4] The exclusive use of one or the other of these terms in this book would be anachronistic and would also cause practical difficulties when dealing with quotations.

In accordance with common usage, I tend to use the term 'Privy Council' to refer to the 'Judicial Committee of the Privy Council'. Practical considerations have also resulted in a tendency to use the term 'Treaty' (always with a capital 'T') when referring to the 'Articles of Agreement for a Treaty between Great Britain

1 The term 'British Empire' is used in Article 1 of the Treaty, while 'British Commonwealth of Nations' is used in the wording of the oath detailed in Article 4.

2 For example, see *Hansard*, House of Commons, vol. 260, col. 362–4, 24 Nov. 1931 and A.B. Keith, *Letters on Imperial Relations, Indian Reform, Constitutional and International Law* (London, Oxford University Press, 1935), pp 111–12.

3 TNA, HO 45/20028, Memorandum No. V in Report of Inter-Imperial Relations Committee of June 4th 1930: Technical Phraseology in Official Documents, Appendix B.

4 H. Duncan Hall, *Commonwealth – A History of the British Commonwealth of Nations* (London, Van Nostrand Reinhold, 1971), p. 641.

and Ireland' signed on 6 December 1921. The practical utility of this term ensured that it was even used by British authorities that firmly denied that the instrument actually constituted an international treaty. Similar motives have resulted in the general use of the term 'Dominion' (always with a capital 'D' in accordance with official usage)[5] in place of 'member of the British Commonwealth of Nations'. Once again, even Irish authorities that denied that the Irish Free State really constituted a Dominion made general use of the term when referring to their country in the context of Commonwealth relations.

I have chosen to use Leo Kohn's term 'repugnancy clause' when referring to the provision that was contained in Section 2 of the Constitution of the Irish Free State (Saorstát Éireann) Act 1922 and in the Preamble of the Irish Free State Constitution Act 1922.[6] This provision placed all Irish law in a subservient position to the 1921 Treaty:

> The said Constitution shall be construed with reference to the Articles of Agreement for a Treaty between Great Britain and Ireland set forth in the Second Schedule hereto annexed (hereinafter referred to as 'the Scheduled Treaty') which are hereby given the force of law, and if any provision of the said Constitution or of any amendment thereof or of any law made thereunder is in any respect repugnant to any of the provisions of the Scheduled Treaty, it shall, to the extent only of such repugnancy, be absolutely void and inoperative and the Parliament and the Executive Council of the Irish Free State (Saorstát Éireann) shall respectively pass such further legislation and do all such other things as may be necessary to implement the Scheduled Treaty.

The oath detailed in Article 4 of the Treaty is always referred to as 'the oath'. The term 'oath of allegiance' is rejected by many historians who argue that the oath was one of allegiance to the Irish Constitution and merely offered fidelity to the King.[7] It should, however, be noted that some opponents of the Treaty held that

5 The use of a capital 'D' when referring to the 'British Dominions' was required by the British government to avoid confusion with the wider term 'His Majesty's dominions' which referred to the British Empire as a whole. See TNA, HO 45/20030.

6 'Repugnancy clause' was the term used by Leo Kohn. See *The Constitution of the Irish Free State* (Dublin, 1932), p. 98. Alternatives include the 'Preliminary Clause' which, for example, was used in *Dáil Debates*, vol. 1, col. 1174–5, 4 Oct. 1922 and letter of 22 Sept. 1922 from Kevin O'Higgins to Thomas Johnson, *Irish Times*, 23 Sept. 1922. The term 'Overhead Clause' was often used at Westminster. For example, see *Hansard*, House of Lords, vol. 52, col. 144 and 166, 30 Nov. 1922. Before the Preamble to the Constitution of the Irish Free State (Saorstát Éireann) Act 1922 was added the repugnancy clause was often referred to as 'the Preamble'. For example, see UCDA, Kennedy Papers, P4/348, Duffy to Kennedy, 12 July 1922.

7 Tom Garvin has argued that the use of the term 'Oath of Allegiance' represents 'a marvellous lie of silence that has become institutionalized in Irish popular culture'. Tom Garvin, *1922: The Birth of Irish Democracy* (Dublin, Gill and Macmillan, 1996), p. 17.

references to the monarch permeated the text of the Constitution and that, therefore, it could be argued that the oath did suggest allegiance to the King.[8]

Finally, this work, as a historical account, will exhibit a tendency to refer to the Judicial Committee of the Privy Council in the past tense. It is important to emphasize that this court remains very much in existence. The Privy Council remains the final court of appeal for cases emanating from the Channel Islands, the Isle of Man and the remaining overseas possessions administered by the United Kingdom such as Gibraltar, the Falkland Islands and Bermuda. It continues to hear appeals from a number of small sovereign states in the Caribbean and in the Pacific and Indian Oceans. At the time of writing these include such states as Jamaica,[9] the Bahamas, Mauritius, Kiribati and the Sultanate of Brunei.[10] Improvements in communications have ensured that, although the jurisdiction of the Judicial Committee of the Privy Council has been much reduced over the past century, the number of appeals it actually hears every year is comparable to its heyday in the late nineteenth and early twentieth centuries.[11]

8 See *Poblacht na hÉireann*, 22 June 1922.

9 In 2005, Jamaica made an unsuccessful attempt to abolish its appeal to the Privy Council. See *Independent Jamaica Council for Human Rights v. Marshall-Burnett* [2005] 2 AC 356.

10 Decisions in appeals from the Sultanate of Brunei take the form of advice to the Sultan rather than advice to the British Sovereign.

11 Kenneth Keith, 'The Interplay with the Judicial Committee of the Privy Council' in Louis Blom-Cooper et al. (eds), *The Judicial House of Lords, 1876–2009* (Oxford, Oxford University Press, 2009), pp 337–8.

Introduction: the Irish appeal to the Privy Council

THE BRITISH EMPIRE in the late nineteenth and early twentieth centuries spanned one-fifth of the land area of the globe and embraced over a quarter of its population. A single court in London held supreme jurisdiction over almost the entire expanse of this global empire. This court, known as the 'Judicial Committee of the Privy Council', was widely perceived as a vital pillar of Imperial unity in this period. One contemporary observer insisted 'The King, the Navy and the Judicial Committee are three solid and apparent bonds of the Empire; for the rest, the union depends on sentiment'.[1]

A general and comprehensive history of this Imperial court in a global context has yet to be written. This book concerns the history of the Privy Council appeal in Ireland, one of the most difficult corners of the Empire. The story of the appeal to the Privy Council from the Irish courts is much more than a history of a legal institution. At its core, this story concerns the first decisive impact of the force of nationalism on this important pillar of Imperial unity.

In 1922 the British government insisted that a court sitting in London should serve as the final court of appeal for the infant Irish Free State. Successive British governments argued that this was required under the terms of the 1921 Anglo-Irish Treaty signed by an Irish delegation led by Arthur Griffith and Michael Collins. The Judicial Committee of the Privy Council, which was largely comprised of British peers, was granted the power to overrule the decisions of all Irish courts including the Supreme Court. Irish nationalists regarded the appeal as a serious affront to Irish sovereignty and also feared that it might be abused to ensure that British institutions would continue to influence the internal affairs of the Irish Free State. In 1922, Professor William Magennis of University College Dublin told the Oireachtas 'So long as there is an appeal of any sort ... Ireland is not independent.'[2]

The hostility felt by many Irish nationalists to this institution was intensified by a widespread belief that the Judicial Committee of the Privy Council was inherently biased against the new self-governing Irish state. Ernest Blythe, minister

1 *Times*, 14 Aug. 1933. Herbert Bentwich (1856–1932) was a barrister and also owner and editor of the *Law Journal*.

2 *Dáil Debates*, vol. 1, col. 1405–6, 10 Oct. 1922.

for finance, spoke for many Irish nationalists when he distinguished the Irish Free State from other parts of the British Empire subject to the Privy Council appeal:

> There are I think, no anti-Canadian and no anti-South African lawyers on the bench in Great Britain, but there are undoubtedly anti-Irish lawyers on the bench in Great Britain, and I do not think that from a court such as that the Irish Free State could have confidence in getting justice that perhaps other countries might have.[3]

Irish commentators also noted that the Judicial Committee included influential judges who had openly opposed the signing of the 1921 Treaty and were hostile to the creation and continued existence of a self-governing Irish state on Britain's doorstep. These unionist judges included Lord Cave, Lord Sumner and the colossus of Irish unionism, Lord Carson.[4] In these unfavourable circumstances it is hardly surprising that this court encountered serious obstacles to winning public confidence in the Irish Free State.

The Irish appeal to the Privy Council had its roots in the settlement that followed the signing of the 'Articles of Agreement for a Treaty between Great Britain and Ireland' signed in London on 6 December 1921. This instrument, popularly known in Ireland as simply 'the Treaty', brought a period of armed conflict between Irish nationalists and crown forces to a close. It is worth emphasizing that no direct reference was made to the Privy Council appeal in any of the provisions of the 1921 Treaty. Nevertheless, in the months that followed, the British government argued that the Irish Free State had accepted the same constitutional status as the self-governing 'Dominions' of the Empire, including Canada, Australia, South Africa and New Zealand, under the provisions of the Treaty.[5] The Privy Council appeal was seen as an essential attribute of Dominion status and, consequently, was an institution that the Irish were obliged to accept.

Other aspects of Dominion status, for example the official roles of the King and the Governor-General, were dismissed as empty colonial symbols. Even the controversial parliamentary oath, often referred to as the 'oath of allegiance', could be dismissed as a mere symbol, albeit one capable of harnessing deep reservoirs of emotion. The appeal to the Privy Council from the Irish courts was an aspect of the settlement that followed the signing of the 1921 Treaty that had obvious practical implications. In 1922 one Irish parliamentarian noted 'the King may be

3 *Seanad Debates*, vol. 13, col. 46, 20 Nov. 1929. See also the remarks made by Kevin O'Higgins with respect to the decision to grant leave to appeal in the case of *Lynham v. Butler* at *Dáil Debates*, vol. 14, col. 134, 27 Jan. 1926 and vol. 14, col. 386, 3 Feb. 1926.

4 See ch. 4, below.

5 Article 1, Articles of Agreement for a Treaty between Great Britain and Ireland, 6 December 1921. Newfoundland, which declined separate representation at the League of Nations, was excluded from the list of Dominions listed in Article 1 of the 1921 Treaty. The status of the Irish Free State was particularly linked to the Dominion of Canada under Article 2 of the 1921 Treaty. See ch. 2, below.

a symbol, the Crown may be a symbol, and there are a whole lot of dead weight symbols in the so-called British Commonwealth of Nations. But the British Privy Council is no symbol; it is a hard fact'.[6] The British government had to overcome considerable Irish resistance before recognition of the appeal was inserted into the final text of the Constitution of the Irish Free State of 1922.[7] A textbook on the 1922 Irish Constitution concluded that the appeal represented 'The one real diminution of National Sovereignty contained in the Constitution'.[8]

Accusations of bias and partiality are among the worst insults that can be made against any court of law. Yet hostility among Irish nationalists towards the Privy Council appeal went even deeper than this. Many feared that the British government would be unable to resist interference in the internal affairs of the Irish Free State after 1922. The Privy Council appeal was seen as offering the potential to make this threat a reality. This perspective was reliant on the assumption that the Judicial Committee was not an independent court of law, an accusation that gained widespread currency in Irish political circles during the 1920s and 1930s. The *Catholic Bulletin* went so far as to accuse the Judicial Committee of being 'The pocket tribunal of the English political party in power'.[9] Irish government ministers echoed this sentiment in language that was scarcely more diplomatic. In 1930 Patrick McGilligan, minister for external affairs, warned of sinister elements that wished to use the Privy Council appeal 'as a means of keeping Ireland a pawn in British party politics'. McGilligan even asked whether 'the appeal to the Privy Council might one day be used as an indirect means for bringing the British back to Ireland?'[10]

British insistence on an appeal to the Privy Council from the Irish courts was really based on a desire to ensure that the Irish would keep to the terms of the Treaty signed in 1921. The Judicial Committee of the Privy Council was intended to be the guardian of the terms of the 1921 Treaty as the institution that would have the final say in interpreting those terms. The legal commentator Arthur Berriedale Keith pointed out, 'there is no doubt whatever that it was the deliberate intention of the British government that the Judicial Committee should have the final voice in the issue of the meaning of the treaty'.[11] Lionel Curtis, a British civil servant and author who played an important role in implementing the 1921 Treaty, made this clear in correspondence with Winston Churchill when he wrote that the Privy Council was the court 'which we have always stipulated must be the supreme arbiter in interpreting the Treaty'.[12]

6 *Dáil Debates*, vol. 1, col. 563, 21 Sept. 1922. 7 See ch. 2, below.
8 Barra Ó Briain, *The Irish Constitution* (Dublin, Talbot, 1929), p. 124.
9 Donal McEgan, 'John Bull's Privy Council', *The Catholic Bulletin*, 23 (1933) 736 at 739.
10 *The Star*, May 1931 and UCDA, McGilligan Papers, P35/166, draft article, 'Who wants the Privy Council?'
11 A.B. Keith, *The Scotsman*, 26 Apr. 1928 and *Letters on Imperial Relations, Indian Reform, Constitutional and International Law, 1916–1935* (London, Oxford University Press, 1935), p. 78.
12 TNA, CO 739/7/47027, Curtis to Churchill, 20 Sept. 1922. For Curtis' considerable contribution to the signing and implementation of the 1921 Treaty see John McColgan,

After 1926 the Irish government embarked on an active policy of limiting the effectiveness of the Privy Council appeal that included measures aimed at blocking appeals and preventing the court's decisions from being enforced. This policy ensured that only a small number of Irish appeals were actually heard by the Judicial Committee of the Privy Council. The modest number of appeals that actually went to London might be used to challenge the significance of this institution in the early history of the self-governing Irish state. Yet it is important to note that Irish observers in the 1920s and 1930s were shocked by the unexpectedly high number of appeals and, almost as important, by the volume of applications for leave to appeal that actually went to London.[13] In 1922 the Irish government had anticipated that appeals from their courts would be extremely rare events.

The significance of the Irish appeal to the Privy Council actually extends beyond the realm of sovereignty. During the inter-war years the Privy Council appeal was also promoted as a purported safeguard for minority rights in the Irish Free State. In particular, British governments asserted that the appeal offered a safeguard for the Protestant population of the Irish Free State, many of whom had held or continued to hold unionist sympathies. In 1922 the British government saw the Privy Council's position as protector of the Protestant minority as part of its wider role as final arbiter of the 1921 Treaty. This ensures that the history of the appeal offers interesting insights into the nature of inter-denominational relations in the early years of the self-governing Irish state. Successive Irish governments insisted that the majority of southern Protestants did not value or desire this purported safeguard of their rights. In fact, there is evidence that the southern Protestant population was far more supportive of the appeal than Irish governments cared to admit.[14] The final abolition of the appeal in the 1930s cannot be completely understood without acknowledgment of sectarian divisions on this subject.

The final abolition of the Irish appeal in the 1930s curtailed the Privy Council's role as arbiter and guardian of the Dominion settlement that was embodied in the 1921 Treaty and the 1922 Constitution. Once the appeal had been abolished the Dominion settlement was doomed and the path was open for the eventual adoption of the current Irish Constitution of 1937. The removal of the Irish appeal also proved to be the first symptom of a global decline in the jurisdiction of the Judicial Committee of the Privy Council that continues to this day.

In 1935 the Irish Free State was recognized as the first part of the British Empire to unilaterally abolish its appeal to the Judicial Committee of the Privy Council.[15] Elsewhere the decline in the jurisdiction of the Judicial Committee began after the conclusion of the Second World War. For example, the appeal

'Implementing the 1921 Treaty: Lionel Curtis and Constitutional Procedure', *Irish Historical Studies*, 20 (1977), 312 and Deborah Lavin, *From Empire to International Commonwealth: A Biography of Lionel Curtis* (Oxford, Clarendon, 1995).

13 TNA, CAB 32/56 E(IR-26) 4th meeting, 2 Nov. 1926.

14 See ch. 5, below.

15 *Moore v. Attorney General for the Irish Free State* [1935] IR 472 and [1935] AC 484.

survived in Canada until 1949, South Africa until 1950, India until 1950, Sri Lanka until 1971, Malaysia until 1985, Australia until 1986, Singapore until 1994 and New Zealand until 2003. This book will examine why the British government resisted the abolition of the Irish appeal whereas it quietly acquiesced to the gradual process of abolition in other parts of the globe.

CHAPTER ONE

The appeal as a pillar of the British Empire

THE ORIGINS AND NATURE OF THE APPEAL

IRISH CIVIL SERVANTS in the inter-war years were not accustomed to write in admiring tones on the history of the Judicial Committee of the Privy Council. Nevertheless, on occasion a sense of wonder at the vastness of its jurisdiction broke through their dismissive tone:

> In the variety of the suitors and the laws between and upon which it adjudicated and in the extent of the jurisdiction which it exercised it stood unique amongst the appellate tribunals of which history has any record … Appeals or applications for leave to appeal come at the present time from one quarter of the inhabited globe.[1]

The growth of the British Empire from the seventeenth century onwards converted a previously obscure institution into a court whose final appellate jurisdiction covered a significant portion of the human race. Yet, the nature and procedure of the Privy Council appeal was intimately connected with its medieval origins.

The jurisdiction of the Judicial Committee of the Privy Council has its roots in institution of the *Curia Regis*, or 'royal council' and the concept of the King as the fount of all justice throughout his dominions. The right to hear and determine appeals in the territories controlled by the King of England was considered to be a crown prerogative. The monarch could not be expected to give every case his own personal attention and appeals were therefore made to the 'King in Council'. During the reign of Henry VI the body of men who officially advised the King became widely known as the 'Privy Council'.[2]

The struggle between King and parliament in the mid-seventeenth century complicated the exercise of appeals to the Privy Council in the three kingdoms of England, Ireland and Scotland. In 1641 the Long Parliament abolished prerogative courts. These were institutions that exercised the King's discretionary powers and

1 NAI, dept. of the Taoiseach, S5340/2, undated memorandum on 'The Judicial Committee Act 1833 and after'.

2 A.V. Dicey, *The Privy Council* (2nd ed. London, Macmillan, 1887), p. 43.

included the Court of Star Chamber, the Court of High Commission, the Council of Wales and the Council of the North. The King's prerogative court in Ireland, known as the Court of Castle Chamber, also seems to have ceased functioning by this date.[3] Although the right to appeal to the Privy Council never completely died in the three kingdoms it only survived in extremely restricted circumstances.[4] However, the right of subjects in overseas territories to take appeals to the Privy Council was relatively unaffected by developments in the three kingdoms. In the early seventeenth century, Privy Council appeals from overseas territories were confined to the Channel Islands of Jersey and Guernsey as remnants of the Duchy of Normandy once held by English monarchs. During the interregnum of 1641–60 appeals from the Channel Islands were heard by a Privy Council-in-exile under the future Charles II. The new authorities in London were not prepared to tolerate this position and Oliver Cromwell's protectorate (1653–9) established a rival Privy Council in London that also began to hear appeals from the Channel Islands.[5] Competing claims of authority came to a close in 1660 with the restoration of Charles II, an event that was followed by a surge of appeals.[6]

After the restoration the appellate jurisdiction of the Privy Council began a period of expansion that mirrored the growth of a colonial empire.[7] Colonial charters issued before 1660 tended to ignore the Privy Council appeal and it seems to have been expected that colonists would seek judicial relief by appealing to the directing body of the company or individual patentee in England overseeing that particular settlement. In any case, it was unlikely that large numbers of litigants from settlements still in the process of formation would have been prepared to send appeals across great expanses of sea. Yet the feudal concept that the crown enjoyed final supervisory jurisdiction was never surrendered. After 1660 references to the right of appeal to the Privy Council began to appear with greater frequency in charters and legislation concerning the American colonies.[8] Despite some initial resistance to the appeal, in particular in the Massachusetts Bay Colony and Jamaica, a steady flow of cases began to flow into London.[9] The Privy Council appeal would have a profound influence on the planting of the common law in the American colonies.[10] It also helped to create an important source of unity between the colonies that would later form the United States of America.[11]

3 16 Charles I c. 10 or Privy Council (Star Chamber Abolition) Act 1640. On the Court of Castle Chamber see Jon G. Crawford, *A Star Chamber Court in Ireland* (Dublin, Four Courts Press, 2005).

4 P.A. Howell, *The Judicial Committee of the Privy Council, 1833–1876* (Cambridge, Cambridge University Press, 1979), p. 4.

5 Joseph Henry Smith, *Appeals to the Privy Council from the American Plantations* (New York, Octagon, 1965), pp 38–41.

6 Howell, *Judicial Committee*, p. 5 and Smith, *Appeals from the American Plantations*, pp 63–4.

7 Smith, *Appeals from the American Plantations*, pp 5–41.

8 Howell, *Judicial Committee*, pp 5–7.

9 Smith, *Appeals from the American Plantations*, pp 45–63.

10 Ibid., pp 3 and 464–522.

11 Loren P. Beth, 'The Judicial Committee of the Privy Council and the Development of Judicial Review', *American Journal of Comparative Law*, 24 (1976), 42.

The recognition of the secession of thirteen colonies in North America in 1783 barely interrupted the steady expansion in the number of appeals and the range of jurisdictions subject to the appeal.[12] By the eighteenth century the expansion of the British Empire obliged the Privy Council to grapple with appeals from India concerning disputes of Hindu and Islamic law. The abolition of the slave trade in 1807 saw a substantial rise in appeals from West Africa.[13] Legal difficulties following the complete abolition of slavery throughout the British Empire in 1833 also resulted in a sharp rise of appeals, in particular from the West Indies.[14] The decline of prosperity in the West Indies in the decades that followed would see a gradual reduction of appeals from these colonies. This decline was easily compensated by the rise of appeals from expanding colonies in British North America and Australasia. The number of appeals from the subcontinent of India rose sharply in the aftermath of the transfer of power from the British East India Company to the crown in 1858.[15] In some cases the jurisdiction of the Privy Council even spread beyond the extensive territories of the British Empire. The Foreign Jurisdiction Act 1890 facilitated appeals from protectorates, protected states and trust territories. The Privy Council could also hear appeals from certain foreign countries such as Japan, China, Siam and the Ottoman Empire that allowed British subjects to be tried by special tribunals that were independent of the local courts.[16]

In the late seventeenth century appeals to the King in Council were heard by *ad hoc* appeals committees composed of at least three privy counsellors who delivered their decisions in the form of advice to the King. Yet by the early nineteenth century it could not be denied that the appeal lacked proper organization. There was a considerable backlog of appeals and the privy counsellors who heard cases often lacked any form of legal training. Finally, lord chancellor Henry Brougham, who also oversaw the enactment of the Reform Act of 1832 and the abolition of slavery in the British Empire in 1833, initiated a radical overhaul of the appeal.[17] The need to improve the Privy Council appeal was an important part of a famous 1828 speech on wider legal reform made by Brougham in the House of Commons. This tour de force lasted six hours with short pauses while Brougham refreshed himself from a hat filled with oranges. Brougham told parliament that the Privy

12 Howell, *Judicial Committee*, pp 7–8.

13 Slave Trade Act 1807. Ibhawoh, *Imperial Justice*, p. 18 and Tara Helfman, 'The Court of Vice Admiralty at Sierra Leone and the Abolition of the West African Slave Trade', *Yale Law Journal*, 115:5 (2006), 1122.

14 Slavery Abolition Act 1833. Howell, *Judicial Committee*, pp 110–11.

15 Government of India Act 1858. Howell, *Judicial Committee*, p. 110.

16 Foreign Jurisdiction Act 1890 and Howell, *Judicial Committee*, p. 78. There was a steady flow of appeals from consular courts to the Judicial Committee of the Privy Council although they were never common. For example, there was just one such appeal in 1897, two in 1898 and four in 1900. TNA, LCO 2/179, correspondence relating to the proposed establishment of a final court of colonial appeal, Oct. 1901.

17 Henry Brougham, First Baron Brougham and Vaux (1778–1868) was a Whig statesman who held the office of lord chancellor between 1830 and 1834. See Robert Stewart, *Henry Brougham, 1778–1868: His Public Career* (London, Bodley Head, 1986).

Council appeal needed to be reformed to achieve justice for the 'countless millions whom you desire to govern all over the world'.[18] He proved instrumental in creating a new 'Judicial Committee of the Privy Council' that came into being in 1833.[19]

Brougham's reforms brought a new order and professionalism to the appeals process[20] and quickly reduced the backlog of cases.[21] The reforms proved so successful that the jurisdiction of the new Judicial Committee was extended in 1844.[22] Yet the reformed court still faced serious practical difficulties. Even judges with extensive learning and experience could not be expected to be experts in all the different legal systems contained within the British Empire. The obvious solution to this difficulty was to appoint colonial judges to the Judicial Committee. The Judicial Committee Act 1833 provided for the appointment of judges who were familiar with the law of India or other colonies[23] and also ensured that repeated efforts were made to facilitate visiting colonial judges to sit on the Judicial Committee.[24] Formidable barriers of time, distance and money ensured that these efforts were never entirely successful. Although the Judicial Committee faced many difficulties in the nineteenth and twentieth centuries, its inability to appear as a genuinely 'Imperial' or 'Commonwealth' institution, as opposed to a body of British judges deciding colonial appeals, was one of its greatest failures.

The Judicial Committee of the Privy Council had a number of unusual features that made it particularly vulnerable to criticism. First, the Judicial Committee gave judgment in the form of advice to the crown that was later enforced through an Order in Council. This allowed some commentators to argue that the Judicial Committee was a mere advisory body and not really a court at all.[25] These

18 Howell, *Judicial Committee*, p. 15.

19 The appeal was placed on a statutory basis with the passage of the Judicial Committee Act 1833. This was later amended by the Judicial Committee Act 1844. John A. Costello argued that this amending legislation did not apply to the Irish Free State. UCDA, Costello Papers, P190/94, memorandum on *Lynham v. Butler*, undated.

20 Brougham's aim at achieving a wholly professional court was not entirely achieved as the lord president of the council and previous holders of that office could also hear appeals. In practice lord presidents seldom sat on appeals and only did so to satisfy the need for a quorum. Howell, *Judicial Committee*, pp 123–5. Section 5 of the Judicial Committee Act 1833 also made it possible for any non-judicial member of the Privy Council to sit on the Judicial Committee if it was considered necessary. This was seen as a measure for breaking an even split in opinion on the Judicial Committee. Howell concludes that, in such circumstances, only judges who already sat on the Judicial Committee were brought in. Howell, *Judicial Committee*, pp 31–2.

21 Howell, *Judicial Committee*, p. 52.

22 Judicial Committee Act 1844.

23 These were retired judges who had sat in India or other colonies who had £400 a year added to their pensions for sitting on the Judicial Committee. These judges were often styled 'assessors' but they were made full members of the Judicial Committee under the Appellate Jurisdiction Act 1887. Howell, *Judicial Committee*, pp 46–8.

24 Section 30 of the Judicial Committee Act 1833. See also the Judicial Committee Amendment Act 1895, Appellate Jurisdiction Act 1908 and Appellate Jurisdiction Act 1929.

25 For example, see NAI, dept. of foreign affairs, 3/1, draft speech on abolition of appeals to the Privy Council, undated 1933. The advice given to the King by the Judicial Committee was seen

conclusions ignored constitutional practice that ensured that the crown always accepted the advice given to it by the Judicial Committee of the Privy Council. Those who tried to cast doubt on the reality of the Judicial Committee as a court of law could also make use of an unusual tradition that saw judges sit without the traditional wigs and gowns. Legal practitioners who appeared before the Judicial Committee were expected to wear wigs and gowns but were permitted to follow the professional etiquette that was customary in their home countries.[26]

Another unusual feature was that it was possible to appeal directly to the Privy Council from an inferior court and bypass the final appellate courts of the colonies and Dominions. This unusual feature could only be limited by legislation passed at Westminster.[27] Dominion legislation seeking to limit appeals often forgot about this reality and focussed entirely on appeals from their highest courts to the Privy Council.[28] Another unusual feature was that the Privy Council delivered its decision in the form of a single judgment and only permitted dissenting judgments after 1966.[29] Dissenting judgments did leak out on a number of occasions before 1966 and caused some embarrassment.[30] The votes of the judges on every decision were carefully recorded, although German bombs destroyed most of these records in 1940.[31] The practice of only producing a single judgment proved to be a source of criticism even among staunch supporters of the Privy Council.[32] Some judges even refused to sit on Privy Council appeals as long as this rule was maintained.[33] However, the 'single judgment rule' also had its supporters and lack of consensus thwarted attempts at reform. For example, consultation on the possibility of removing the single judgment rule in 1912 revealed that there was a lack of consensus even within particular Dominions. In Canada the provinces of Ontario, Quebec, Prince Edward Island, New Brunswick and Saskatchewan favored the

as having binding effect. The Privy Council was anxious to emphasize this in *British Coal Corporation v. R*: 'according to constitutional convention it is unknown and unthinkable that His Majesty should not give effect to the report of the Judicial Committee, who are thus in truth an appellate Court of law'. [1935] AC 500 at 510–11. See also *Dáil Debates*, vol. 14, col. 331, 3 Feb. 1926.

26 Howell, *Judicial Committee*, p. 215.

27 Judicial Committee Act 1844.

28 A.B. Keith, *Imperial Unity and the Dominions* (Oxford, Clarendon, 1916), p. 368.

29 This rule was established by Order in Council of 22 Feb. 1627 and confirmed by Order in Council of 4 Feb. 1878. A.B. Keith, *Responsible Government in the Dominions*, 3 vols (Oxford, Clarendon, 1912), iii, p. 1376. Dissenting judgments were finally allowed by the Judicial Committee (Dissenting Opinions) Order, 1966 (S.I. 1966, No. 1100).

30 Howell, *Judicial Committee*, pp 201–3.

31 Ibid., at pp 203–4. See also Alan C. Cairns, 'The Judicial Committee and its Critics', *Canadian Journal of Political Science*, 4:3 (1971) 301 at 331–2 and 345.

32 For example, see Sir Josiah H. Symon, 'Australia and the Privy Council', *Journal of Comparative Legislation and International Law*, 4 (1922), 147. On the perceived disadvantages of the practice of delivering a single judgment see A.B. Keith, *Responsible Government in the Dominions*, 2 vols (2nd ed. Oxford, Clarendon, 1928), ii, pp 1104–5. See also David Swinfen, *Imperial Appeal: The Debate on the Appeal to the Privy Council, 1833–1986* (Manchester, Manchester University Press, 1987), pp 221–46.

33 Howell, *Judicial Committee*, pp 222–3.

publication of dissenting judgments while British Columbia and Alberta had no objection to the change. However, Nova Scotia and Manitoba supported the continuance of the single judgment rule. The absence of consensus between the provinces on reform ensured that the Canadian government favored the maintenance of the status quo.[34] The rule was one of a number of idiosyncrasies that were a source of endless fascination to legal academics but, no doubt, contributed to impressions of the Privy Council as 'an archaic and effete institution'.[35]

The Judicial Committee of the Privy Council sat for most of its history in a room known as the 'Council Chamber' on Downing Street, London. Although the Judicial Committee never had exclusive use of this room it was seen as having pre-eminent rights over it. This position was solidified by the expansion of a large library dedicated to the laws of the British Empire that gradually filled parts of the adjacent building.[36] The Council Chamber was originally decorated by the architect John Soane in a style so extravagant that it was described as 'splashed with a splendid sickness of marble, murals, red carpeting and plaster decorations'.[37] Accusations of poor taste led to the removal of this decoration in 1845 and its replacement by plain white surfaces that were, in turn, criticized for their excessive austerity.[38] This consideration, coupled with the modest size of the room, sometimes led to criticism that it was ill-suited as the location of a final appellate court of a global empire. Several lord chancellors wanted to move the court into the Palace of Westminster or construct a new imposing building in order to give the Imperial court the prominence that it deserved.[39] Others maintained that the modest nature of the room was an asset and in keeping with British tradition.[40] Nevertheless, the location of the court on Downing Street did little to refute the perceived connection between the Judicial Committee and the British government that was particularly common among Irish nationalists.

THE PRIVY COUNCIL APPEAL IN THE UNITED KINGDOM

The Judicial Committee of the Privy Council does hear appeals from the United Kingdom itself but its jurisdiction is limited to a few obscure and archaic areas of jurisdiction. For example, the Privy Council is empowered to hear appeals from

34 TNA, LCO 2/3464, Report of the Privy Council of Canada, 8 Oct. 1912.

35 NAI, dept. of foreign affairs, file 3/1, draft speech on abolition of appeals to the Privy Council, undated 1933.

36 The pressure of business required the Judicial Committee to sit in separate divisions that often had to be accommodated in venues other than the Council Chamber. Howell, *Judicial Committee*, p. 168.

37 Howell, *Judicial Committee*, p. 171. 38 Ibid., at p. 175.

39 TNA, LCO 2/3464, 'Memorandum on the Imperial Court of Appeal', Lord Haldane, 30 July 1918; unsigned memorandum of 28 Feb. 1919, memorandum by Claud Schuster, 10 July 1923 and PC 8/1095, report of the supreme tribunals (additional judges) committee, 12 May 1927.

40 TNA, LCO 2/3464, memorandum by Claud Schuster, 10 July 1923.

the Court of Admiralty of the Cinque Ports, although the last full sitting of this court occurred in 1914. Other areas of jurisdiction that are rarely used include appeals from Prize Courts and the High Court of Chivalry. The Privy Council continues to hear certain types of appeal from ecclesiastical courts of the Church of England such as the Arches Court of Canterbury and the Chancery Court of York.[41] Appeals from ecclesiastical courts were one of the few areas of the Privy Council's jurisdiction over the United Kingdom that did attract significant public attention in the nineteenth century.[42] Although these appeals were common at the time of the creation of the modern Judicial Committee in 1833 they suffered a serious decline in the decades that followed.[43] More recent additions to the Privy Council's jurisdiction include disputes under the House of Commons Disqualification Act 1975, which prohibits certain groups of people from sitting in the lower house of the British parliament. In the 1990s the Privy Council was empowered to hear appeals relating to the devolution of powers to legislative assemblies in Scotland, Wales and Northern Ireland.[44] This important role proved short-lived and it has since been transferred to the new Supreme Court of the United Kingdom that was established in October 2009.[45]

The existence of a separate appellate court for the United Kingdom, the Appellate Committee of the House of Lords, and a different appellate court for the remainder of the Empire, the Judicial Committee of the Privy Council, was a product of history but left a poor impression. Australian prime minister William Hughes described the United Kingdom and the rest of the Empire as sheep being driven into two separate pens.[46] This poor impression was exacerbated by the position that judgments of the Privy Council did not enjoy binding authority over the courts of the United Kingdom.[47] These realities allowed some commentators in the Dominions and elsewhere to claim that they were being fobbed off with a second-class appellate court. Some even claimed that they would prefer an appeal to the House of Lords instead of the Privy Council.[48] Unfavourable comparisons between the Judicial Committee of the Privy Council and the House of Lords

41 The Privy Council now hears certain appeals from the Disciplinary Committee of the Royal College of Veterinary Surgeons and from the Church Commissioners under the Pastoral Measure 1983. http://www.jcpc.uk/about/role-of-the-jcpc.html#UK (accessed 21 Oct. 2015).

42 Howell, *Judicial Committee*, pp 2–3.

43 Ibid., p. 110.

44 Scotland Act 1998; Government of Wales Act 1998 and Northern Ireland Act 1998.

45 Established under Part 3 of the Constitutional Reform Act 2005.

46 TNA, LCO 2/3464, minutes of the 1918 Imperial war conference, 17 July 1918. William Morris 'Billy' Hughes (1862–1952) was prime minister of Australia from 1915 to 1923.

47 The Privy Council itself was not bound by its own previous decisions, although it only departed from them in exceptional circumstances. *Cushing v Dupuy* (1880) 5 AC 409. See also H.H. Marshall, 'The Binding Effect of Decisions of the Judicial Committee of the Privy Council', *International and Comparative Law Quarterly*, 17 (1968), 743.

48 For example, see Keith, *Responsible Government* (1912), iii, pp 1376–7 and Sir Frederick Pollock, 'The Judicial Committee and the Interpretation of the New Constitution' in J.H. Morgan (ed.), *The New Irish Constitution* (London, Hodder and Stoughton, 1912), pp 88–9.

tended to ignore the reality that the membership of both courts was almost identical after 1876.[49] The main difference in terms of membership was the occasional addition of Dominion and colonial judges on the Judicial Committee of the Privy Council. Nevertheless, there is no doubt that the continued existence of separate courts of appeal for the United Kingdom and the rest of the British Empire damaged the prestige of the Privy Council appeal.[50]

THE PRIVY COUNCIL APPEAL IN THE DOMINIONS AND COLONIES

It is important to note that the Irish Free State was not the only entity in the British Empire to experience difficulties with its appeal to the Judicial Committee of the Privy Council. Arthur Berriedale Keith, a leading authority on British Imperial law, wrote in the 1920s that the appeal was increasingly seen in the Dominions as 'a badge of inferiority'.[51] Nevertheless, the Privy Council appeal also retained a significant amount of support in this period. Serious efforts to completely abolish the appeal were rare. One of the few attempts to abolish it, before the successful removal of the Irish appeal, occurred in Canada in the late nineteenth century.

The Canadian Liberal government that came to power in 1873 created a new Supreme Court for their Dominion. This important development led to efforts to prevent further Canadian appeals going to London. One of the key features of the Canadian appeal to the Privy Council was its role in interpreting the division of provincial and Dominion powers.[52] The perception that the Privy Council tended to favour the provinces proved an important consideration in seeking abolition of the appeal in the 1870s.[53] However, the legal provision designed to achieve abolition, popularly known as the 'Irving Amendment', proved to be flawed and inoperative.[54] Support for abolition had shallow roots, the main supporter being Edward Blake, the Canadian minister for justice. Determined opposition from the Canadian Conservative party strengthened the hand of an unsympathetic British government.[55] The fall of the Liberal administration in Ottawa in 1878 put an end to serious attempts to abolish the Canadian appeal for decades to come.

It was far more common for Dominions to seek to limit Privy Council appeals instead of the radical and internally divisive solution of complete abolition. Even

49 Appellate Jurisdiction Act 1876. This reality was, however, recognized in a series of undated Irish government memoranda dealing with the history of the Judicial Committee of the Privy Council. NAI, dept. of the Taoiseach, S5340/2, undated memorandum on 'The Judicial Committee Act 1833 and after'.
50 For example, see *Hansard*, House of Commons, vol. 83, col. 101, 14 May 1900.
51 Keith, *Responsible Government* (1928), ii, pp 1149–50.
52 See Sections 91 and 92 of the British North America Act 1867
53 Swinfen, *Imperial Appeal*, pp 27–8 and pp 45–9.
54 Clause 47 of the Supreme Court Act 1875.
55 Swinfen, *Imperial Appeal*, pp 27–53.

here the Dominions could encounter obstacles if they attempted to limit appeals by unilateral measures. After 1878 Canadian governments preferred to try to limit the appeal rather than seeking its complete abolition. For example, Canada created a criminal code in 1888 that purported to abolish all appeals to the Privy Council in criminal cases.[56] This measure had its roots in the public outrage that followed the decision of the Privy Council to consider granting leave to appeal to Louis Riel, the messianic leader of the Métis rebellion in Saskatchewan in 1885, even though he was finally refused leave to appeal his conviction for treason.[57] In 1926 the Privy Council declared the resulting Canadian ban on criminal appeals invalid in circumstances that were closely linked with the Irish appeal.[58] This will be described in a later chapter.[59]

In 1900 a determined effort was made to abolish all federal and state appeals in constitutional matters from the embryonic Commonwealth of Australia. Many proponents of Australian unity wanted a strong federal government with a final court of appeal on constitutional issues that was located in Australia itself. This desire for greater judicial autonomy may have been boosted by awareness of some of the unpopular decisions made by the Privy Council in Canada. It might also have had its roots in the experience of the important colonies of New South Wales, Queensland and Western Australia that, as a consequence of a number of administrative blunders, had enjoyed substantial periods in the nineteenth century in which no appeals had gone to London.[60]

In 1900 Australian delegates brought the draft legislation that would later become the Commonwealth of Australia Constitution Act to London prior to its enactment by Westminster. It contained a proposal to give final appellate jurisdiction to a new High Court of Australia in constitutional affairs with the possibility of gradual exclusion of Privy Council appeals concerning other areas of law. This challenge to the Privy Council appeal met with firm opposition from colonial secretary Joseph Chamberlain. Chamberlain stressed the importance of the Privy Council appeal as a pillar of unity that maintained the uniformity of the common law throughout the territories of the British Empire. He appealed to supporters of the appeal in Australia, in particular to the leaders of the colonies that were about to become states within the Commonwealth of Australia. Chamberlain stressed that the Australian effort to abolish the appeal to the Privy Council had come at a particularly unfortunate time as proposals were under consideration for creating a reformed Imperial court of appeal. This proposed Imperial court of appeal was intended to replace the House of Lords as the final appellate court in the United Kingdom and so end the position under which the

56 Section 1025, Canadian Criminal Code 1888.

57 *Riel v. The Queen* (1885) 10 AC 675.

58 *Nadan v. The King* [1926] AC 482.

59 See ch. 4, below.

60 The High Court of Australia stated that it was 'common knowledge' when the Australian Constitution was being drafted that 'the decisions of the Judicial Committee in Canadian cases had not given widespread satisfaction'. *Baxter v. Commissioners of Taxation, New South Wales* (1907) 4 CLR 1087 at 1111. See also Howell, *Judicial Committee*, pp 81–7.

'mother country' and the remainder of the British Empire had different appellate courts. The proposed Imperial court was to be more representative of the Empire as a whole and include permanent judges from the colonies. The final result was a compromise in which Australia retained the Privy Council appeal in constitutional cases subject to certain limitations.[61]

Chamberlain's reformed Imperial court never actually materialized due to absence of support within the United Kingdom and in most of the Dominions. The Australians continued to campaign for a reformed appellate court in the coming decades but without any real success. Although the Privy Council appeal did have its supporters in Australia its reputation was damaged by a number of unpopular decisions in the early twentieth century.[62] In 1918 prime minister William Hughes was reported as telling the Imperial war conference that there was a strong demand among his people that 'there should be no appeal to the Privy Council or to any Imperial Court of Appeal at all' and that if a vote were taken on the matter in Australia 'it would be carried overwhelmingly'.[63]

The Union of South Africa created in 1910 was, like the Irish Free State, a unitary state. This meant that there was no necessity for an external court to adjudicate on the relationship between a federal government and state or provincial governments. In addition, the difficult birth of the Union of South Africa in the aftermath of the Second Boer War (1899–1902) ensured that the British government had to tread very carefully when the Privy Council appeal was enshrined in the Constitution passed in 1909. The Privy Council only heard cases from the South African courts 'by special leave', a more restrictive form of appeal than appeals 'as of right'.[64] In addition, the South African Constitution provided that 'Parliament may make laws limiting the matters in respect of which such special leave may be asked'.[65] In fact, the South Africans never found it necessary to use these powers to restrict the appeal.

The Privy Council appeal was generally popular in the small Dominions of New Zealand and Newfoundland. No serious effort was made to abolish the appeal

61 Under this compromise there could be no appeals to the Privy Council from the Australian High Court 'as to the limits inter se of the constitutional powers of the Commonwealth and those of any State or States' unless the High Court issued a certificate allowing it. The Commonwealth parliament was also authorized to make laws limiting the appeal to the Privy Council although these laws would be automatically reserved for Royal Assent. Article 74, Commonwealth of Australia Constitution Act 1900.

62 For example, *Deakin v. Webb* (1904) 1 CLR 585, *Webb v. Outrim* [1907] AC 81 and *Baxter v. Commissioners of Taxation, New South Wales* (1907) 4 CLR 1087.

63 NAI, dept. of foreign affairs, 3/1, draft speech on abolition of appeals to the Privy Council, undated 1933. H. Duncan Hall, *The British Commonwealth of Nations* (London, Methuen, 1920), pp 263–70

64 Section 106, South Africa Act 1909.

65 The bills limiting matters in which special leave could be asked were subject to compulsory reservation by the Governor-General before they could come into force under Section 106 of the South Africa Act 1909 and Article 74 of the Australian Constitution. No such limiting legislation was passed by either South Africa or Australia in the first half of the twentieth century.

from their courts in the nineteenth and early twentieth centuries. New Zealand kept the appeal until the early years of the twenty-first century.[66] The impact of the Great Depression forced Newfoundland to surrender responsible government in 1933. In 1949 Newfoundland became the tenth province of the Dominion of Canada.

The remaining British colonies could not seriously contemplate ending the Privy Council appeal as long as they lacked powers of self-government. In many colonies abolition was not desirable, as it would ensure the final court of appeal would be the colonial 'governor in council', which was seldom a body of professional judges.[67] The most common source of Privy Council appeals came from India after the transfer of power from the British East India Company to the crown in 1858. However, the numbers of appeals from the subcontinent continued to lag far behind other colonies and Dominions when differences of population are taken into account.[68] Nevertheless, India played a particularly important role in the history of Privy Council appeals in the late nineteenth and early twentieth centuries. A popular story detailed in many histories of this court involved a nineteenth-century traveller coming across an Indian village in which the people were offering a sacrifice to the Judicial Committee of the Privy Council in gratitude for returning their land to them.[69] Proposals to create a dedicated Indian Supreme Court that would sit in India and entirely replace the Privy Council appeal were occasionally mooted before independence but had little prospect of adoption.[70]

The presence of India in the Empire actually proved to be a stumbling block in creating a more representative Imperial court to replace the Privy Council appeal. In 1909 Syed Ameer Ali became the first native Indian judge to be eligible to sit on the Judicial Committee of the Privy Council.[71] Although the multi-racial nature of the litigants who appeared before the Judicial Committee was often celebrated, a multi-racial judiciary was an entirely different matter.[72] Ameer Ali, a Muslim, was

66 Sections 42 and 50, Supreme Court Act 2003.

67 Keith, *Imperial Unity*, p. 368.

68 Howell, *Judicial Committee*, pp 110 and 117–18. Although Howell's analysis ends in 1876 the same trend persisted in the years that followed. See the following figures for appeals between the years 1912 and 1918: India 360; Canada 139; Australia 45; New Zealand 14; Newfoundland 6; South Africa 5; Crown Colonies and Others 76; Special References 3; Prize Appeals 53. TNA, LCO 2/3464, memorandum by Lord Finlay on House of Lords and Privy Council Appeals, 1918. The population of these entities in the early twentieth century was estimated as follows: India 312.6 million; Canada 7.2 million; Australia 4.7 million; New Zealand 1 million; Newfoundland 0.2 million and South Africa 5.9 million. Lionel Curtis, *The Problem of the Commonwealth* (London, Macmillan, 1915), p. 59.

69 Lord Haldane, 'The Work for the Empire of the Judicial Committee of the Privy Council', *Cambridge Law Journal*, 1:2 (1922), 153. Other sources for this popular story are provided in Howell, *Judicial Committee*, p. 1.

70 Swinfen, *Imperial Appeal*, pp 107, 137 and 168–9.

71 Bonny Ibhawoh, *Imperial Justice: Africans in Empire's Court* (Oxford, Oxford University Press, 2013), pp 151–2.

72 Haldane, 'The Work for the Empire of the Judicial Committee of the Privy Council', 144.

privately accused of judicial bias in favour of other Muslims who found themselves engaged in litigation with persons of other faiths.[73] Dominion governments that continued to oppose non-white immigration had little enthusiasm for seeing significant numbers of Asian judges hearing appeals from their courts. Canadian prime minister Sir Robert Borden made it clear to British officials that Canada could not contemplate a court that heard Canadian appeals in which Hindus or Muslims held equal status with the other judges.[74]

SUPPORT FOR THE PRIVY COUNCIL APPEAL

Most histories of the Judicial Committee of the Privy Council tend to focus on the decline of the appeal and opposition to it in different parts of the Empire. The nature of the Irish appeal ensures that this book is no exception to this trend. However, it is important to emphasize that the Privy Council appeal did enjoy substantial support throughout the British Empire. The appeal was promoted in the Dominions as providing necessary reassurance for British firms to invest in them. This argument was seldom raised in the Irish Free State but was used to support accusations that the Privy Council was biased in favour of British firms and creditors.[75] More importantly, the Privy Council was seen as a vital pillar of Imperial unity and was also credited with maintaining a measure of uniformity between the laws of the parts of the Empire that followed the common law tradition.[76] A.F. Pollard compared the unification of England by 'the hammering out in the Courts of a common English law' to the unification of the British Empire through the work of the Privy Council.[77] This was an obvious exaggeration but the belief that the Privy Council operated as the 'sheet-anchor of Imperial unity' was widely held.[78] These perceptions were echoed in the analyses of Irish legal experts who concluded that the appeal was 'the only operative Imperial institution which can be said to make of the Commonwealth a legal and constitutional unit'.[79]

73 TNA, LCO 2/533, Claud Schuster to George Coldstream, 7 Dec. 1954.
74 TNA, LCO 2/3464, memorandum by Claud Schuster, 10 July 1923.
75 For Irish claims that the Privy Council favoured British moneyed interests see Hector Hughes, *National Sovereignty and Judicial Autonomy in the British Commonwealth of Nations* (London, P.S. King, 1931), pp 9, 94–100, 104–5 and 126. An Australian judge, Stephen J, accused the Privy Council of acting 'in the interests of the great fleet-owning nations' in merchant shipping cases. *Port Jackson Stevedoring v. Salmond and Spraggon* (1978) 139 CLR 231 at 258. See also Hall, *British Commonwealth*, pp 269–70.
76 Swinfen, *Imperial Appeal*, pp 60–1, 148 and 163.
77 A.F. Pollard, *The Commonwealth at War* quoted in Hall, *British Commonwealth*, pp 266–7
78 NAI, dept. of foreign affairs, file 3/1, draft speech on abolition of appeals to the Privy Council, undated 1933.
79 NAI, dept. of foreign affairs, unregistered papers, preliminary note on the 1930 Imperial conference, undated, Sept. 1930. *Documents on Irish Foreign Policy*, vol. III (Dublin, Royal Irish Academy, 2002), p. 631.

Criticism and demands for the abolition of the Privy Council appeal tended to rise in the aftermath of an unpopular decision in a case emanating from a particular region of the British Empire or Commonwealth.[80] The occasional delivery of unpopular decisions is, of course, the fate of any court of law. Yet, the sheer size of the jurisdiction of the Privy Council and the variety of legal systems over which it presided also presented judges with serious challenges in interpreting unfamiliar law. An analysis of the appeal to the Privy Council written in the 1930s emphasized the vastness of the jurisdiction of this court and concluded 'The task which is superhuman excites one's pity for the judge who has to attempt it and one's admiration that it is so often accomplished successfully.'[81]

The appeal to the Privy Council was often promoted as an effective safeguard for minority groups throughout the Empire in the early twentieth century. These groups included the French-speaking population of Canada, the Protestant population of the Irish Free State and the English-speakers of South Africa.[82] In Canada this perception of the appeal as a safeguard for minorities was augmented by Privy Council decisions that supported provincial autonomy.[83] Pierre Trudeau, prime minister of Canada, would later argue that without the Privy Council's support for provincial autonomy 'Quebec separation might not be a threat today; it might be an accomplished fact'.[84] The perception that the Judicial Committee of the Privy Council was a neutral party between the white majority and the Maori minority is often stated to be one of the factors behind the retention of the appeal in New Zealand until the early twenty-first century.[85] Assertions that the Privy

80 Examples of decisions of this nature include *Webb v. Outrim* [1907] AC 81, *Deakin v. Webb* (1904) 1 CLR 585 and *Baxter v. Commissioners of Taxation, New South Wales* (1907) 4 CLR 1087 in Australia; *Nadan v. The King* [1926] AC 482 in Canada; *Pearl Assurance Co. Ltd v. Government of the Union* [1936] AC 570 in South Africa; *Wigg and Cochrane v. Attorney General* [1927] IR 285, 293 in the Irish Free State; *Lesa v. Attorney General* [1982] 1 NZLR 165 in New Zealand and *Pratt and Morgan v. AG of Jamaica* [1993] 4 All ER 769 in the Caribbean.

81 Hughes, *National Sovereignty*, pp 96–7.

82 For example, see Keith, *Responsible Government* (1928), ii, p. 1230 and TNA, LCO 2/3465, W.H. Clark, high commissioner, to J.H. Thomas, 25 Mar. 1935.

83 For example, *Attorney General for Ontario v Attorney General for Canada* [1896] AC 348 and *Attorney General for Canada v. Attorney General for Ontario* [1937] AC 326.

84 Peter W. Hogg, 'Canada: From Privy Council to Supreme Court' in Jeffrey Goldsworthy (ed), *Interpreting Constitutions: A Comparative Study* (Oxford, Oxford University Press, 2006), p. 76.

85 For example, see Megan Richardson, 'The Privy Council and New Zealand' *International and Comparative Law Quarterly*, 46 (1997), 908 and John William Tate, 'Hohepa Wi Neera: Native Title and the Privy Council Challenge', *Victoria University of Wellington Law Review*, 35 (2004), 73. See also http://executive.govt.nz/MINISTER/wilson/privy-council/change.htm and http://www. converge.org.nz/pma/cra0409.htm (accessed 28 Nov. 2009). There were other reasons put forward for retaining the New Zealand appeal to the Privy Council. See 'New Zealand's link with the Privy Council and the Proposed Supreme Court', New Zealand Parliamentary Research Papers 2003/02, 8 May 2003. http://www.parliament.nz/en-NZ/ParlSupport/ResearchPapers/9/a/c/9ac228b4a 27949008d1bee6f84ff7e45.htm (accessed 24 June 2010). The decision to abolish the Privy Council appeal was followed by feelings of regret in certain quarters of opinion in New Zealand. Nevertheless, it was deemed impractical to attempt

Council acted as the protector of vulnerable communities often created hostility to that court from the dominant community of a colony or Dominion. This was true of white-dominated Rhodesia where the appeal was seen as a safeguard for a vulnerable black majority, in particular after the unilateral declaration of independence in 1965.[86] The prospect of the Privy Council adjudicating on laws that concerned racial status was a rallying cry for those in the white community who wished to abolish the appeal from South Africa.[87]

Opinion on the quality of the judgments delivered by the Privy Council has always been divided. Jawaharlal Nehru, future prime minister of India, was a staunch supporter of the appeal before independence and concluded that 'inconvenience and expense were no high price to pay for the justice obtainable at the Privy Council'.[88] Frequent praise from statesmen and commentators from Canada was also important as Canadian litigants provided the great majority of Dominion appeals. For example, one Canadian delegate at the 1911 Imperial conference, Louis-Philippe Brodeur KC, who would be appointed a judge of the Supreme Court on his return from London, praised the competence displayed by the Privy Council in interpreting the Quebec civil code and admitted 'litigants prefer sometimes to come before the Privy Council rather than go before the Supreme Court of Canada'.[89]

The Dominion that most valued the appeal was New Zealand, if longevity is seen as a reliable guide. A statute passed in 2003 finally abolished the appeal from the New Zealand courts, although the Privy Council could still hear cases in which the appeal process had been started before formal abolition came into force.[90] The Judicial Committee of the Privy Council has survived into the twenty first century and continues to hear cases from 27 British territories and Commonwealth members that have chosen to retain the appeal.[91]

CONCLUSION

The Irish Free State had no monopoly on difficulties with the Privy Council appeal. In these circumstances, can the Irish appeal really be distinguished from its equivalent in the other self-governing Dominions? Irish nationalists who

to revive the appeal. http://www.nzherald. co.nz/catherine-masters/news/article.cfm?a_id=49&objectid=10439301 (accessed 23 June 2010).

86 See Thomas Mohr, 'A British Empire Court: An Appraisal of the History of the Judicial Committee of the Privy Council' in Anthony McElligott et al. (eds), *Power in History: Historical Studies XXVII* (Dublin, Irish Academic Press, 2011), pp 130–2.

87 TNA, LCO 2/3465, W.H. Clark, high commissioner, to J.H. Thomas, 25 Mar. 1935.

88 Swinfen, *Imperial Appeal*, p. 168.

89 (1862–1924) Brodeur attended the 1911 Imperial conference as Canadian minister of marine and fisheries. See TNA, CO 886/5B, meeting of 12 June 1911.

90 Sections 42 and 50, Supreme Court Act 2003.

91 http://www.jcpc.uk/about/role-of-the-jcpc.html (accessed 29 July 2014).

opposed the appeal in the 1920s and 1930s stressed the wider context of Irish history and even emphasized parallels with the struggle for Irish judicial sovereignty in the eighteenth century between the Irish House of Lords and its British counterpart.[92] The physical proximity of the Irish Free State to the United Kingdom was often used to distinguish it from the Dominions in the new world.[93]

British governments seldom made determined efforts to prevent a Dominion or former colony from abolishing its appeal to the Privy Council. The failure of the half-hearted attempt to abolish Canadian appeals in the 1870s can be attributed to the shallowness of domestic support in addition to resistance from London. The British did refuse to accept abolition of the appeal from Rhodesia in the 1960s and 1970s.[94] This refusal was, of course, part of a much wider dispute between the United Kingdom and the white minority government in Rhodesia that attempted to preserve its dominance by declaring independence.[95] In 2005 Jamaica encountered resistance from the Judicial Committee of the Privy Council itself in transferring its appeal to the new Caribbean Court of Justice. Although the Judicial Committee recognized the power of the Jamaican parliament to abolish the appeal it held that it could not be substituted by an appeal to the new Caribbean Court of Justice on the grounds that the judges of that court lacked the protection of tenure.[96]

The determined and persistent resistance to Irish attempts to abolish the appeal certainly had no parallel in terms of relations between London and the Dominions in 1920s and 1930s. British statesmen openly admitted this reality. Lord Birkenhead discussed what might happen if the United Kingdom received requests from the Dominions for legislation to abolish the Privy Council appeal and concluded, 'if Canada, or Australia, or New Zealand, or South Africa, desired such legislation, in the end and after discussion such legislation would be passed'.[97] The Irish Free State was conspicuously absent from this list. A British memorandum on the Privy Council appeal that had been prepared for the 1926 Imperial conference admitted 'there are particular considerations applicable to the Irish Free State alone'.[98]

What were these particular considerations that justified separating the Irish Free State from the other Dominions? Its geographic position and its status as a

92 For example, see UCDA, Kennedy Papers, P4/340, memorandum by Henry Harrison on 'The Draft Constitution of the Irish Free State', 18 Sept. 1922; UCDA, Costello Papers, P190/97, J.J. Hearne to John A. Costello, 22 Oct. 1931; J.G. Swift MacNeill, *Studies in the Constitution of the Irish Free State* (Dublin, Talbot, 1925), pp 56–9; Henry Harrison, *Ireland and the British Empire, 1937* (London, R. Hale, 1937), p. 181; *Dáil Debates*, vol. 1, col. 1406 and 1414, 10 Oct. 1922; *Dáil Debates*, vol. 14, col. 348, 3 Feb. 1926 and *Irish Independent*, 10 Oct. 1922.

93 For example, Eamon de Valera wrote to Lloyd George on 10 August 1921: 'The freedom which the British Dominions enjoy is not so much the result of legal enactments or of treaties as of the immense distances which separate them from Britain and have made interference by her impractical'. Eamon de Valera to Lloyd George, 10 Aug. 1921, *Documents on Irish Foreign Policy*, vol. I (Dublin, Royal Irish Academy, 1998), p. 255.

94 Section 62 of the Rhodesia Act 1969.

95 See Mohr, 'British Empire Court', pp 130–2.

96 *Independent Jamaica Council for Human Rights v. Marshall-Burnett* [2005] 2 AC 356.

97 TNA, CAB 32/56 E(IR-26) 4th Meeting, 2 Nov. 1926.

98 Ibid.

former part of the United Kingdom distinguished it from Canada, Australia, South Africa and New Zealand. There was also a minority within the Irish Free State that had never desired separation from the United Kingdom. However, the main distinction between the Irish appeal to the Privy Council and its equivalent in the other Dominions lies in its association with the 'Articles of Agreement for a Treaty' signed by British and Irish representatives in London on 6 December 1921. The Irish Free State might have seceded from the United Kingdom but the terms of the 1921 Treaty ensured that it remained an integral part of the British Empire as a self-governing Dominion. It was imperative for the British government that the Irish Free State be seen to be a Dominion by the international community and, perhaps more importantly, by the other constituent parts of the Empire. In addition, the Privy Council, as guardian of the terms of the Treaty, also offered the means of ensuring that the Irish Free State would continue to be a Dominion in defiance of the policies of future Irish governments.

The legal nature of the 'Articles of Agreement' or 'Treaty' has always been disputed.[99] Whether this agreement is seen as an international treaty or as some form of intra-imperial contract does not diminish the absence of any satisfactory precedent for it among the other Dominions. The settlement contained within the 1921 Treaty and fleshed out in greater detail in the Irish Constitution of 1922 proved to be the most divisive issue in Irish politics in the inter-war years. The British government in 1921 was well aware of this reality and insisted that the Irish Free State accept the appeal with the clear intention that the Privy Council would decide the meaning of any provision of the 1921 Treaty in case of dispute.[100] A firm declaration that the Irish were acting illegally would justify additional repercussions for breaking the terms of the 1921 Treaty. The Privy Council appeal was intended to serve as both arbiter and guardian of the Treaty settlement. This is the most important feature that separates the history of the Irish relationship with the Judicial Committee of the Privy Council from experiences elsewhere. In addition, the history of the Irish appeal reveals a consistent reluctance on the part of successive British governments to treat the Irish Free State in the same manner as the other Dominions. To understand the reasons for these realities it is important to examine the Privy Council appeal in the wider context of Irish history.

99 For example, see Harrison, *Ireland and the British Empire*, pp 43–7.
100 See ch. 3, below.

CHAPTER TWO

The Privy Council appeal and the Irish question, 1886–1922

THE PRIVY COUNCIL APPEAL AND IRELAND BEFORE 1922

POLITICAL LINKS BETWEEN the islands of Great Britain and Ireland date back to the Anglo-Norman invasion of the twelfth century. Yet, the two islands were only unified into a single 'United Kingdom of Great Britain and Ireland' in 1801 when the Irish parliament in Dublin was formally abolished and Irish representatives began to attend the parliament at Westminster. The union also saw the abolition of the judicial functions of the Irish House of Lords that sat in College Green, Dublin. Instead, the House of Lords that sat in Westminster became the new ultimate court of appeal for Ireland. This put an end to a long history of rivalry between the parliaments and appellate courts in Dublin and London that had reached an unprecedented intensity in the eighteenth century.[1]

Irish nationalists in the twentieth century would later place a great deal of emphasis on the claim that the island of Ireland had not in any way been subject to the jurisdiction of the Judicial Committee of the Privy Council before the birth of the Irish Free State in 1922. Although the Privy Council was the final court of appeal for most of the British Empire, the United Kingdom, with a few increasingly obscure exceptions, was not subject to its jurisdiction.[2] Yet, it must be admitted that there were legal and historical links between Ireland and the Judicial Committee of the Privy Council that preceded the creation of the Irish Free State. For example, there was an appeal from the orders of the lord chancellor of Ireland in matters of lunacy that survived until the passage of the Supreme Court of Judicature Act 1873.[3] Between 1835 and 1907 the Judicial Committee had jurisdiction over applications for the extension of Irish patents in relation to new inventions.[4] Section 5 of the Copyright Act 1842, a statute that was also applicable to Ireland, gave the Judicial Committee jurisdiction over applications for a licence to print a book when the owner of the copyright refused to republish it after the death of the author. The famous case of *Swift v. Kelly* (1835) that concerned the validity of a marriage between members of two landed families in Ireland who had

1 Andrew Lyall, *The Irish House of Lords: A Court of Law in the Eighteenth Century* (Dublin, Clarus, 2013), pp 17–52.
2 See ch. 1, above.
3 Section 18 of the Supreme Court of Judicature Act 1873.
4 Patents Act 1835 and Patents and Designs Act 1907.

both converted from Protestantism to Catholicism was finally decided by the Judicial Committee of the Privy Council.[5]

Lord Brougham tried unsuccessfully to make the lord chancellors of Ireland, together with former holders of this office, permanent members of the Judicial Committee in London.[6] Despite this failure several Irish lord chancellors, such as Sir John Campbell and Joseph Napier, did sit on the Judicial Committee by reason of special commission or as a consequence of appointment to the British Privy Council.[7] The passage of the Appellate Jurisdiction Act 1876 made it easier for Irish judges to sit on the Judicial Committee of the Privy Council. In addition, Irishmen who rose to high judicial office in Great Britain did sit on the Judicial Committee. Lord Cairns, a native of county Down, was one of the most notable Irishmen to become lord chancellor of Great Britain and sat on the Judicial Committee. Cairns' appointment in 1868 was hardly a cause for celebration for Irish nationalists as he was described as a 'Protestant of the Protestants' and 'a most vigilant and effective champion of the Irish Establishment'.[8] It should be noted that judges of Irish descent from the colonies and Dominions were also entitled to sit on the Judicial Committee. These included Frank Gavan Duffy, chief justice of the Australian High Court and brother of George Gavan Duffy of the Irish High Court, who was sworn in as a privy counsellor in 1932.[9]

Irish involvement with the Judicial Committee of the Privy Council made little impact on Irish popular opinion for much of the nineteenth century. Yet the institution of the Privy Council gained new prominence when it became associated with Irish attempts to win 'home rule'. By the late nineteenth century it was believed that the establishment of an autonomous parliament in Dublin would be sufficient to satisfy the demands of Irish nationalists and keep Ireland within the embrace of the United Kingdom. The Privy Council appeal was an integral part of all legislative proposals for home rule. Although this reality inspired Irish commentators to pay greater attention to the institution of the Privy Council appeal, attention tended to wane in the aftermath of the defeat of two home rule bills at Westminster in 1886 and 1893. The 1886 bill was defeated in the House of Commons while the 1893 bill passed in the House of Commons but was defeated in the House of Lords. A third home rule settlement was approved by the House of Commons in 1912 but delayed until 1914 by the continued opposition of the House of Lords.[10] The outbreak of the First World War resulted in further delay as the proposed settlement was frozen for the duration of the conflict.[11]

5 (1835) 3 Knapp 284–302. Paul Ward, *Family Law in Ireland* (Leiden, Kluwer Law International, 2010), para. 144.
6 P.A. Howell, *The Judicial Committee of the Privy Council, 1833–1876* (Cambridge, Cambridge University Press, 1979), p. 48.
7 Ibid., at pp 128–9 and 134–6.
8 Ibid., at pp 134–5.
9 The *Law Journal: Irish Free State Section*, 18 June 1932 and the *Tablet*, 4 June 1932.
10 Government of Ireland Act 1914.
11 Suspensory Act 1914.

What was the envisaged role of the Privy Council under the proposals for Irish home rule? The Irish Government Bill 1886, better known as the first home rule bill, would have empowered the Privy Council to decide whether legislation passed by the proposed Irish parliament was within its powers. In other matters the appeal from the Irish courts to the House of Lords would have remained intact.[12] The Irish Government Bill 1893 and the Government of Ireland Act 1914 would have completely replaced the jurisdiction of the House of Lords with that of the Privy Council. They also contained provisions that would have allowed for the 'speedy determination' by the Privy Council of constitutional questions including the validity of laws passed by the Irish legislature.[13] The Government of Ireland Act 1920 retained the appeal to the House of Lords but gave special jurisdiction to the Privy Council to decide certain constitutional matters.[14] It is clear from the terms of all four proposals for Irish home rule that the Judicial Committee of the Privy Council was intended to be the arbiter of these settlements. Erskine Childers, in his 1911 book *The Framework of Home Rule*, supported the proposed role of the Privy Council as the final arbiter of the limits of devolved power under a future home rule settlement.[15] Childers might have preferred to forget this position after the signing of the 1921 Treaty when he became one of the most vociferous critics of the Irish provisional government's decision to accept the appeal to the Privy Council.[16]

Some proposals that the Privy Council act as arbiter of any home rule settlement even proposed that this court decide whether or not Ulster should be included or excluded from the embrace of an autonomous parliament in Dublin. For example, Horace Plunkett, politician and agricultural reformer, proposed the inclusion of Ulster in a home rule settlement with the option of exclusion by referendum after the completion of a trial period.[17] Plunkett's proposal also provided for an earlier exclusion of Ulster during the trial period if the Judicial Committee of the Privy Council determined that Ulster was 'suffering from misgovernment, or that permanent injury to its economic interests was reasonably apprehended'.[18] These proposals ignored the difficulties that would face any court

12 Sections 25 and 36 of the Irish Government Bill 1886. http://multitext.ucc.ie/d/Home_Rule_Bill_1886 (accessed 21 Oct. 2015).

13 Sections 28 and 29 of the Government of Ireland Act 1914 were virtually identical to Sections 22 and 23 of the Irish Government Bill 1893. Section 30 of the 1914 Act contained additional provisions that were not found in the 1893 bill. For the full text of the 1893 bill see 'The Home Rule Bill, 1893', *Pall Mall Gazette Extra*, no. 67, 1893. See also http://www.dippam.ac.uk/eppi/documents/18825/ (accessed 21 Oct. 2015).

14 Sections 49 to 53 of the Government of Ireland Act 1920.

15 Erskine Childers, *The Framework of Home Rule* (London, E. Arnold, 1911), p. 335. See also Frederick Pollock, 'The Judicial Committee and the Interpretation of the New Constitution' in J.H. Morgan (ed.), *The New Irish Constitution* (London, Hodder and Stoughton, 1912), pp 81–9.

16 *Poblacht na hÉireann*, 3 Apr., 4 May and 22 June 1922.

17 Sir Horace Plunkett (1854–1932) was a leading figure in establishing agricultural cooperatives in Ireland. He was also a unionist MP from 1892 to 1900, chairman of the Irish convention 1917 to 1918, founder of the Irish Dominion League in 1919 and a member of Seanad Éireann from 1922 to 1923.

18 Sir Horace Plunkett, *A Better Way: An Appeal to Ulster not to Desert Ireland* (Dublin, Hodges,

of law in deciding what misgovernment or permanent economic injury actually entailed. In any case, unionist opponents of granting home rule to Ireland were convinced that future Irish governments would take extraordinary measures to block the enforcement of unpopular decisions and undermine the position of the Privy Council as final arbiter of any settlement.[19] Although these prophets might be accused of cynicism, their predictions proved to be accurate in the later context of the 1920s and 1930s.[20]

The delay in granting autonomy caused by the outbreak of the First World War doomed any prospect of home rule in Ireland. In 1916 an armed uprising in Dublin declared the creation of an Irish republic. The surge in popular support for the executed leaders of the rising rendered home rule obsolete, a reality that was consolidated by election victories for Sinn Féin in 1918 and 1920. It became increasingly apparent that a majority of Irish nationalists would no longer be satisfied with autonomy within the United Kingdom. By 1919 a low level, but vicious, conflict began between a self-proclaimed Irish republican government and crown forces.

The Government of Ireland Act 1920 offered home rule but created two autonomous Irish parliaments in place of one within the United Kingdom. A parliament in Belfast was created for the six Protestant and unionist-dominated counties of 'Northern Ireland'. The remaining twenty-six counties were supposed to form 'Southern Ireland' with a bicameral parliament in Dublin that offered Irish nationalists an alternative to complete secession from the United Kingdom. The sincerity or otherwise of the offer was irrelevant given its unacceptability to the majority of Irish nationalists. No form of autonomy within the United Kingdom was acceptable to a population that had now come to expect a great deal more. Yet if 'Southern Ireland' was lost to the United Kingdom it was imperative that it not be allowed to secede from the British Empire. The precedent that this would create for vast colonial populations overseas was too calamitous for any British government to contemplate. A compromise was needed that would allow the parts of the island dominated by Irish nationalists to secede from the United Kingdom yet remain within the Empire. By 1921 the British administration led by David Lloyd George gradually came to the conclusion that the solution lay in granting Dominion status, the constitutional position enjoyed by the white-dominated colonies, to the twenty-six counties. On 6 December 1921 British and Irish

Figgis, 1914), p. 23. See also John Kendle, *Ireland and the Federal Solution* (Kingston and Montreal, McGill-Queen's University Press, 1989), p. 169.

19 These prophets included the future Lord Cave (George Cave), who would play a major role in the history of the Irish appeal to the Privy Council, and the future Lord Glenavy (James H. Campbell), who would play a major role in the creation of the courts of the future Irish Free State and become the first Cathaoirleach or 'Chairman' or the Irish Seanad or 'Senate'. See George Cave, 'The Constitutional Question' and J.H. Campbell, 'The Control of the Judiciary and Police' in S. Rosenbaum (ed.), *Against Home Rule – The Case for the Union* (London, Frederick Warne, 1912), pp 81–106 at 95 and pp 153–61 at 161.

20 See ch. 4, below.

representatives signed the 'Articles of Agreement for a Treaty' which granted the new 'Irish Free State' the same legal status as Canada, Australia, New Zealand and South Africa.[21]

The Dominion of Canada was singled out by the Anglo-Irish Treaty as the model on which to base Irish connections with the remainder of the British Empire.[22] For many Irish nationalists this Imperial link was encapsulated in a controversial parliamentary oath whose wording mentioned fidelity to King George V.[23] In addition, the King was recognized as head of state of the infant Irish Free State and was an integral part of the 'Oireachtas' or parliament.[24] The King's representative in Dublin was known as the 'Governor-General', and this mirrored an identical office in Ottawa.[25] Although the oath became a particular focus of attention during the bitter civil war that marred the birth of the Irish Free State, there were other more substantial Imperial links that received far less attention from the general public.

IMPERIAL LINKS UNDER THE DOMINION SETTLEMENT

One of the more significant Imperial links concerned nationality and consular affairs. Lawyers argued that the nascent status of Irish citizenship was only effective within the territory of the twenty-six counties and that once persons travelled beyond its frontiers they reverted to the common status of the British subject.[26] In addition, all British subjects remained reliant on British embassies and consulates when they travelled outside the Empire. It was also argued that Dominion parliaments could not make laws for matters that fell outside the frontiers of that Dominion, for example, ships on the high seas or the transfer of prisoners from other countries.[27]

The greatest fear of Irish opponents of the 1921 Treaty was that geographic realities would ensure that the Irish Free State would not be treated in identical fashion to Canada notwithstanding the constitutional link that had been established between these two countries. It was feared that legal powers that were considered obsolete with respect to Canada would be used to influence the internal affairs of the Irish Free State. These legal powers were considerable. For example,

21 Article 1, Articles of Agreement for a Treaty between Great Britain and Ireland, 6 December 1921. See second schedule, Constitution of the Irish Free State (Saorstát Éireann) Act 1922 (Dublin) and Irish Free State Constitution Act 1922 (Westminster).

22 Ibid., at Article 2.

23 Ibid., at Article 4.

24 Article 12 and 51, Constitution of the Irish Free State.

25 Ibid., at Article 60.

26 Article 3, Constitution of the Irish Free State and UCDA, FitzGerald Papers, P80/603, J.J. Hearne to Stephen Roche, 21 Aug. 1930. Legislation passed by the de Valera government made sure to provide that the status of Irish citizenship was effective in both the municipal and international spheres. See the long title and Section 34 of the Irish Nationality and Citizenship Act 1935.

27 Thomas Mohr, 'The Foundations of Irish Extra-Territorial Legislation', *Irish Jurist*, 40 (2005), 86.

in 1922 the United Kingdom still claimed the power to pass 'Imperial legislation' for the Dominions. It also claimed that this Imperial legislation outranked that passed by Dominion parliaments, a position established under common law and symbolized by a key Imperial statute known as the Colonial Laws Validity Act 1865. The crown even claimed powers to delay and veto Dominion statutes, powers that would be reflected in the provisions of the 1922 Constitution of the Irish Free State.[28] In short, many Irish nationalists feared that the granting of Dominion status to the Irish Free State would not prevent continued interference by the British government in internal Irish affairs.

The prospect of an appeal to the Privy Council from the courts of the Irish Free State raised particular concerns. Irish nationalists were offended by the very idea of their courts being subject to an appellate court in London. Yet, they also feared that it offered the most obvious means for London to influence the internal affairs of the future Irish Free State. In fact, the main motivation behind British insistence that the Irish accept the appeal was based on ensuring that the Irish Free State would not attempt to breach or unilaterally withdraw from the settlement based on the 1921 Anglo-Irish Treaty. The Judicial Committee of the Privy Council was intended by the British government to act as guardian of the 1921 Treaty, just as it had been previously intended to act as guardian of the proposed home rule settlements.

THE PRIVY COUNCIL APPEAL AND THE 1921 TREATY

Was the issue of the Privy Council appeal actually raised during the negotiations in London that preceded the signing of the Anglo-Irish Treaty in 1921? Had the issue already been settled between the British government led by Lloyd George and the Irish delegation led by Arthur Griffith and Michael Collins before the Irish began drafting their own constitution? These questions became the subject of some dispute in the years that followed. Death, defection to the anti-Treaty camp and withdrawal from politics deprived the Irish government of the mid-1920s of access to all members of the Irish delegation that had signed this historic instrument. Lord Birkenhead, a member of the British delegation that had signed the Treaty, insisted that the appeal had indeed formed part of the negotiations. Birkenhead even went so far as to claim that the Irish delegation had accepted the Privy Council appeal during the 1921 negotiations, but had specifically requested that no reference be made to it in the text of the Treaty to save them from unnecessary embarrassment.[29] It should be emphasized that this claim was made

28 Article 41, Constitution of the Irish Free State.

29 TNA, CAB 32/56 E(IR-26) 4th meeting, 2 Nov. 1926. Birkenhead insisted that the negotiations that preceded the signing of the Treaty had not focused on whether or not there should be an appeal, but on whether the appeal should be to the House of Lords or to the Judicial Committee of the Privy Council.

some years after the signing of the Treaty and in the context of partisan arguments concerning the survival of the Irish appeal.

Why was this issue so important? Irish governments would later claim that the Privy Council appeal had not really been part of the Treaty settlement and, consequently, that it was possible to abolish it without enduring accusations of breaking the Treaty.[30] British governments rejected this argument and maintained that acceptance of the Privy Council appeal was an integral part of the settlement that led to the creation of the self-governing Irish state.[31]

The Irish government faced an uphill task in attempting to prove a negative, that the Irish appeal to the Privy Council had *not* been settled during the 1921 Treaty negotiations. It could be stated with confidence that issues other than the appeal had dominated the Treaty negotiations, including the role of the crown, the oath and the status and boundaries of Northern Ireland. Yet there can be no doubt that the Privy Council appeal was an important consideration during these negotiations irrespective of whether or not it formed part of the substantive talks. The prospect of an Irish appeal to the Privy Council was certainly high on the agenda of the British delegation in 1921.

The nature of Dominion status was such that it could only be defined by means of analogy. The 1921 Treaty made it clear that key aspects of the constitutional status of the Irish Free State would be linked to those pertaining in Canada, a Dominion that was, in many ways, a good choice as a constitutional model.[32] Canada was the closest Dominion to the Irish Free State in geographic terms and had made important advances in terms of autonomy. Hugh Kennedy, who would later become the first attorney general and later the first chief justice of the Supreme Court of the Irish Free State, wrote soon after the signature of the Treaty that 'Canada is chosen as the type because of the great advance made by that Dominion on the road to liberty in association'.[33] While this may have been the reason held out to the Irish for choosing Canada as a constitutional model, the British had additional reasons that were not disclosed during the Treaty negotiations. British cabinet papers reveal that Canada was chosen with the express purpose of ensuring that the Irish Free State would be subject to Canadian practice with respect to the Privy Council appeal.[34]

30 TNA, CAB 32/79 PM(30)5.

31 TNA, CAB 32/56 E(IR-26) 4th meeting, 2 Nov. 1926 and TNA, LCO 2/3465, Imperial conference 1926, Appeals to the King in Council, 1 Nov. 1926.

32 Article 2 of the Articles of Agreement for a Treaty, 6 December 1921, provided 'the position of the Irish Free State in relation to the Imperial Parliament and Government and otherwise shall be that of the Dominion of Canada, and the law, practice and constitutional usage governing the relationship of the Crown or the Representative of the Crown and of the Imperial Parliament to the Dominion of Canada shall govern their relationship to the Irish Free State.'

33 UCDA, Kennedy Papers, P4/301.

34 TNA, CAB 43/1 SFB, 25th meeting of the British signatories to the Treaty with Ireland, 29 May 1922; TNA, CO 532/257, Lionel Curtis to Sir James Masterson Smith, 8 Oct. and 1 Nov. 1923 and TNA, LCO 2/910, memorandum by Sir Claud Schuster, 6 Nov. 1930.

There were two types of appeal to the Judicial Committee of the Privy Council. These were appeals 'as of right' and appeals 'by special leave'. In the case of appeals 'as of right' the Judicial Committee was, subject to certain limitations, under an obligation to admit and determine the appeal. Appeals 'by special leave', sometimes called appeals 'as of grace', were more restrictive in that the Privy Council had discretion as to whether to grant or refuse leave to appeal. Appeals from Canada were 'as of right' which helped to ensure that appeals from that Dominion were far more numerous than from any other part of the Empire with the exception of India. Moreover, Canadian appeals were not subject to constitutional limitations as was the case in Australia and in South Africa. In fact, the number of Canadian cases heard every year by the Privy Council in the early twentieth century usually surpassed the combined total heard from all the other Dominions.[35]

The final text of the Anglo-Irish Treaty signed in 1921 contained no reference to the Judicial Committee of the Privy Council. This was not the result of a mere oversight. The British delegation decided not to push for a direct reference to the Privy Council appeal in the text of the Treaty. This was a pragmatic decision since it avoided adding another controversial question to negotiations that were already overburdened with other difficult issues. However, the decision to omit the Privy Council appeal from the text of the Treaty was also motivated by a belief that it was possible to insert the appeal into the Anglo-Irish settlement by a backdoor route.

Lionel Curtis, a British official who would play an important role in implementing the Anglo-Irish settlement, later described a meeting during the 1921 Treaty negotiations in which it was decided to secure an Irish appeal to the Privy Council by establishing a constitutional link with Canada instead of pressing for an explicit reference to the appeal in the text of the Treaty.[36] According to Curtis the decision was made at a private meeting that was only attended by British delegates.[37] Curtis did not mention whether the British delegates ever communicated this decision to their Irish counterparts.

Evidence from subsequent Anglo-Irish negotiations on the draft Irish Constitution in the summer of 1922 strongly suggests that the issue was not settled in 1921 as suggested by Birkenhead. In 1922 the Irish negotiating team, that included Michael Collins and Arthur Griffith, made a determined effort to avoid any reference to the Privy Council appeal being inserted into the text of the draft Irish Constitution. If the matter had already been settled six months earlier in the

35 See the following figures for Dominion appeals between the years 1912 and 1918: Canada 139; Australia 45; New Zealand 14; Newfoundland 6; South Africa 5. TNA, LCO 2/3464, memorandum by Lord Finlay on House of Lords and Privy Council Appeals, 1918.

36 For Curtis' contribution to the signing and implementation of the 1921 Treaty see John McColgan, 'Implementing the 1921 Treaty: Lionel Curtis and Constitutional Procedure', *Irish Historical Studies*, 20 (1977), 312 and Deborah Lavin, *From Empire to International Commonwealth: A Biography of Lionel Curtis* (Oxford, Clarendon, 1995).

37 TNA, CO 532/257, Curtis to Sir James Masterson Smith, 8 Oct. and 1 Nov. 1923.

negotiations on the 1921 Treaty the British delegation would surely have raised this argument to counter Irish resistance. No such argument was ever raised in 1922. Instead, Lloyd George emphasized that the Irish had to accept the Privy Council appeal as a consequence of the constitutional link with Canada established by the Treaty. No reference was made in 1922 to any prior discussions on this subject during the Treaty negotiations. If the matter had really been settled in 1921 and left out of the text of the Treaty to save the Irish from unnecessary embarrassment the British could have saved a great deal of time and effort in 1922 by reminding the Irish delegation. The British had good reason to know that Arthur Griffith was particularly sensitive to charges of breaking faith on past agreements.[38] The entire argument that the Irish had accepted the Privy Council appeal during the 1921 negotiations, but had specifically requested that no reference be made to it in the text of the Treaty, was only raised at a time when leading members of the Irish delegation – Collins and Griffith – were no longer in a position to contradict this version of events.

It is clear that the origins of the Irish appeal were not without elements of stealth and deception. Nevertheless, this does not necessarily mean that the Irish delegation in the 1921 Treaty negotiations was unaware of the likelihood that the decisions of future Irish courts might be subject to appeals to London. The Privy Council appeal had, after all, been an integral part of the various proposals for Irish home rule. As mentioned earlier, the secretary to the Irish delegation that negotiated the 1921 Treaty, Erskine Childers, had written about this issue at some length.[39] The Irish Dominion League, a movement that tried to persuade both sides in the Anglo-Irish conflict of 1919 to 1921 to seek a solution based on compromise, had recognized that the Privy Council would be the arbiter of any Dominion settlement in Ireland. This was made clear in an unsuccessful bill moved by leading figures of the Irish Dominion League at Westminster that would have offered Dominion status to Ireland in 1920.[40] In addition, it had to be admitted that the appeal operated in all of the existing Dominions including, of course, Canada. This was made clear in textbooks on British Imperial law, including the one used for guidance by the Irish delegation during the Treaty negotiations.[41] The Irish certainly confronted the issue of the Privy Council appeal when the time came to draft a constitution for their self-governing state.

38 For example, see the events of 5 December 1921 that preceded the signing of the 1921 Treaty. Frank Pakenham (Lord Longford), *Peace by Ordeal* (London, Sidgwick and Jackson, 1972), pp 236–42.

39 Childers, *Framework of Home Rule*, pp 334–5.

40 *Hansard*, House of Lords, vol. 40, col. 693, 22 June 1920, and col. 1113–62, 1 July 1920. Draft bills for a Dominion settlement drafted by the Irish Dominion League provided 'on all matters concerning the interpretation of this Act an appeal shall lie from the ultimate Irish tribunal so established to the Judicial Committee of the Privy Council of Great Britain'. National Library of Ireland, Monteagle Papers, MS 13,417, Section 6 of draft of a bill to constitute the Dominion of Ireland. See also Section 16(1) of instructions to draftsman, Section 13 of Draft B and Section 12 of draft of 31 May 1920 annotated by Henry Harrison.

41 H. Duncan Hall, *The British Commonwealth of Nations* (London, Methuen, 1920), pp 263–70.

DRAFTING THE CONSTITUTION OF THE IRISH FREE STATE

In early 1922 it was agreed that the Irish could draft their own Constitution but that the British government would get a confidential preview of the text before it was made public.[42] On 24 January 1922 a constitution committee was formally appointed and held its first meeting at the Mansion House on Dublin's Dawson Street.[43] Michael Collins made himself chairman of the small group charged with creating the preliminary draft of the Irish Constitution. However, Collins had many other responsibilities and Darrell Figgis, a prominent Dublin literary figure, took effective control of the workload of the committee. The remaining membership included four lawyers, Hugh Kennedy,[44] John O'Byrne,[45] Kevin O'Shiel[46] and Clement J. France,[47] a businessman, James Douglas,[48] a former civil servant, James McNeill,[49] and two academics, professor Alfred O'Rahilly[50] and professor James Murnaghan.[51] Collins told members of the committee that they 'were now the people charged with the most important task – more important than the Treaty itself'.[52] Although Collins seldom attended committee meetings, his instructions proved decisive in determining the nature of the draft Constitution that would finally emerge from its deliberations.[53] He is reported to have told the other members:

> You are not to be bound up by legal formalities but to put up a constitution of a Free State and then bring it to the Provisional Government who will

This text was used by the Irish delegation in 1921 and was also used during the drafting of the 1922 Constitution. James G. Douglas, *Memoirs of Senator James G. Douglas (1887–1954): Concerned Citizen*, ed. J. Anthony Gaughan (Dublin, UCD Press, 1998), p. 80.

42 NAI, cabinet minutes, G1/1, 2 February 1922 and TNA, CAB 43/6 22/N/60(6), meeting between the British and Irish signatories, approval of draft constitution, 26 February 1922.

43 NAI, dept. of the Taoiseach, S8952, constitution committee, report of first meeting, 24 Jan. 1922.

44 Kennedy would later become the first person to hold the offices of legal adviser to the provisional government, attorney general of the Irish Free State and chief justice of the Irish Supreme Court.

45 Later attorney general and judge of the High Court and Supreme Court.

46 O'Shiel was appointed as assistant legal adviser to the provisional government on 6 September 1922 and subsequently served as a land commissioner.

47 France was an American lawyer who had come to Ireland on behalf of the American committee for relief in Ireland. He declined to be a formal member of the committee on the basis that he was not Irish. For this reason his name was not mentioned when the membership of the committee was made public on 31 January 1922. Nevertheless, he attended committee meetings and was a signatory of Draft B that formed the basis of the future constitution.

48 Later vice-chairman of the Seanad of the Irish Free State.

49 Later high commissioner in London and second Governor-General of the Irish Free State.

50 Professor of mathematical physics at University College Cork. He was a late addition to the committee, joining it on 30 January 1922. NAI, dept. of the Taoiseach, S8952 and S8953.

51 Professor of jurisprudence and Roman law at University College Dublin and later judge of the Supreme Court.

52 NAI, dept. of the Taoiseach, S8952, Constitution Committee, report of first meeting, 24 Jan. 1922.

53 According to Farrell he only attended one meeting apart from the inaugural session. Brian Farrell, 'The Drafting of the Irish Free State Constitution: I', *Irish Jurist*, 5 (1970), 115 at 117.

> fight for the carrying of it through. It is a question of status and we want definitely to define and produce a true democratic constitution. You are to bear in mind not the legalities of the past but the practicabilities of the future.[54]

Arthur Griffith also attended the opening session although he was never a member of the constitution committee. He supported Collins' approach to drafting the Constitution by instructing the committee 'not to stand on legal formalities but to make the Constitution as free as possible'.[55] He is also reported to have remarked 'as little of that as possible' while indicating a copy of the Canadian Constitution.[56]

It is clear that Michael Collins anticipated that the Irish Free State would evolve towards a position of full sovereignty. This can be seen in instructions given by Collins to the constitution committee:

> The Constitution should be as simple as possible. In the simple form suggested, it would serve as our permanent Constitution which need never be altered, but could be added up to, as the final stages of complete freedom were gained.[57]

The members of the constitution committee seemed only too happy to follow Collins' instructions on these points.[58] However, over the next few weeks some members of the committee came round to the view that it might be prudent to make some very limited references to the terms of the 1921 Treaty in the Constitution.[59] The committee scrupulously examined the Constitutions of the existing Dominions. Nevertheless, the committee never felt obliged to follow Dominion precedents in drafting a Constitution for the Irish Free State.[60]

The draft Constitution that was finally produced made no mention of any appeal from the Supreme Court to the Judicial Committee of the Privy Council,

54 NAI, dept. of the Taoiseach, S8952, constitution committee, report of first meeting, 24 Jan. 1922.
55 Ibid.
56 Padraic Colum, *Arthur Griffith* (Dublin, Browne and Nolan, 1959), p. 356.
57 NAI, dept. of the Taoiseach, S8952, constitution committee, report of first meeting, 24 Jan. 1922. James Douglas confirms in his memoirs that these instructions, which were attached to an outline constitution drafted by an unnamed solicitor, were authored by Collins himself. Douglas, *Memoirs*, pp 85–6.
58 O'Rahilly only agreed to serve on the committee on the understanding that he did not recognize the Treaty as being constitutionally binding and that there would be no mention of the King in the text produced. J. Anthony Gaughan, *Alfred O'Rahilly: II, Public Figure* (Dublin, Kingdom, 1989), p. 155. For Figgis' views on Dominion precedents see Darrell Figgis, *The Irish Constitution Explained* (Dublin, Mellifont, 1922), pp 7–10. For Douglas' views see his article of 2 April 1922 in the *Daily News* and NAI, dept. of the Taoiseach, S8954A.
59 This was reflected in the sections on 'External Affairs' that appeared in Drafts A and B. See NAI, dept. of the Taoiseach, S8953.
60 For the views of Hugh Kennedy and James MacNeill on this question see UCDA, Kennedy Papers, P4/308, memorandum on relationship between the Treaty and the Constitution, 1922 and P4/320, memorandum on the powers and duties of the Governor-General, 1922.

the appellate court common to all the existing Dominions. Indeed, the constitution committee was not content to simply ignore the Privy Council appeal but decided to create a provision that was intended to prevent its imposition on the Irish Free State. This provision stated:

> The decision of the Supreme Court shall in all cases be final and conclusive, and shall not be reviewed or capable of being reviewed by any other Court, Tribunal or Authority whatsoever.[61]

The inclusion of this provision guaranteed a confrontation with the British government over the text of the draft Irish Constitution.

NEGOTIATIONS ON THE CONSTITUTION OF THE IRISH FREE STATE

On 27 May 1922, the Irish delegation presented the British with their draft Constitution. Later that day Collins and Griffith met the British signatories of the Treaty and were immediately placed on the defensive. The British response was overwhelmingly negative. Lloyd George asserted that the draft was merely the Constitution of a republic in disguise. He highlighted the diminution of the position of the King, the lack of any reference to the oath, the inclusion of provisions allowing the Irish Free State to make its own treaties independently of the common foreign policy of the Empire and, of course, the absence of an appeal to the Judicial Committee of the Privy Council. These were all matters that struck at the very heart of Imperial unity. The British were particularly alarmed at the exclusion of the Privy Council appeal by the assertion that the decisions of the Irish Supreme Court would be 'final and conclusive'. British legal advisers warned that the Irish might claim that their own courts could act as arbiters of the terms of the 1921 Treaty under the provisions of the draft Constitution.[62] This had to be resisted at all costs.

The formal British response to the draft Irish Constitution asked the Irish negotiators six key questions.[63] These concerned the position of the Irish Free State in the British Empire, the position of the crown, the powers of the Irish Free State to make treaties, the place of the controversial parliamentary oath, whether all Irish ministers would be prepared to sign a declaration accepting the 1921

61 Article 65 of the provisional government's draft. TNA, CAB 43/3 SFC 34, draft Constitution.

62 TNA, CAB 43/2, SF(B) 54, notes by the law officers on the draft Irish Constitution, 27 May 1922.

63 TNA, CAB 43/2, SFB 54, notes by the law officers on the draft Irish Constitution, 27 May 1922; CAB 43/2, SFB 55, note on the draft Irish Constitution, 27 May 1922; CAB 43/7 22/N/163, twenty-fifth meeting of the British signatories, 29 May 1922; CAB 43/3 SFC 35, memorandum on the draft Irish Constitution, 29 May 1922 and CAB 43/2, SFB 59, memorandum on the draft Constitution for the Irish Free State, 29 May 1922.

Treaty and acceptance of the Privy Council appeal.[64] The Irish answered almost all of these questions to the satisfaction of the British negotiators. There was some quibbling over matters concerning the position of the crown that were soon resolved.[65] The British government was generally satisfied with the Irish responses and the sense of tension that had characterized the negotiations began to diminish. The only exception was the Irish response to the question that concerned the Privy Council appeal. When Michael Collins reported back to the Irish cabinet on the issue of the appeal he made it clear that the British 'could go to hell on that'.[66]

Collins used more diplomatic language when he returned to London. He told the British negotiators that there was strong feeling in Ireland against allowing Irish cases to go to this tribunal because some of its judges had publicly taken up a very hostile attitude to the embryonic Irish Free State. These judges were later named as Lords Carson, Sumner and Cave. Carson had long been the leading figure in Irish unionism and his inclusion on the list of unacceptable judges was hardly surprising. Sumner and Cave were also strong unionists and had unwisely made clear their hostility to the 1921 Treaty and the creation of the Irish Free State during debates in the House of Lords.[67] Lloyd George was prepared to offer reassurance on this point and insisted that such individuals would be precluded by the part they had taken in political debates from sitting on Irish appeals.[68]

In private Lloyd George expressed his frustration with the three judges and told his cabinet that they had placed the British government in an 'awkward and indefensible position'.[69] Churchill raised the possibility of making a public declaration that 'certain judges', a reference to Carson, Sumner and Cave, had disqualified themselves by their political actions from hearing Irish cases. He even went so far as to question whether the Privy Council could be purged.[70]

The Irish made other objections to the appeal. Griffith claimed that the appeal was unpopular in many quarters in the Dominions and speculated that it might be abolished in the near future. He also raised the argument of the expense of taking a case to the Privy Council, insisting that 'It is a rich man's appeal which may well be used to the destruction of a man not well off'.[71] Griffith even went so far as to question whether the appeal to the Privy Council was really demanded by the terms of the Treaty.[72]

64 TNA, CAB 43/2 SFB 62 and CAB 43/3 SFC 40, letter from the prime minister to Mr. A. Griffith, 1 June 1922.
65 TNA, CAB 43/3 SFC 40, letter from Mr. Arthur Griffith to the Prime Minister, 2 June 1922.
66 UCDA, Gavan Duffy Papers, P152/204, cabinet meeting of 2 June 1922.
67 For example, see *Hansard*, House of Lords, vol. 52, col. 147, 30 Nov. 1922 and Thomas Mohr, 'Lord Cave, the British Empire and Irish Independence', *Oxford University Commonwealth Law Journal*, 12:2 (2013), 229.
68 TNA, CAB 43/7 22/N/163, interview between the prime minister and Mr Griffith and Mr Collins, 1 June 1922.
69 TNA, CAB 23/30, CAB 32(22), conclusions of cabinet meeting, 2 June 1922.
70 Ibid.
71 TNA, CAB 43/3 SFC 40, Griffith to Lloyd George, 2 June 1922.
72 Ibid.

The British were confident that they could wear the Irish down on this issue. It seemed unlikely that the Irish negotiators were going to throw away the entire Treaty settlement and the creation of a self-governing Irish state for the sake of the single issue of the Privy Council appeal. The British knew that they were negotiating on solid ground since the Irish had accepted Dominion status under the Treaty and all of the existing Dominions were subject to the appeal to the Privy Council. They were also prepared to offer concessions in order to secure their core objective. Under the 1921 Treaty they had persuaded the Irish to accept a constitutional link between the Irish Free State and Canada. The British had selected Canada as a constitutional model because that Dominion was subject to appeals 'as of right', a relatively unrestricted procedure that ensured that a large number of Canadian cases went to London every year. The British abandoned this position during the 1922 negotiations on the draft Irish Constitution. They conceded that Irish appeals could be 'by special leave', a more restrictive formula that was also used with respect to South Africa.[73] This allowed the Irish to save some face as they could now claim that they had wrested a concession from the British that was better than the strict terms of the 1921 Treaty.[74]

The final format of the Irish Constitution of 1922 was largely settled during a series of one-to-one negotiations between Hugh Kennedy, legal adviser to the Irish provisional government, and Lord Hewart, lord chief justice of England and Wales and one of the British signatories of the 1921 Treaty. By 9 June, Hewart had secured reluctant agreement to place a reference to the Privy Council appeal into the draft Constitution.[75] Although Kennedy would soon become the leading legal figure in the Irish Free State he seemed unfamiliar with the nature or significance of the Privy Council appeal in 1922.[76] This made Hewart's task all the easier.

The final wording of what would become Article 66 of the 1922 Constitution parodied the initial Irish resistance to the appeal. It may be recalled that this provision had originally been drafted by the Irish provisional government with the specific intention of preventing appeals.[77] It provided:

73 On 12 June the Irish cabinet urged Kennedy to try to insert a reference to the constitutional practice in the Dominions with respect to appeals to the Privy Council. This initiative failed as the law, and consequently the practice, differed in each Dominion with respect to the appeal. In this case a reference to practice followed with respect to Canada was clearly undesirable as the Privy Council gave leave to appeal in more cases from Canada in most years than from all the other Dominions combined. NAI, cabinet minutes, G1/2, 12 June 1922.

74 *Dáil Debates*, vol. 1, col. 1402–10, 10 Oct. 1922.

75 TNA, CAB 43/1 SFB, 28th draft Irish Constitution, 9 June 1922.

76 Kennedy reported to the provisional government during the negotiations with Hewart that 'There is to be no appeal from the Irish Courts to the Privy Council in London, only some old supposed right of anyone personally to petition the King being reserved.' NAI, dept. of the Taoiseach, S4285A, Hugh Kennedy to provisional government, 11 June 1922. This confusion was probably caused by the established practice of referring to the institution as a direct appeal to the monarch without reference to the existence of an established court in London that made the decision and communicated it in the form of 'advice' to the King. This was not the last Irish misconception with respect to the Privy Council appeal.

77 Article 65 of the provisional government's draft.

> The decision of the Supreme Court shall in all cases be final and conclusive, and shall not be reviewed or capable of being reviewed by any other Court, Tribunal or Authority whatsoever:

This provision was not deleted in the first redraft but was instead given an addition that contradicted its original intent:

> Provided that nothing in this Constitution shall impair the right of any person to petition His Majesty for special leave to appeal from the Supreme Court to His Majesty in Council or the right of His Majesty to grant such leave.[78]

Irish commentators in the 1920s and 1930s attacked the legitimacy of the Irish appeal to the Privy Council by pointing to the internal contradiction in the wording of Article 66.[79] In 1922 the British government was not interested in textual elegance and focused its efforts on closing potential loopholes in the draft Constitution that could be used by future Irish governments to undermine the appeal.[80] It soon became clear that distrust of future Irish intentions lay at the foundations of the appeal to the Privy Council from the Free State courts.

78 Note that the provisions for the establishment of the Privy Council appeal were put in place in the redraft of 8 to 9 of June and were slightly altered in the second or third redrafts. TNA, CAB 43/7 22/N/163, report on draft Irish Constitution.

79 For example, see *Dáil Debates*, vol. 1, col. 1407–8, 10 Oct. 1922; Leo Kohn, *The Constitution of the Irish Free State* (Dublin, Allen and Unwin, 1932), p. 355 and D.W. Harkness, *The Restless Dominion* (New York, New York University Press, 1969), p. 24. This internal contradiction was also found in other Dominion constitutions when dealing with the appeal to the Judicial Committee of the Privy Council. Section 106 of the South Africa Act 1909 had a similar structure. See also Section 47 of the Supreme Court of Canada Act 1875.

80 The first potential loophole was contained in Article 65 where it was provided that the Supreme Court should have appellate jurisdiction from all decisions of the High Court with certain exceptions. As Articles 64 and 65 stood after the first redraft it would have been possible, under these exceptions, to exclude cases coming before the High Court that involved questions as to the validity of any law from the jurisdiction of the Supreme Court. This would have the additional effect of excluding the Privy Council since only cases coming before the Supreme Court could be appealed to that body. In order to safeguard against this, the following words were inserted in Article 65: 'not including cases which involve questions as to the validity of any law'. TNA, CAB 43/1 SFB, 29th amendments to draft Constitution, 10 June 1922. The second loophole appeared in Article 64 of the provisional government's draft that had provided that the judicial power of the High Court extended to the interpretation of treaties. This draft had not provided for any appeal to the Judicial Committee of the Privy Council. The provisional government's draft seemed to ensure that the Irish courts would have had sole jurisdiction over questions as to whether Irish legislation conflicted with the 'Articles of Agreement' or 'Treaty' of 1921. Although the British did not consider the Articles of Agreement to constitute an international treaty, they were well aware that their Irish counterparts believed otherwise. The reference to the High Court's role in the interpretation of treaties was removed from the final text of the Constitution at British insistence. TNA, CAB 43/1 SFB, 28th draft Constitution, 9 June 1922 and CAB 43/2 SFB, 63 draft Constitution, 1 June 1922.

THE IRISH CONSTITUENT ASSEMBLY

'We do not like this Appeal. We tried not to have this Appeal'. Kevin O'Higgins, minister for justice, appealed for understanding during the debates of the special Constituent Assembly as he justified and defended his government's acceptance of the appeal.[81] The Constituent Assembly was a special parliamentary assembly of the 'third Dáil Éireann' called in late 1922 in order to enact the Constitution of the Irish Free State.[82] The appeal to the Judicial Committee of the Privy Council was the most vigorously contested of all the provisions inserted in the draft Constitution at the insistence of the British government. The Irish provisional government was now faced with the disagreeable task of securing approval for a provision that it had found difficult to swallow only a few months earlier. It was clear that the appeal would have to be steamrolled through the Constituent Assembly notwithstanding opposition complaints.[83] The importance placed on the appeal by the British was made clear when Winston Churchill took the trouble to write to the Irish leader W.T. Cosgrave, who had succeeded the recently deceased Griffith and Collins, to remind him of Irish commitments on the Privy Council appeal while the Constituent Assembly was considering the draft Constitution.[84]

The reaction in the Constituent Assembly could scarcely have been worse. Professor William Magennis, an independent TD representing the National University of Ireland, insisted that the appeal undermined the reality of Irish independence and felt that this was an issue of such seriousness that it justified reopening negotiations with the British government.[85] The Labour party distinguished the appeal from the other concessions made by the Irish negotiators on the ground that it represented a genuine threat to the reality of Irish sovereignty.[86]

O'Higgins insisted that the appeal was a prerogative of the crown in Canada and was, therefore, required by the provisions of the 1921 Treaty.[87] He deliberately played down the importance of the appeal and placed considerable emphasis on its unpopularity in some quarters of the Dominions. O'Higgins stressed that the Irish had received assurances in London that the Privy Council would follow the restrictive practice followed in South Africa in allowing appeals from the Irish Free State. The provisional government presented these assurances as a significant negotiating triumph. O'Higgins was confident that the adoption of South African practice with respect to Privy Council appeals ensured that no appeal would be

81 *Dáil Debates*, vol. 1, col. 1414–15, 10 Oct. 1922.

82 The Constituent Assembly had a number of special features that were designed to free it from both the burdens of the past and of the future. Its members were not required to take the republican oath of previous incarnations of Dáil Éireann or the oath demanded by the 1921 Treaty. See *State (Ryan) v. Lennon* [1935] IR 170 at 205, 226 and 241.

83 For example, see *Dáil Debates*, vol. 1, col. 365, 18 Sept. 1922.

84 TNA, CAB 43/1 SFB 33rd, appendix III, and NAI, dept. of the Taoiseach, S4285A, Winston Churchill to W.T. Cosgrave, 11 Oct. 1922.

85 *Dáil Debates*, vol. 1, col. 1405–6, 10 Oct. 1922.

86 Ibid., at col. 563, 21 Sept. 1922.

87 Ibid., at col. 1402–3, 10 Oct. 1922.

heard in cases involving domestic Irish affairs. He expected that special leave would only be given in cases where 'international issues of the first importance' were concerned.[88] O'Higgins even predicted, with unrestrained optimism, that there would be no more than two or three appeals in the next century.[89] George Gavan Duffy, a signatory of the 1921 Treaty, went further by claiming that no appeal would ever go to the Judicial Committee of the Privy Council from the Irish Free State.[90] These optimistic projections were not borne out by the events of the coming decade and the British would even dispute the Irish claim that they had been offered exactly the same practice as applied to South Africa with respect to appeals to the Privy Council.

Did the British promise that all aspects of the Irish appeal would operate in exactly the same manner as in South Africa or did they merely promise that Irish appeals would be 'by special leave', a position that also happened to be followed in South Africa? The Irish government claimed the former while the British government insisted on the latter. In 1926 the lord chancellor, Lord Cave, ordered a search of British government files to discover the nature of any undertakings that might have been made during the 1922 negotiations. The search yielded no concrete results.[91] There is evidence that some form of link between the Irish and South African appeals could have been made orally outside the main meetings of the negotiations.[92] Even if it is accepted that such an undertaking was made, it is difficult to pin down exactly what could have been promised. The Irish seemed convinced that the British government had promised that all aspects of the Irish appeal would operate in exactly the same manner as in South Africa and in 1926 Kevin O'Higgins declared that this formed part of the 'unwritten Constitution' of the Irish Free State.[93] However, it could not be denied that the South African Constitution contained express provisions allowing the limitation of the appeal that were not replicated in the text of its Irish equivalent.[94] This did not prevent the Irish from arguing that they too enjoyed these powers.[95]

88 Ibid., at col. 1404, 10 Oct. 1922.

89 Ibid. See also letter of 22 Sept. 1922 from Kevin O'Higgins to Thomas Johnson, *Irish Times*, 23 Sept. 1922.

90 *Dáil Debates*, vol. 1, col. 1413–14, 10 Oct. 1922.

91 *Hansard*, House of Lords, vol. 63, col. 403–4, 3 Mar. 1926 and TNA, LCO 2/910, Dominions secretary to lord chancellor, 17 Feb. 1926. L.S. Amery informed the lord chancellor that Sir John Anderson (1852–1924), under-secretary for Ireland, 1920–2, believed that the Irish representatives had indeed been assured that leave to appeal would only be granted in exceptional cases. Amery was unable to give any further details. TNA, LCO 2/910, Dominions secretary to lord chancellor, 17 Feb. 1926.

92 Thomas Jones, *Whitehall Diary*, 3 vols (London, Oxford University Press, 1971), iii, p. 204.

93 *Seanad Debates*, vol. 6, col. 415, 24 Feb. 1926.

94 Section 106 of the South Africa Act 1909 provided that 'Parliament may make laws limiting the matters in respect of which such special leave may be asked'. This power was also granted to the Australian parliament under Article 74 of the Australian Constitution.

95 UCDA, Kennedy Papers, P4/342, proposed amendments to the Constitution, undated and P4/842, memorandum on Privy Council appeals, undated.

In reality South African practice did not mean that appeals would be limited to 'international issues of the first importance' as understood by members of the Irish government.[96] This claim went far beyond any kind of restriction on the appeal that existed in South Africa or, for that matter, in any other Dominion. All South African appeals to the Privy Council from 1910 to 1921 concerned domestic matters. The subject matter of these appeals included several land disputes, a number of mining cases, the interpretation of an immigration statute, an unsuccessful attempt to circumvent the operation of racially discriminatory legislation relating to market stands and a case that involved an allegation of negligence in the supply of sheep dip.[97] Between 1920 and 1922 the Privy Council granted leave to appeal in four South African cases.[98] Although this number was small it should have told the Irish government in 1922 that the appeal from the South African courts was far from being a matter of theory rather than fact.[99] Irish legal experts created an exaggerated picture of what 'South African practice' would mean by focusing on sources that told them what they wanted to hear.[100]

The gap between 'South African practice' as understood by members of the Irish government and as understood by the Judicial Committee of the Privy Council lay at the heart of future controversies concerning the Irish appeal.[101] It ensured that the Irish government would accuse the Privy Council of breaching faith as soon as it gave Irish litigants leave to appeal.[102] The Irish appeal would never entirely escape the serious complications that had accompanied its birth.

96 *Dáil Debates*, vol. 1, col. 1404, 10 Oct. 1922.

97 See *South African Breweries Limited v. Durban Corporation* [1912] AC 412; *British Chartered Company of South Africa v. Lennon (Limited)* (1915) 31 TLR 585 and 85 LJPC 11; *Union of South Africa (Minister of Railways and Harbours) v. Simmer and Jack Proprietary Mines* [1918] AC 591; *Marshall's Township Syndicate Limited v. Johannesburg Consolidated Investment Company Limited* [1920] A.C. 420; *Thomas v. Malan* [1921] 1 AC 726; *Indian Immigration Trust Board of Natal v. Govindasamy* [1921] 1 AC 433; *Madrassa Anjuman Islamia v. Municipal Council of Johannesburg* [1922] 1 AC 500.

98 Leave to appeal was refused in a fifth case in *Whittaker v. Durban Corporation* (1920) 36 TLR 784 and 90 LJPC 119.

99 TNA, CAB 43/3 SFC 40, Griffith to Lloyd George, 2 June 1922.

100 The Irish assumption that 'South African practice' meant the near abolition of Privy Council appeals was largely reliant on certain *obiter* remarks made by the Privy Council itself in *Whittaker v. Durban Corporation* (1920) 36 TLR 784. See UCDA, Kennedy Papers, P4/842, memorandum on Privy Council appeals, undated; *Dáil Debates*, vol. 14, col. 341, 3 Feb. 1926; *Seanad Debates*, vol. 6, col. 407–8, 24 Feb. 1926; *Hull v. M'Kenna* [1926] IR 402 at 406; Barra Ó Briain, *The Irish Constitution* (Dublin, Talbot, 1929), pp 120–1 and Henry Harrison, *Ireland and the British Empire, 1937* (London, R. Hale, 1937), pp 188–9.

101 See ch. 6, below.

102 *Lynham v. Butler* [1925] 2 IR 82.

CHAPTER THREE

The Privy Council as arbiter and guardian of the Anglo-Irish Treaty

MAINTAINING THE TREATY SETTLEMENT

IT IS IMPORTANT TO RE-ITERATE that the main reason for British insistence on maintaining an Irish appeal to the Privy Council was as a means of securing the settlement imposed by the 1921 Treaty. The appeal was part of a wider legal structure aimed at maintaining the integrity of the Treaty from potentially unscrupulous Irish governments. This included (i) a power known as reservation that permitted the crown to veto bills passed by Dominion parliaments; (ii) a legal provision that placed all Irish law in a subservient position to the 1921 Treaty; (iii) the supremacy of Imperial legislation passed at Westminster over legislation enacted by the Dominions; and (iv) the appeal to the Judicial Committee of the Privy Council.

(i) Reservation

The final text of the 1922 Constitution included provisions in Article 41 declaring that the crown held powers of withholding assent and reserving legislation for the King's pleasure. These powers were often called the crown 'veto' and allowed the Governor-General to withhold the King's assent to a bill passed by a Dominion legislature pending the signification of the King's pleasure.[1] This was a delaying measure that could be converted into a permanent veto. A bill could be reserved for a limited period of time in order to permit its transmission to London where the measure could be examined. A reserved bill was terminated unless the King's assent was signified within a specified period of time.

In 1932 a prominent textbook on the Constitution of the Irish Free State dismissed the power of reservation as an anachronism.[2] It has to be remembered that this conclusion was written with the benefit of a decade of hindsight and knowledge of the significant reforms contained within the 1931 Statute of Westminster. This issue looked very different in 1922. The provisional government placed a great deal of emphasis on British assurances that the power of reservation

1 *Dáil Debates*, vol. 1, col. 1168–84, 4 Oct. 1922. Roberts-Wray rejects the accuracy of the term 'veto' when referring to the King's assent but admits that it has long been in common use. Sir Kenneth Roberts-Wray, *Commonwealth and Colonial Law* (London, Stevens, 1966), p. 225.

2 Leo Kohn, *The Constitution of the Irish Free State* (Dublin, Allen and Unwin, 1932), pp 203–10.

would not be used with respect to legislation concerning Irish internal affairs.[3] Irish delegates had received assurances on this point from their British counterparts during the negotiations on the draft Irish Constitution.[4] Yet the Irish government was forced to admit to the Constituent Assembly that the power of reservation could still be exercised with respect to legislation that concerned external affairs, in particular matters that affected Great Britain or the existing Dominions.[5] Lloyd George and the British law officers emphasized this reality during the negotiations on the 1922 Constitution.[6] This power of veto would certainly have included legislation that was incompatible with the provisions of the 1921 Treaty. In 1920 General Jan Smuts, prime minister of South Africa, had recognized that the veto could be used with respect to laws aimed at secession from the Empire. Kevin O'Higgins was forced to admit that 'if an Act were passed repealing this Treaty or an Act were passed repudiating the Crown, you cannot write it down as part and parcel of the function of the Representative of the Crown to signify the King's assent to that'.[7]

In 1922, British ministers speaking in parliament promoted the presence of the crown veto in the text of the Irish Constitution as a possible safeguard for the 1921 Treaty.[8] The British government sought assurances from T.M. Healy, who had recently been proposed as the first Governor-General of the Irish Free State, that he would exercise his powers to refuse assent to legislation that broke the Treaty. Healy replied that he would 'keep a watchful eye on Bills and Amendments or proposed Amendments to Bills which may in any way conflict with the Treaty, or may be such as may affect the relations of His Majesty with foreign States or other parts of the Empire'.[9]

In fact, the British government did consider making use of the power of reservation in the years that followed the creation of the Irish Free State. For example, the cabinet discussed its use to prevent the enactment of the Land Act 1926. This legislation was passed by the Oireachtas with the open intention of blocking an appeal from the Irish Supreme Court to the Privy Council in the case of *Lynham v. Butler*.[10] The British backed away from this radical course of action when it became clear that the Land Act 1926 was only aimed at blocking this particular appeal.[11] Lord Cave, the lord chancellor, was reluctant to make use of

3 *Dáil Debates*, vol. 1, col. 1168–9, 4 Oct. 1922.
4 TNA, CAB 43/3 SFC 35, memorandum by British representatives, 29 May 1922, CAB 43/3 SFC 40, Griffith to Lloyd George, 2 June 1922 and CAB 43/2 SFB 3, memorandum on Dominion status, by Lionel Curtis, 17 Oct. 1921.
5 *Dáil Debates*, vol. 1, col. 1168–9, 4 Oct. 1922.
6 TNA, CAB 43/3 SFC 35, British memorandum on draft Irish Free State Constitution, 20 May 1922.
7 *Dáil Debates*, vol. 1, col. 1168–9, 4 Oct. 1922.
8 *Hansard*, House of Commons, vol. 159, col. 373, 27 Nov. 1922.
9 TNA, CO 739/15, T.M. Healy to Duke of Devonshire, 2 Dec. 1922.
10 [1921] IR 185; [1925] 2 IR 82 and [1925] 2 IR 231. See also *Irish Law Times and Solicitors' Journal*, 60 (1926), 31 and 43 and *Dáil Debates*, vol. 14, col. 389–90, 3 Feb. 1926.
11 TNA, DO 117/3, memorandum on the Irish Free State and the Privy Council, 29 Jan. 1926.

the power of reservation until it became clear that the Irish were contemplating a wider assault on the Privy Council appeal.[12]

(ii) The subservience of Irish law to the 1921 Treaty

Perhaps the most significant amendment to the draft Irish Constitution that emerged from the Anglo-Irish negotiations of 1922 was the insertion of legal provisions that placed all Irish law in a subservient position to the terms of the 1921 Treaty. The main provision that enforced this position was known as the 'repugnancy clause', a term derived from the reality that any law that was found to be repugnant to the Treaty was to be considered null and void.[13] It provided '[I]f any provision of the said Constitution or of any amendment thereof or of any law made thereunder is in any respect repugnant to any of the provisions of the Scheduled Treaty, it shall to the extent only of such repugnancy, be absolutely void and inoperative'.[14] Once again, this provision reflected the British government's distrust of Irish intentions to keep to the terms of the 1921 Treaty. It might be argued that, in this case, the sense of distrust had been heightened by the nature of the draft Irish Constitution brought to London in the summer of 1922 that almost entirely ignored the terms of the Treaty. In fact, the British had planned to insert a provision of this nature from the very beginning. A British memorandum, drafted just four days after the signing of the Treaty, suggested that a provision be placed in the future Irish Constitution that tied its interpretation to the terms of the Treaty.[15] The Irish government initially accepted the repugnancy clause during the Anglo-Irish negotiations on the draft 1922 Constitution. Later, having realized its full significance, an eleventh-hour attempt was made to reverse this position. The Irish had left it too late to object and their efforts proved unsuccessful.[16]

The significance of the repugnancy clause as a limit on Irish sovereignty was inextricably connected with the Privy Council appeal. The repugnancy clause that finally appeared in the 1922 Constitution could only be enforced through the courts. The appeal to the Judicial Committee of the Privy Council was essential in ensuring that this repugnancy clause could not be ignored.

(iii) The supremacy of Imperial statutes

In 1922 the parliament at Westminster was still popularly known as the 'Imperial parliament'. For centuries this Imperial parliament enjoyed the right to legislate

12 TNA, LCO 2/910, lord chancellor to Dominions secretary, 3 Feb. 1926. For Irish attitudes towards the power of reservation see *Dáil Debates*, vol. 1, col. 1168–9, 4 Oct. 1922.

13 The term 'repugnancy clause' was created by Kohn, *Constitution of the Irish Free State*, p. 98.

14 See Section 2 of the Constitution of the Irish Free State (Saorstát Éireann) Act 1922 (Dublin) and the Preamble to the Irish Free State Constitution Act 1922 (Westminster). Article 50 of the Constitution provided that all constitutional amendments had to be compatible with the 1921 Treaty.

15 TNA, CAB 43/2 SFB 40, memo by Lionel Curtis, 10 Dec. 1921.

16 Thomas Towey, 'Hugh Kennedy and the Constitutional Development of the Irish Free State, 1922–1923', *Irish Jurist*, 13 (1977), 355 at 362–4.

for all of Britain's far-flung possessions scattered around the globe. Nevertheless, the sheer size of the Empire ensured that no one legislature could satisfy all its legislative needs. The crown had the power to create local legislatures in British territories whether conquered, ceded or settled.[17] Yet the Imperial parliament reserved the right to intervene directly if the circumstances required it.[18]

When the Imperial parliament passed legislation that extended to the Dominions these 'Imperial statutes' enjoyed an overriding status over the other laws of the Dominions. This higher status was recognized by the common law and had been restated in an important Imperial statute called the Colonial Laws Validity Act 1865. This statute clarified that a Dominion law that conflicted with an Imperial statute that extended to that Dominion could be declared void and inoperative to the extent of such repugnancy.[19] This was of particular importance to the Constitution of the Irish Free State, which had been enacted in a statute passed by the Constituent Assembly in Dublin but also passed as an Imperial statute by the parliament at Westminster. The British Imperial statute, known as the Irish Free State Constitution Act 1922, included the repugnancy clause and many provisions that reflected the settlement reached in the 1921 Treaty.[20] The supremacy of Imperial statutes ensured that these restrictive provisions could never be unilaterally removed at the instigation of any future Irish government. Once again the final word on these matters would rest with the Judicial Committee of the Privy Council as the court with final appellate jurisdiction over the Irish Free State.

(iv) The Judicial Committee of the Privy Council as arbiter and guardian of the Treaty

It was clear that the British did not trust the Irish courts to ensure that Irish legislation and the Irish Constitution would remain compatible with the terms of the 1921 Treaty. Nevertheless it was not always clear to Irish observers in 1922 which institution would be the final arbiter of the Treaty. Some Irish commentators seemed to fear that the British government itself might claim that it had unfettered competence to decide whether Irish laws complied with the Treaty.[21] Liam de Róiste, a TD in the Constituent Assembly representing Cork city, proposed an

17 *Phillips v. Eyre* (1870) LR 6 QB 1.

18 Alpheus Todd, *Parliamentary Government in the British Colonies* (London, Longmans, Green, 1880), p. 172.

19 Section 2 of the Colonial Laws Validity Act 1865 provided 'Any Colonial Law, which is, or shall be in any respect repugnant to the Provisions of any Act of Parliament extending to the Colony to which such Law may relate, or repugnant to any Order or Regulation made under Authority of such Act of Parliament, or having in the Colony the Force and Effect of such Act, shall be read subject to such Act, Order, or Regulation, and shall, to the Extent of such Repugnancy, but not otherwise, be and remain absolutely void and inoperative.' The 1865 Act also made it clear that a colonial law could no longer be declared void for being repugnant to the English common law or for being inconsistent with the instructions given to a Governor-General. See Thomas Mohr, 'The Colonial Laws Validity Act and the Irish Free State', *Irish Jurist*, 43 (2009), 21.

20 Preamble, Irish Free State Constitution Act 1922.

21 *Dáil Debates*, vol. 1, col. 1485, 11 Oct. 1922.

amendment that would have allowed questions of compatibility with the Treaty to be decided at an Imperial conference, a regular gathering of representatives of the governments of the United Kingdom and the Dominions.[22] Kevin O'Higgins and Ernest Blythe seemed unwilling to place their faith in the Dominions at this stage. They made it clear that their preferred arbiter of the 1921 Treaty was the League of Nations. In this respect O'Higgins and Blythe were influenced by the nascent Irish 'department of foreign affairs', that would soon be renamed the 'department of external affairs' in accordance with Dominion usage. This department advocated the registration of the Treaty with the League of Nations in the near future. Among the reasons given for doing so was the desire to ensure that a non-British tribunal, in the form of the Permanent Court of International Justice, might adjudicate on the provisions of the Anglo-Irish Treaty.[23] This possibility was not available in 1922 as the Irish Free State was not yet a member of the League. It was left to independent TD Professor William Magennis to point out to the Constituent Assembly that, as matters stood, such disputes would clearly fall within the final jurisdiction of the Judicial Committee of the Privy Council.

Magennis stressed the important influence that Lord Watson's decisions in the Privy Council had had on constitutional law in Canada.[24] Watson's decisions in a number of key cases, for example an appeal popularly known as the 'local prohibition case', had significantly boosted the powers of the parliaments of the provinces at the expense of the Canadian parliament at Ottawa.[25] Could an active Privy Council have a similar influence over Irish affairs? Many members of the Constituent Assembly took little comfort from O'Higgins' claim that the Privy Council would only deal with 'international issues of the highest importance'. Such matters would surely include questions of whether Irish laws were compatible with the 1921 Treaty, which the Irish insisted was an international agreement. Many members of the Constituent Assembly saw the risk of Privy Council interference in such matters as a greater threat to Irish sovereignty than appeals concerning routine domestic disputes.[26]

Irish newspapers that opposed the Treaty had long anticipated British intentions that the Privy Council appeal be considered an indispensable requirement of the Treaty.[27] These newspapers had predicted that the appeal would

22 Ibid., at col. 1484.

23 NAI, dept. of the Taoiseach, S3332, memorandum on Irish membership of the League of Nations by Patrick Sarsfield O'Hegarty with covering note by J.J. Walsh, 15 Sept. 1922.

24 *Dáil Debates*, vol. 1, col. 1414, 10 Oct. 1922.

25 *Attorney General for Ontario v. Attorney General for Canada* [1896] AC 348. For more details on the impact of decisions of William Watson, Baron Watson (1827–99), on Canadian constitutional law see David Schneiderman, 'A.V. Dicey, Lord Watson, and the Law of the Canadian Constitution in the Late Nineteenth Century', *Law and History Review*, 16 (1998), 495.

26 *Dáil Debates*, vol. 1, col. 1411–13, 10 Oct. 1922.

27 A.B. Keith also anticipated the imposition of the Privy Council on the Irish Free State before the publication of the 1922 Constitution. A.B. Keith, 'Notes on Imperial Constitutional Law', *Journal of Comparative Legislation and International Law*, 4 (1922), 104 at 105.

extend to the Irish Free State long before the draft Irish Constitution was actually published. They also noted that if the Privy Council were intended to serve as the arbiter of the Treaty, it would, by extension, become the final arbiter of the Irish Constitution. As Erskine Childers' anti-Treaty newspaper, *Poblacht na hÉireann*, made clear, 'The tribunal that decides what the Constitution means rules the Constitution'.[28] *Poblacht na hÉireann* shared the common Irish perception that the Privy Council was an instrument under the direct control of the British government. This allowed the paper to conclude that the Privy Council appeal would ensure that the British government would act as 'judge, jury and executioner in their own cause'.[29] Henry Harrison, a former MP who had supported Irish home rule, wrote that the contention that the appeal was an essential component of the Treaty implied that the Privy Council 'was placed permanently and irrevocably astride of the Irish Constitution'. Harrison felt that the draft Irish Free State Constitution gave the Privy Council powers that were analogous to those held by the United States Supreme Court with respect to constitutional interpretation. He warned that, unless these provisions were altered, the Irish Free State would be placed 'not merely in a subordinate position but at a most serious disadvantage in its international relationship with Great Britain'.[30] Harrison later added:

> Britain was to be judge in her own case – or, rather, to be more precise, a British tribunal, sitting in a British atmosphere, manned by judges appointed and paid by the British Government, applying British standards of thought and public policy and administering British law and the statutes of the 'Imperial Parliament' was to decide all questions arising out of Britain's contract or Treaty with Ireland.[31]

Harrison compared this loss of control on the part of the Irish Free State to a person who had voluntarily committed himself to supervision on the grounds of lunacy.[32]

Fears that the Privy Council might serve as the final arbiter of the Irish Constitution in addition to the 1921 Treaty were not so far-fetched when it is remembered that the two were inextricably linked as a consequence of the repugnancy clause. These fears resulted in an interesting amendment to one of the provisions on which the Irish provisional government placed most importance. Article 2 of the draft Constitution that came back from London provided 'All powers of government and all authority legislative, executive and judicial, are derived from the people'. During the debates in the Constituent Assembly a number of TDs argued that it was necessary that this provision be amended to

28 *Poblacht na hÉireann*, 3 Apr. 1922.
29 Ibid., at 3 Apr. 1922 and 22 June 1922.
30 UCDA, Kennedy Papers, P4/340, memorandum by Henry Harrison on 'The Draft Constitution of the Irish Free State', 18 Sept. 1922.
31 Harrison, *Ireland and the British Empire, 1937*, p. 140. 32 Ibid.

declare that these powers be derived from 'the *Irish* people'.[33] The provisional government initially rejected this as a spurious amendment.[34] As a provision of the Irish Constitution, what other people could have been intended? However, George Gavan Duffy, a signatory of the 1921 Treaty, pointed out that the day would come when the provisions of the Irish Constitution would be interpreted by the Judicial Committee of the Privy Council 'and heaven knows what they may discover there'.[35] Duffy and others felt that it was possible that the Privy Council might interpret the term 'the people' as referring to the people of the Empire or Commonwealth on the basis of their common status as British subjects rather than the people of the Irish Free State alone.[36] In spite of their initial scoffs, the provisional government eventually took these arguments sufficiently seriously to amend the article to read 'All powers of government and all authority legislative, executive and judicial in Ireland, are derived from the people of Ireland'.[37]

The British government, unlike their Irish counterpart, was never in any doubt as to the identity of the arbiter of the Treaty. As Arthur Berriedale Keith pointed out, 'there is no doubt whatever that it was the deliberate intention of the British government that the Judicial Committee should have the final voice in the issue of the meaning of the treaty'.[38] Lionel Curtis made this clear in correspondence with Winston Churchill when he wrote that the Privy Council was the court 'which we have always stipulated must be the supreme arbiter in interpreting the Treaty'.[39] Although the British seem to have been careful not to raise this issue during the Treaty negotiations their intentions were soon revealed once they were concluded. Winston Churchill and others made repeated assurances during the debates on the Irish Constitution at Westminster that the Privy Council would act as the final arbiter of the Treaty.[40]

The need to enshrine the Privy Council as the arbiter of the Treaty together with the desire to provide a safeguard for the Protestant community of the Irish Free State were the main motivating factors behind the clandestine methods used to impose the Irish appeal. Indeed, the two safeguards were heavily intertwined in the sense that the British saw the Treaty as the ultimate source of rights for southern Protestants. In addition, aggrieved southern unionists were the most obvious potential litigants in taking legal proceedings that would determine the compatibility of Irish government policy with the provisions of the Treaty. Once the matter had made its way through the Irish courts the final judgment would lie in the hands of the Privy Council. It was always open to the British government, in

33 *Dáil Debates*, vol. 1, col. 655–6, 25 Sept. 1922 and UCDA, Kennedy Papers, P4/341.

34 *Dáil Debates*, vol. 1, col. 656, 25 Sept. 1922 and UCDA, Kennedy Papers, P4/340.

35 *Dáil Debates*, vol. 1, col. 656, 25 Sept. 1922.

36 Ibid., at col. 655–6.

37 Ibid., at col. 661.

38 A.B. Keith, *The Scotsman*, 26 Apr. 1928 and *Letters on Imperial Relations, Indian Reform, Constitutional and International Law, 1916–1935* (London, Oxford University Press, 1935), p. 78.

39 TNA, CO 739/7/47027, Curtis to Churchill, 20 Sept. 1922.

40 *Hansard*, House of Commons, vol. 155, col. 1664, 26 June 1922 and House of Lords, vol. 52, col. 166–7, 30 Nov. 1922 and House of Lords, vol. 52, col. 181, 1 Dec. 1922.

the absence of such a protagonist, to initiate legal proceedings before the Privy Council by making use of a special provision in Section 4 of the Judicial Committee Act 1833. This option was not ideal as it would be much easier for an Irish government to ignore a decision that resulted from this procedure as opposed to one that had emerged from a case originating in the Irish courts. British cabinet discussions reveal that they were prepared, if necessary, to make use of an *agent provocateur* who would initiate an action in the Irish courts that could eventually be appealed to the Privy Council.[41]

It is true that the Privy Council would not be able to directly enforce its decisions in the face of a hostile Irish administration. In 1922 Ernest Blythe, minister for finance, attempted to soothe Irish concerns about the appeal by suggesting that the Irish government might simply ignore unpopular decisions emanating from this court in London.[42] Nevertheless, a decision in which the Irish were found to be in breach of the 1921 Treaty would strengthen the hand of those seeking compliance in the eyes of the Dominions and the international community.

The intended role of the Privy Council as the arbiter and guardian of the Treaty gave a powerful incentive to the Irish government to seek alternatives in the Permanent Court of International Justice or even in the Imperial conference. The prospect of a new and more representative Imperial court was often raised as an additional alternative.[43] After all, the creation of the Judicial Committee of the Privy Council pre-dated the existence of Dominion status and the new 'Commonwealth' that was supposed to be based on principles of equality of status between the United Kingdom and the Dominions. The Judicial Committee had never been designed to adjudicate on Anglo-Irish disputes in the changed circumstances of the twentieth century.

PROPOSALS FOR A REFORMED GUARDIAN OF THE TREATY

In the autumn of 1922 Alfred Cope, unofficial representative of the British government in Dublin and a important figure in securing the 1921 Treaty settlement, was struck by the extreme unpopularity of the Privy Council appeal in Ireland.[44] This moved him to submit a plan to his government for a more inclusive Judicial Committee that would consider Irish appeals and settle disputes as to the interpretation of the Treaty. Cope wanted to create a new Judicial Committee of the Irish Privy Council that would hear appeals that were not related to the Treaty. He also proposed an agreed court composed of the Judicial Committees that sat in London and in Dublin to hear questions involving the Treaty.[45] In a similar vein,

41 TNA, CAB 43/1 22/N/148(4), 15 June 1922.

42 *Dáil Debates*, vol. 1, col. 1408, 10 Oct. 1922.

43 For example, see *Dáil Debates*, vol. 1, col. 1407 and 1411–15, 10 Oct. 1922.

44 Sir Alfred William ('Andy') Cope (1877–1954), *Dictionary of Irish Biography*, vol. 2, pp 836–7.

45 TNA, CAB 43/1 SFB 33rd, Alfred Cope to Sir Francis Greer and Lionel Curtis, 10 Oct. 1922.

Arthur Berriedale Keith recommended in 1922 that a special tribunal composed of British, Irish and Dominion representatives consider alleged violations of the Treaty in place of the Judicial Committee of the Privy Council.[46] Although these were certainly imaginative ideas, they never won the approval of the British government.

The role of the Privy Council as the intended arbiter and guardian of the 1921 Treaty has been largely overlooked in existing historical accounts of this period. Yet, this position was wholly in accordance with Irish historical precedent, since the Privy Council had also been intended to act as arbiter and guardian of the various home rule settlements. This element of continuity between the proposals for home rule and the settlement reached in 1921 has similarly failed to attract attention. Such neglect might be justified by the argument that the Privy Council appeal from the Irish Free State failed to live up to expectations. It might also be argued that, notwithstanding the intentions of the British in 1921 and 1922, the Privy Council never actually found itself in the position of arbiter of the Treaty. Yet, as subsequent chapters will make clear, in spite of the brevity of the existence of the Irish appeal, it is clear that the Privy Council *did* act as arbiter of the Treaty on a number of different occasions.[47]

CONCLUSION

Opponents of the 1921 Treaty made extensive reference to the Privy Council appeal to support their conclusion that the Constitution of the Irish Free State was an 'abject surrender' by the provisional government. Anti-Treaty commentators in Ireland were in no doubt that the Privy Council would be the arbiter of the Treaty and were also confident that this court would be unable to resist interfering in the internal affairs of the Irish Free State.[48] The provisional government could not ignore criticism of this nature. Ernest Blythe, minister for finance, set out the policy of successive Irish governments towards the Privy Council with characteristic bluntness. He declared that 'If His Majesty in Council were to give a decision that the Irish people thought to be unjust, that decision would be a dead letter absolutely, and we all know it'.[49] External interference would be resisted whatever the cost.

46 A.B. Keith, 'Notes on Imperial Constitutional Law', *Journal of Comparative Legislation and International Law*, 4 (1922), 104.
47 See chs 4 and 8, below.
48 *Poblacht na hÉireann*, 3 Apr. 1922.
49 *Dáil Debates*, vol. 1, col. 1408, 10 Oct. 1922.

CHAPTER FOUR

Lord Cave and the early appeals

HULL v. M'KENNA

IN 1926 KEVIN O'HIGGINS, the Irish minister for justice, asked the Dáil to consider the worth of the Irish appeal to the Judicial Committee of the Privy Council. He asked 'whether it is a good court, whether it is a useful court, whether it is a necessary court'.[1] His own answers to these questions left little room for compromise, concluding that the Privy Council was 'a bad court, a useless court, an unnecessary court'.[2]

The Irish appeal to the Privy Council had been imposed by compulsion. Yet it is important to note that not all aspects of the unhappy events that followed were inevitable and the Irish appeal actually had a good start in the early 1920s. In 1923 the Privy Council heard three Irish petitions for leave to appeal including one concerning the case of *Hull v. M'Kenna*.[3] These were preliminary hearings that determined whether the Privy Council would allow full appeals. One of the presiding judges, Lord Haldane, made use of these proceedings to reassure Irish nationalists on the nature of the Privy Council appeal.

Haldane was a Scottish judge whose career was particularly intertwined with the Privy Council appeal. As a struggling young barrister, the Privy Council appeal had provided him with a career breakthrough that ensured that he received a great deal of work from litigants appearing before this Imperial court.[4] As a Liberal MP he took a particular interest in parliamentary debates concerning the Privy Council appeal, which he considered a key institution of the British Empire.[5] As a judge Haldane referred to the Privy Council as one of his 'spiritual homes' and attempted to sit on as many appeals as possible concerning constitutional questions.[6] Most encouraging from an Irish perspective was that Haldane was a strong supporter of Dominion autonomy and had also been a strong supporter of Irish home rule when he sat in parliament. Haldane had even undertaken a mission to achieve a peaceful settlement of the Anglo-Irish conflict in 1919.[7]

1 *Dáil Debates*, vol. 14, col. 331–4, 3 Feb. 1926. 2 Ibid., at 334. 3 [1926] IR 402.

4 Richard Burdon Haldane, *An Autobiography* (London, Hodder and Stoughton, 1929), pp 35–9 and 42–3.

5 For example, see *Hansard*, House of Commons, vol. 83, col. 101, 14 May 1900.

6 Lord Haldane, 'The work for the Empire of the Judicial Committee of the Privy Council', *Cambridge Law Journal*, 1:2 (1922), 246.

7 Haldane saw Irish home rule and Dominion autonomy as related issues. He wrote in his

Nobody could have been surprised when Haldane took a leading position as the first Irish petitions came before the Judicial Committee of the Privy Council. In his opening remarks he stressed that the Privy Council was always reluctant to interfere if the legal question involved was one that could be 'best determined on the spot'. Haldane added that 'it is obviously proper that the Dominions should more and more dispose of their own cases'.[8] He also tried to calm the fears of Irish nationalists with respect to the objectivity of the Judicial Committee of the Privy Council by stressing 'we have nothing to do with politics, or policies, or party considerations'.[9] Most reassuring of all, he dismissed all three Irish petitions for leave to appeal. Haldane noted that the Irish Free State 'must in a large measure dispose of her own justice'.[10] Lord Buckmaster, who had served as lord chancellor under prime minister Asquith, added that the Irish Constitution made it plain that 'as far as possible, finality and supremacy are to be given to the Irish Courts'.[11] These welcome conclusions were greeted with relief by Irish observers, including the Irish attorney general, Hugh Kennedy. He noted 'if they had been so dishonestly minded, the British side could have eaten into our rights very substantially'.[12]

Although the Privy Council declined to hear the first Irish petitions for leave to appeal this event was significant in the context of Imperial and Irish history. Lord Haldane's introductory remarks stressed the Privy Council's identity as an institution that spanned the entirety of the British Empire. He stressed:

> The Judicial Committee of the Privy Council is not an English body in any exclusive sense. It is no more an English body than it is an Indian body, or a Canadian body, or a South African body, or, for the future, an Irish Free State body ... [T]he Judicial Committee of the Privy Council is not a body, strictly speaking, with any location. The Sovereign is everywhere throughout the Empire in the contemplation of the law. He may as well sit in Dublin, or at Ottawa, or in South Africa, or in Australia, or in India as he may sit here, and it is only for convenience ... that we do sit here [in London].[13]

These words were later quoted throughout the Empire to support contentions that acceptance of the Privy Council appeal did not necessarily imply subservience to the United Kingdom.[14] Haldane also tried to break the stereotype of the Judicial

autobiography 'We were strong Home Rulers because we held that it was only by giving Ireland freedom to govern herself that we could hope to satisfy her. But we felt not less the necessity of studying how the sense of liberty might be made to reach Canada, Australasia, and even India'. Haldane, *Autobiography*, pp 93–4, 109, 315–17.

8 [1926] IR 402 at 404. 9 Ibid., at 403. 10 Ibid., at 407–8.

11 Ibid., at 409. Stanley Owen Buckmaster, first Viscount Buckmaster (1861–1934), served as lord chancellor between 1915 and 1916. See R.F.V. Heuston, *Lives of the Lord Chancellors, 1885–1940* (Oxford, Clarendon, 1964), pp 243–310.

12 UCDA, Kennedy Papers, P4/516, Hugh Kennedy to W.T. Cosgrave, 30 July 1923.

13 *Hull v. M'Kenna, 'Freeman's Journal' v. Fernstrom* and *'Freeman's Journal' v. Traesliberi* [1923] IR 402 at 403–4.

14 For example, see TNA, LCO 2/3465, W.H. Clark, British high commissioner to the Union of

Committee of the Privy Council as an exclusive body of British judges by pointing to the policy of inviting Dominion judges to hear petitions. Although Haldane was trying to placate the Irish Free State, his words reflected principles that he had uttered in private for many years.[15] They had a powerful impact on all of the Dominions as they extended far beyond the particular circumstances of the Irish Free State. For example, one South African commentator declared that Haldane's remarks represented 'unwritten law' in that Dominion.[16] Sadly, Haldane's vision of the Judicial Committee of the Privy Council, as an institution that was not dependent on British dominance or characterized by its physical location in London, was not shared by all his judicial colleagues.[17]

The refusal of the Privy Council to grant leave to appeal to the first Irish petitions also sealed the fate of the *Freeman's Journal*, the most influential Irish newspaper of the nineteenth century, which had lodged the other two petitions for leave to appeal that accompanied *Hull v. M'Kenna*.[18] A disastrous attempt to dominate the market in newsprint led to a dispute with its creditors that ended in litigation that finally went against the *Freeman's Journal*. The possibility of a Privy Council appeal represented a last throw of the dice for a newspaper that had been in existence since 1763. Ironically, the *Freeman's Journal* had become a staunch supporter of the Cosgrave government and the 1921 Treaty. Its closure in 1924 deprived both of an important voice in rallying public support.[19]

THE BOUNDARY COMMISSION REFERENCE

The next case concerning Ireland that came before the Privy Council was unusual as it was not an appeal involving private litigants but a special reference made at the behest of the British government under Section 4 of the Judicial Committee Act 1833. This provision allowed the crown to refer any matter for consideration

South Africa, to J.H. Thomas, 25 Mar. 1935 and UCDA, Blythe Papers, P24/217, memorandum on appeals to the Judicial Committee of the Privy Council, 1926.

15 TNA, LCO 2/3464, untitled memorandum by Lord Haldane, 30 July 1918.

16 TNA, LCO 2/3465, W.H. Clark, high commissioner, to J.H. Thomas, 25 Mar. 1935.

17 The judgment of the Privy Council delivered by Lord Cave in the Canadian case of *Nadan v. The King* held that the powers of the Canadian parliament were confined to matters falling within the frontiers of that Dominion. [1926] AC 482 at 492. This suggested that Canadian legislation could not circumscribe the jurisdiction of a tribunal that sat in London and therefore outside the frontiers of the Dominion of Canada. The territorial aspect to the *Nadan* decision was rejected by the Privy Council itself in *British Coal Corporation v. R* [1935] IR 487 and [1935] AC 500 in a decision that once again emphasized the 'Imperial' nature of the Judicial Committee of the Privy Council as envisioned in *Hull v. M'Kenna* [1923] IR 402. See also *Woolworths (NZ) v Wynne* [1952] NZLR 496.

18 *The 'Freeman's Journal' Limited v. Erik Fernstrom* and *The 'Freeman's Journal' Limited v. Follum Traesliberi* [1926] IR 402.

19 Felix M. Larkin, '"A great daily organ": the *Freeman's Journal*, 1763–1924', *History Ireland*, 14:3 (May/June 2006), 44.

by the Privy Council.[20] The great advantage of this procedure was that it could be used to decide issues that could not otherwise be the subject of ordinary judicial proceedings such as boundary disputes between Dominions or between the constituent parts of Dominions. Special references had been used to settle boundary disputes between Victoria and New South Wales in 1872[21] and between Manitoba and Ontario in 1885.[22] This procedure would perform a similar function with respect to the Labrador boundary between Canada and Newfoundland in 1927.[23] The Irish reference concerned the interpretation of Article 12 of the Anglo-Irish Treaty that dealt with the boundary that was to be drawn between Northern Ireland and the Irish Free State.[24]

On 26 April 1924, the Irish government formally requested the immediate constitution of the Boundary Commission specified in the provisions of the 1921 Treaty. This body was to consist of three persons; one appointed by the government of the Irish Free State, another appointed by the government of Northern Ireland and a chairman appointed by the British government. Legal difficulties arose when the Northern government refused to nominate a representative. On 4 June 1924 the British prime minister, Ramsay MacDonald, announced his government's intention to seek clarification as to the legal consequences of this refusal by means of a special reference to the Judicial Committee of the Privy Council.[25] This means of breaking the deadlock was the brainchild of the influential British official, Lionel Curtis.[26] The British government did not seek the consent of the government of Northern Ireland or that of the Irish Free State before imposing this solution. Both of these governments were presented with a *fait accompli.*

The special reference asked the Judicial Committee to provide answers to a number of key questions that focused on whether the Boundary Commission could be properly constituted without a representative appointed by the Northern government.[27] Although the government of Northern Ireland sent lawyers to make submissions to the Judicial Committee, the government of the Irish Free State declined to do so. The Governor-General of the Irish Free State, T.M. Healy, did advise the Irish government to send counsel to argue against the Privy Council's competence to hear this case. Instead, the Irish government refused to consider itself a party to the action.[28] It insisted that the special reference was an internal

20 See Howell, *Judicial Committee*, pp 40–3.

21 W. Harrison Moore, 'The Case of Pental Island', *Law Quarterly Review*, 20 (1904), 236. The Privy Council also heard a boundary dispute between South Australia and Victoria but this was an appeal from the Australian High Court and not a reference under Section 4 of the Judicial Committee Act 1833. *South Australia v. Victoria* [1911] 12 CLR 667.

22 A.B. Keith, *The Constitutional Law of the British Dominions* (London, Macmillan, 1933), p. 275.

23 (1927) 43 TLR 289.

24 Cmd. 2214. See also Cmd. 2155, 2166 and 2264.

25 *Hansard*, House of Commons, vol. 174, col. 1257–61, 4 June 1924.

26 Deborah Lavin, *From Empire to International Commonwealth: A Biography of Lionel Curtis* (Oxford, Clarendon, 1995), p. 222.

27 Cmd. 2214.

28 NAI, dept. of the Taoiseach, S1801I, despatch from T.M. Healy, 5 July 1924.

British matter that merely concerned the British government seeking advice as to its own legal and constitutional powers.[29] Nevertheless, the Irish disliked the special reference to the Privy Council in principle and objected to any further delay in dealing with the issue of the border.[30] The delay was exacerbated when the British government insisted on bringing judges from Australia and Canada to hear the case in order to create a genuinely 'Imperial' tribunal.[31] Although the insistence on bringing in Dominion judges was generally perceived as a delaying measure in the Irish Free State, there were those who saw its advantages. The *Church of Ireland Gazette* concluded that it ensured that 'the most distinguished body of legal opinion in the whole world' would settle the legal issues connected to the boundary question.[32] The *Irish Statesman*, a moderate nationalist newspaper, argued that prime minister James Craig of Northern Ireland, who had often claimed to be a champion of Empire, would find it more difficult to defy the Privy Council if it were representative of the Empire as a whole.[33] Edward Carson, himself a judge who sat on the Privy Council, was accused of insulting the Dominion judiciary when he expressed regret that the British government could not get anyone from the United Kingdom to settle these issues and instead had to go to 'Timbuctoo or somewhere or other'.[34]

The Irish government did not regard itself as a party to these proceedings and, therefore, also refused to consider itself as being bound by any eventual decisions.[35] Nevertheless, there was no doubt that the final decision would have an impact on the Irish Free State. The Judicial Committee finally held that the Northern government could not be compelled to appoint a representative and, consequently, the Boundary Commission could not operate. This decision caused a brief period of panic in London and Dublin as both the British and Irish governments feared that their positions were in danger. The Cosgrave administration feared that its opponents would declare a breach of the Treaty, hold that all elected representatives were now free to enter the Oireachtas without taking the oath and so cause the Irish government to fall. The minority Labour government in London feared that special legislation amending the provisions of the 1921 Treaty concerning the

29 NAI, dept. of the Taoiseach, S1801I, T.M Healy to the registrar of the Privy Council, 10 July 1924. See also *Dáil Debates*, vol. 7, col. 2023–4, 6 June 1924 and vol. 8, col. 1716–24, 18 July 1924.

30 *Dáil Debates*, vol. 7, col. 2611, 18 June 1924.

31 These were Sir Adrian Fox (1863–1932), chief justice of the High Court of Australia, and Sir Lyman P. Duff (1865–1955), a judge of the Canadian Supreme Court who would be appointed chief justice in 1933. The only other occasion in which a Dominion judge sat on an Irish case before the Privy Council occurred when Francis Anglin (1865–1933) sat on the Judicial Committee for *In re Compensation to Civil Servants under Art. X of the Treaty* [1929] IR 44. Anglin was appointed to the Canadian Supreme Court in 1909 and was chief justice from 1924 to 1933.

32 *Church of Ireland Gazette*, 13 June 1924.

33 *Irish Statesman*, 14 June 1924.

34 *Times*, 9 June 1924 and *Irish Statesman*, 14 June 1924.

35 The Irish government argued that the King had not acted on the advice of Irish ministers in referring the matter to the Privy Council. NAI, dept. of the Taoiseach, S1801I, T.M Healy to the registrar of the Privy Council, 10 July 1924. See also *Dáil Debates*, vol. 8, col. 1722, 18 July 1924.

Boundary Commission, that would allow the decision of the Privy Council to be circumvented, might be stalled or defeated in the House of Lords and so lead to a general election.[36] These fears proved to be exaggerated and confidence was soon restored. This allowed the parliaments in Dublin and Westminster to pass parallel legislation providing for the first amendment of the terms of the 1921 Treaty and allowing the British government to appoint a representative for Northern Ireland to sit on the Boundary Commission.[37]

The unusual circumstances surrounding this special reference have resulted in its omission from most accounts of the operation of the Privy Council appeal in Ireland. Nevertheless, it was a significant incident in establishing the relationship between the Irish Free State and the Privy Council appeal. First, the association of the Privy Council appeal with the fiasco of the Boundary Commission, which collapsed in 1924 leaving the border unchanged, did nothing to enhance its reputation in Ireland. Second, the decision itself – that Northern Ireland could not be forced to engage with the Boundary Commission – did little to win Dublin's confidence in having Irish disputes heard by judges from many parts of the British Empire.

The special reference also raised a number of worrying precedents for the future. Irish statesmen noted the absence of any limitations on the subject matter that could be referred to the Privy Council under Section 4 of the Judicial Committee Act 1833.[38] The circumstances of the special reference were used to support the common Irish stereotype of the Judicial Committee of the Privy Council as an instrument of the British government despite the efforts made to include Australian and Canadian judges. Some members of the Oireachtas insisted that the special reference was a blocking device that had been raised at the instigation of the British Colonial Office. It was even claimed that the British had used the special reference as a means of evading the terms of the Treaty while retaining Dominion support.[39] Most important of all, this incident was the first occasion that the Judicial Committee of the Privy Council acted as arbiter of the terms of the Anglo-Irish Treaty, a disturbing prospect for Irish nationalists.[40]

LIMITED TOLERATION OF THE APPEAL

The special legislation passed in Dublin and Westminster permitted the work of the Boundary Commission to continue and so limited the impact of the Privy Council's decision on public consciousness. The decision was eclipsed even within legal circles by its separateness from the ordinary appeal recognized by Article 66

36 TNA, CAB 23/48, 46(24), meeting, 4 Aug. 1924.

37 Treaty (Confirmation of Supplemental Agreement) Act 1924 (Dublin) and Irish Free State (Confirmation of Agreement) Act 1924 (Westminster).

38 NAI, dept. of the Taoiseach, S1801I, despatch from T.M. Healy, 5 July 1924.

39 *Seanad Debates*, vol. 3, col. 671–4, 3 July 1924. 40 Ibid.

of the Irish Constitution and, more importantly, by the dramatic collapse of the work of the Boundary Commission in 1924. The status quo of the border, that followed the established county boundaries, was to remain intact.

The impact of the remarks made by Lords Haldane and Buckmaster in the 1923 applications for leave to appeal, including *Hull v. M'Kenna*, proved more enduring than the special reference on the border. By the mid-1920s there were signs that Irish suspicions with respect to the Privy Council appeal were actually beginning to thaw. The rejection of the first petitions for leave to appeal to the Privy Council ensured that a textbook on Irish constitutional law published in 1925 predicted that the appeal would 'raise no difficulties in the development of the Irish Constitution under conditions of good-will between Ireland and Great Britain'.[41]

The Privy Council appeal even enjoyed a brief 'honeymoon period' in the Irish Free State in the early 1920s. Of course, the appeal won little more than a limited form of toleration and never came close to winning support from the entire population. Irish nationalists remained suspicious of the appeal and the position of relative tolerance was based on the perception that Irish appeals to the Privy Council would be very exceptional events. In 1923 the Seanad was informed by its chairman that the Privy Council would decline to grant leave to appeal to litigants from the Irish Free State unless there was 'some question of national importance involved or except the case raises grave constitutional issues'.[42] Irish governments favoured the ending of appeals to London but did not necessarily advocate formal abolition in the early 1920s. Instead, Irish statesmen predicted that the appeal would gradually be rendered obsolete through non-usage.[43]

The early 1920s even saw signs of positive engagement with the Privy Council appeal. The Irish government did not object when the Privy Council granted leave to appeal in the case of *Wigg and Cochrane v. Attorney General* in 1926.[44] The Irish government engaged with the appeal and appointed lawyers to argue the Irish government's position before the Privy Council. Kevin O'Higgins explained that this case, which raised a dispute over the interpretation of a provision of the 1921 Treaty, concerned relations between members of the British Commonwealth and, as such, was considered to be 'one of the kind of cases that could be admitted'.[45] The Irish government seemed willing to acquiesce in the role of the Privy Council as arbiter of the Treaty.

A few weeks after this example of positive engagement saw Kevin O'Higgins condemn the Judicial Committee of the Privy Council as 'a bad court, a useless

41 John G. Swift MacNeill, *Studies on the Constitution of the Irish Free State* (Dublin, Talbot, 1925), pp xxiii and 83–9.

42 *Seanad Debates*, vol. 1, col. 1570, 30 July 1923.

43 *Dáil Debates*, vol. 1, col. 1402–3, 10 Oct. 1922, vol. 14, col. 124–5 and 132, 27 Jan. 1926, vol. 14, col. 384–5, 3 Feb. 1926 and *Seanad Debates*, vol. 6, col. 401, 24 Feb. 1926.

44 [1925] 1 IR 149; [1927] IR 285 and [1927] IR 293.

45 *Dáil Debates*, vol. 14, col. 134, 27 Jan. 1926. See also *Dáil Debates*, vol. 14, col. 342 and 386, 3 Feb. 1926 and *Seanad Debates*, vol. 6, col. 439 and 386, 24 Feb. 1926.

court, an unnecessary court'. A few months later the Irish government began to openly state its objective to secure eventual abolition of the appeal.[46] What had caused this dramatic change of fortune? How had the limited goodwill that had built up as a result of *Hull v. M'Kenna* been squandered so quickly? The answer to both of these questions lies in the career of one of the most prominent judges who heard Irish appeals to the Privy Council. This judge was Lord Cave, who was widely accused of being biased against the Irish Free State.

LORD CAVE

George Cave (1856–1928) was a barrister and also a Conservative MP between 1906 and 1918. He was appointed solicitor general in 1915 and served as home secretary between 1916 and 1918. Immediately after the conclusion of the First World War Cave was appointed a lord of appeal, which allowed him to sit as a judge in the House of Lords and the Judicial Committee of the Privy Council. In 1925 he defeated former prime minister H.H. Asquith, then Lord Oxford, in the election for the chancellorship of the University of Oxford. Cave became chancellor as a result of party political considerations and solid support from supporters who called themselves 'cavemen'.[47]

Although Cave had originally come from a Liberal background, he broke with that party after Gladstone embraced the cause of Irish home rule in 1885. The related objectives of maintaining the integrity of the British Empire and resistance to Irish nationalism were important features of Cave's political life. He was at the forefront of resistance to Irish home rule in the years before the outbreak of the First World War and openly contributed to publications that opposed granting greater autonomy to Dublin.[48] Cave was also a firm supporter of Ulster's right to secede if the rest of the island of Ireland were granted home rule.[49] His strong unionist sympathies had important consequences for his political and legal careers.

Cave was horrified at the consequences of the Irish rising of Easter 1916. He visited Dublin soon after the event and witnessed the destruction it had wrought on the city at first hand. As a barrister he participated in the prosecution of Roger Casement, one of the leading figures behind the rising. As home secretary, Cave was responsible for the decision to circulate Casement's notorious 'black diaries', containing references to homosexual inclinations, to journalists and other influ-

46 UCDA, Blythe Papers, P24/217, memorandum on the Judicial Committee of the Privy Council and TNA, CAB 32/56 E(IR-26) 4th meeting, 2 Nov. 1926.

47 Thomas S. Legg, Marie-Louise Legg, 'Cave, George, Viscount Cave (1856–1928)', *Oxford Dictionary of National Biography* (Oxford University Press, 2004; online edn, Jan. 2011) http://www.oxforddnb.com/view/article/32329 (accessed 11 Feb. 2015).

48 For example, George Cave, 'The Constitutional Question' in S. Rosenbaum (ed.), *Against Home Rule – The Case for the Union* (London, Frederick Warne, 1912), pp 81–106.

49 Charles Mallet, *Lord Cave: A Memoir* (London, John Murray, 1931), pp 154–5 and 163–5.

ential figures.[50] This decision destroyed Casement's reputation and undermined calls for clemency. Casement was hanged at Pentonville Prison in August 1916.

One of Cave's last duties as home secretary was to assist in drafting a bill intended to extend conscription to Ireland in 1918. The scheme collapsed in the face of mass demonstrations that did much to boost the popularity of the anti-conscription Sinn Féin party. Cave's reputation in Ireland did not improve after he became a judge in 1918.[51] He soon became notorious for refusing a writ of prohibition against a military court that had sentenced two Irishmen to death in 1921.[52] Most important of all, it was widely known that Cave was a firm opponent of the Anglo-Irish Treaty of 1921.[53] L.S. Amery, colonial and Dominions secretary in the late 1920s, wrote in private that Cave was widely perceived to be 'no friend of the [Irish] Free State'.[54]

Cave initially refrained from following the examples set by Lords Carson and Sumner who, despite being lords of appeal, openly condemned the Anglo-Irish Treaty during parliamentary debates in early 1922. Although Cave had some sympathy with their sentiments he felt constrained by the undesirability of serving judges making open declarations on matters of political controversy.[55] His scruples on this matter were overcome by a vigorous campaign waged by his adoring wife and mother.[56] They persisted despite a warning from Lord Birkenhead that a speech on Irish politics would undermine Cave's position as a lord of appeal. The remainder of the story can be told by Lady Cave:

> Mother and I agreed it was not sense to suppose such men should have no voice in that which concerned the country for which they made laws. Mother was so frail and lovely, and also so insistent, that between us we left him in no doubt as to our convictions. For some days he held out. He could not bring himself to break down traditions, but he was most unhappy. He had congratulated Lord Sumner on his very fine speech on the question, although he said 'it was wrong' at the time. Lord Carson was speaking in no uncertain voice. George did not discuss the matter with either Lord Carson or Lord Sumner, but thought out the wrongs and rights in his own mind ... [57]

Cave's wife and mother's determination that he express his opinions on the state of affairs in Ireland eventually bore fruit on 16 March 1922. Cave made a speech to the House of Lords that made it clear that he opposed the Anglo-Irish Treaty

50 Mallet, *Lord Cave*, p. 183.

51 There was an unusual period of overlap between 13 November 1918 and 14 January 1919 when Cave was a lord of appeal and also held office as home secretary.

52 *Re Clifford and O'Sullivan* [1921] 2 AC 570 and Mallet, *Lord Cave*, p. 229.

53 Mallet, *Lord Cave*, p. 253.

54 John Barnes and David Nicholson (eds), *The Leo Amery Diaries*, 2 vols (London, Hutchinson, 1980), i, p. 530.

55 Mallet, *Lord Cave*, p. 27 and pp 251–3.

56 Ibid., at pp 27–8.

57 Ibid.

and identified the embryonic Irish Free State as an entity that was 'far from friendly' to the United Kingdom.[58] The speech received a great deal of attention from a largely hostile press.[59] Cave also had to endure the embarrassment of a detailed debate in the House of Lords concerning political statements made by judges. Partisan interventions by persons holding judicial office were condemned as breaches of constitutional convention.[60] Lord Cave's wife and mother remained unrepentant for their intervention.[61] Nevertheless, their actions had disastrous consequences for Cave's reputation and for the Irish appeal to the Privy Council.

Cave's public stance on the Treaty and the creation of the Irish Free State ensured that he was named, along with Lords Carson and Sumner, during the negotiations on the 1922 Constitution as a hostile judge who was unsuited to hear Irish appeals to the Privy Council.[62] Lionel Curtis wrote, while serving as an official at the colonial office, that it was nothing less than a constitutional calamity 'that at this juncture the Court, which we have always stipulated must be the supreme arbiter in interpreting the Treaty, should have been exposed to the profound distrust of a most suspicious people by the fact that three of its members plunged into party politics'.[63] It may be recalled that Lloyd George assured the Irish delegation in 1922 that judges would be excluded from hearing Irish appeals if they had made politically compromising statements.[64] This was a promise that the British government proved unable to keep.

A new Conservative government under Andrew Bonar Law came to power in October 1922. The new administration selected Lord Cave as its lord chancellor. This office gave Cave extensive powers to select judges to hear particular appeals to the House of Lords and the Judicial Committee of the Privy Council. The exclusion of Lord Cave against his own will from hearing Irish appeals had now been rendered impossible. Of course, Cave could still have excluded himself. Lords Carson and Sumner refrained from sitting on any Irish appeal to the Privy Council in the 1920s and 1930s.[65] Lord Cave showed no such restraint.

58 *Hansard*, House of Lords, vol. 49, col. 606–7, 16 Mar. 1922.
59 Mallet, *Lord Cave*, pp 27–8.
60 *Hansard*, House of Lords, vol. 49, col. 943–4, 29 Mar. 1922.
61 Mallet, *Lord Cave*, pp 27–8.
62 TNA, CAB 23/30 32(22), conclusions of cabinet meeting, 2 June 1922.
63 TNA, CO 739/7/47027, Curtis to Churchill, 20 Sept. 1922.
64 TNA, CAB 23/30, CAB 32(22), conclusions of cabinet meeting, 2 June 1922, TNA, CAB 43/1 SFB 33rd, conference, the Irish situation, 10 Oct. 1922 and NAI, dept. of the Taoiseach, S4285A, Winston Churchill to W.T. Cosgrave, 11 Oct. 1922.
65 In 1925 Lord Carson and Lord Cave did hear an appeal to the Judicial Committee of the House of Lords that directly concerned the Irish Free State. The case of *Attorney General v. Great Southern and Western Railway Company of Ireland* concerned the payment of compensation for the removal of rails and sleepers during the First World War. The House of Lords held that this liability was now vested in the government of the Irish Free State. Cave's judgment included consideration of the railway company's claim that it would have difficulty recovering the sum in question from the Irish government. Cave insisted that this was improbable and added that he did not doubt that the liability imposed on the Irish Free State would be fully honoured. [1925] AC 754 at 766–7. Lord Carson did no more than concur with the judgments of Lord Haldane and Lord Dunedin. [1925] AC 754 at 775.

Cave would hold the office of lord chancellor from 1922 until 1928, with a short interval in 1924 when the first Labour government was in power.[66] This ensured that he was inextricably linked with the Judicial Committee of the Privy Council throughout the formative years of the Irish appeal. His earliest speeches as lord chancellor made repeated references to the importance of the Irish appeal to the Privy Council as arbiter and guardian of the 1921 Treaty.[67] These considerations contributed to the crystallization of a disastrous public image for the Judicial Committee of the Privy Council in Ireland. Darrell Figgis, one of the most prominent figures on the committee that drafted the first Irish Constitution, wrote that the expectation of impartiality from a tribunal with such political links was 'a fool's dream'.[68]

LYNHAM v. BUTLER

The initial period of calm in the history of the Irish appeal to the Privy Council appeal came to an end in 1926 when Lord Cave and his colleagues granted leave to appeal in the case of *Lynham v. Butler*.[69] This case concerned the interpretation of provisions of the Irish Land Act 1923 that were of purely domestic significance. Fears raised in 1922 of the appeal serving as a device for British interference in the internal affairs of the Irish Free State were rapidly revived. The Irish government responded by sending what it termed a 'constitutional protest' to London.[70] A special statute, known as the Land Act 1926, was rushed through the Oireachtas. This legislation confirmed the Irish Supreme Court's interpretation of the Land Act 1923 when it had given judgment in *Lynham v. Butler*. The 1926 Act did not appear to violate the provisions of the 1921 Treaty or any Imperial legislation and so the Privy Council seemed obliged to accept the Irish Supreme Court's interpretation of the 1923 Act. This ensured that there was no longer any useful purpose in continuing the appeal which was withdrawn at the request of the appellants. The incident appeared to show that a grant of leave to appeal to the Privy Council that was contrary to the wishes of the Irish Free State could, as one commentator noted, 'be defeated by the Oireachtas any time it wishes'.[71] Irish opponents of the Treaty were unimpressed with the Land Act 1926 and dismissed it as an electoral stunt.[72] The Irish government could still afford to ignore such begrudgery in 1926.

66 In fact, Cave retained the judicial functions of lord chancellor throughout 1924 as Labour's lord chancellor, Lord Haldane, preferred to devote himself to government business. Haldane, *Autobiography*, pp 324–5.

67 *Hansard*, House of Lords, vol. 52, col. 166–7, 30 Nov. 1922 and col. 181, 1 Dec. 1922.

68 Darrell Figgis, *The Irish Constitution* (Dublin, Mellifont, 1922), p. 54.

69 [1925] 2 IR 82. 70 *Dáil Debates*, vol. 14, col. 339, 3 Feb. 1926.

71 Barra Ó Briain, *The Irish Constitution* (Dublin, Talbot, 1929), p. 124.

72 *Dáil Debates*, vol. 14, col. 387, 3 Feb. 1926.

The Irish government had found an effective method of blocking Privy Council appeals. No attempt at subtlety or stealth was made and the Irish government openly admitted that the purpose of the Land Act 1926 had been designed to undermine the proposed appeal to the Privy Council. There were voices in the Oireachtas that worried that the precedent established by the Land Act 1926 would allow the legislature to interfere with the independence of any court by means of blocking pending litigation.[73] These concerns were drowned out by accusations that the British had broken faith. Kevin O'Higgins insisted that the decision violated undertakings given by the British government in 1922 that had placed definite limits on appeals from the Irish Free State. He condemned the decision to hear this case on the basis that it was nothing less than the first attempt at external intervention in the domestic affairs of the Irish Free State.[74]

There were predictable calls in the Irish Free State for the complete abolition of the Privy Council appeal in place of the temporary solution represented by the Land Act 1926. Yet the Irish government remained uncertain as to its prospects of success in unilaterally abolishing the appeal. Ernest Blythe was obliged to raise the difficult point that abolition would be ineffective as a consequence of the constitutional link with Canada.[75] The *Church of Ireland Gazette* reassured its flock that the Land Act 1926 had not abolished the institution of the Privy Council appeal, which many southern Protestants considered an important minority safeguard.[76] In 1926 the Irish government did not believe that it was within the powers of domestic institutions to abolish the appeal. In time, it would abandon this position.

Cave was always unrepentant for the part he played in initiating the controversy in *Lynham v. Butler*. He had not been a party to the 'assurances' and 'undertakings' given in 1922 on which the Irish government placed so much emphasis. Cave was unimpressed when informed of the existence of these claims. He argued that even if the Lloyd George government had given such assurances in 1922 it was clear that they were making promises that they simply could not keep. The jurisdiction of the Privy Council could not be limited by secret promises that had no basis in law.[77] The Irish negotiators had failed to take this basic consideration into account in 1922.

Cave was unable to prevent the enactment of the Land Act 1926. He and his colleagues seriously considered the possibility of using the crown's power of reservation to effectively veto its enactment.[78] Cave backed away from this radical

73 *Seanad Debates*, vol. 6, col. 415–16 and 437, 24 Feb. 1926 and *Dáil Debates*, vol. 14, col. 342–50, 3 Feb. 1926.

74 *Dáil Debates*, vol. 14, col. 389–90, 3 Feb. 1926.

75 *Dáil Debates*, vol. 14, col. 377–8, 3 Feb. 1926.

76 *Church of Ireland Gazette*, 5 Mar. 1926. See ch. 5, below.

77 TNA, LCO 2/910, lord chancellor to Dominions secretary, 3 Feb. 1926.

78 TNA, CAB 23/52/2, meeting of 29 Jan. 1926; CAB 23/52/8, meeting of 26 Feb. 1926 and DO 117/3, lord chancellor to Dominions secretary, 29 Jan. 1926.

course of action when it became clear that the Land Act 1926 was only aimed at blocking the particular appeal in *Lynham v. Butler*.[79] The lord chancellor was reluctant to make use of the power of reservation until it became clear that the Irish were contemplating a wider assault on the Privy Council appeal.[80] He was convinced that the use of this blunt tool against the Land Act 1926 would radicalize Irish opinion and lead to a vigorous campaign to abolish the Irish appeal. Cave also feared that this agitation might spread to the other Dominions.[81] Nevertheless, it was clear that a dangerous precedent had been set. Cave concluded that the blocking measures used by the Irish Free State against appeals were both 'ingenious and effective'.[82] He told the British cabinet 'if a similar course were followed with regard to other appeals it might be necessary to take action; but that time has not yet arrived'.[83] Cave was soon presented with a method of preventing the prospect of total abolition of the Irish appeal by means other than the controversial power of reservation. This opportunity presented itself in the context of another appeal to the Privy Council.

NADAN v. THE KING

One of the most important cases concerning the relationship between the Irish government and the appeal to the Privy Council did not actually originate in the Irish Free State. In 1926 Lord Cave delivered judgment on behalf of the Privy Council in the Canadian case of *Nadan v. The King*.[84] Canadian appeals to the Privy Council were of direct interest to the Irish Free State because the two countries shared a constitutional link under the 1921 Treaty.

Nadan v. The King concerned a challenge to the legality of Section 1025 of the Canadian Criminal Code 1888 that prohibited appeals to the Privy Council in criminal cases. The legality of this provision had always been dubious as it appeared to be inconsistent with superior Imperial legislation.[85] Nevertheless, the British government had declined to take any real action when the Canadian Criminal Code was enacted in 1888.[86] The Privy Council itself developed a policy

79 TNA, DO 117/3, memorandum on the Irish Free State and the Privy Council, 29 Jan. 1926.
80 TNA, LCO 2/910, lord chancellor to Dominions secretary, 3 Feb. 1926. For Irish attitudes towards the power of reservation see *Dáil Debates*, vol. 1, col. 1168–9, 4 Oct. 1922.
81 TNA, CAB 24/178 SFC 54 (26), memorandum by the lord chancellor, 25 Feb. 1926.
82 TNA, CAB 32/56 E(IR-26) 4th meeting, 2 Nov. 1926. Cave is often misquoted in this capacity as having described the Irish measures as 'effective and ingenious'. For example, see NAI, dept. of the Taoiseach, S4285B, undated memorandum for the Imperial conference, 1930.
83 TNA, CAB 24/178 SFC 54 (26), memorandum by the lord chancellor, 25 Feb. 1926.
84 [1926] AC 482. The other judges who heard the appeal were Viscount Dunedin, Lord Shaw, Lord Phillimore and Lord Blanesburgh.
85 Judicial Committee Acts 1833 and 1844.
86 For example, see TNA, TS 27/678, colonial secretary to Governor-General of Canada, 12 Nov. 1888 and TS 27/678, Risley to Greenwood, 24 July 1925.

of tacit toleration of Section 1025 and declined to grant leave to appeal in criminal cases from Canada. The validity of this provision remained unchallenged for thirty-eight years.

Almost four decades of tacit toleration came to an abrupt close in 1926 in the case of *Nadan v. The King*. In 1924 Lord Cave himself had declined to consider the legality of Section 1025 in another Canadian appeal to the Privy Council.[87] Yet, just two years later, Cave declared that it was 'very desirable that a decision upon the question [of Section 1025] should now be reached'.[88] Cave never explained why such a decision was suddenly so desirable after almost four decades of toleration. Nevertheless, on 25 February 1926 the Privy Council found that Section 1025 of the Canadian Criminal Code was null and void on the grounds that it was incompatible with superior Imperial legislation.

Although the Privy Council had always had the power to strike down Canadian legislation it had not done so for a very long time. The reaction in Canada to the decision in *Nadan v. The King* was a mixture of shock and outrage. The *Manitoba Free Press* concluded that the judgment 'makes short work of the claim that Canada has, in law, any claim to national status'.[89] A few months later the Canadian chief justice concluded 'while this subordination of our courts is maintained, while this badge of inferiority is attached to them, our vaunted Dominion status as a full partner in the Empire seems an idle boast, a sop thrown to our vanity'.[90] The negative reaction to the decision in *Nadan v. The King* was heightened by the belief that this decision was not really aimed at Canada but at the Irish Free State.

There are a number of considerations suggesting that the Privy Council may have had one eye on the Irish Free State when making its decision in *Nadan v. The King*. First, it should be recalled that the Irish Free State had come into existence with the same constitutional status within the Empire as enjoyed by the Dominion of Canada. If Canada could not limit or abolish the appeal to the Privy Council the same position must also apply to the Irish Free State. Second, it should be noted that the constitutional link between the Irish Free State and Canada was actually raised during the pleadings in *Nadan*.[91] The third consideration is that there was no practical necessity to reverse four decades of toleration and strike down the Canadian provision. The Privy Council rarely heard criminal appeals and the subject matter of *Nadan v. The King* was hardly of exceptional significance.[92] It concerned small-scale possession and transportation of intoxicating liquor in

87 *Attorney General for Ontario v. Daly* [1924] AC 1011. This appeal was heard by Lord Cave, Lord Haldane, Lord Dunedin, Lord Shaw and Lord Phillimore. See also *Toronto Railway Company v. The King* [1917] AC 630.

88 [1926] AC 482, 491.

89 *Manitoba Free Press*, 18 Mar. 1926. Quoted in Jacqueline D. Krikorian, 'British Imperial Politics and Judicial Independence: The Judicial Committee's Decision in the Canadian Case *Nadan v. The King*', *Canadian Journal of Political Science*, 33:2 (2000), 291 at 313.

90 David Swinfen, *Imperial Appeal: The Debate on the Appeal to the Privy Council, 1833–1986* (Manchester, Manchester University Press, 1987), p. 17.

91 Krikorian, 'British Imperial Politics' at 308–11.

92 Howell, *Judicial Committee*, pp 103–8.

violation of statutes passed by the Province of Alberta. Once the Privy Council had taken the opportunity to invalidate Section 1025 it then declined to hear the actual appeal in *Nadan*. There was no greater need to strike down Section 1025 of the Canadian Criminal Code in *Nadan v. The King* than at any other time since 1888. The fourth factor that supported the belief that the decision in *Nadan* was really aimed at the Irish Free State was the identity of the person who delivered the judgment. This was Lord Cave.[93] The final consideration that convinced many people that the judgment in *Nadan v. The King* was really aimed at the Irish Free State was the timing of the decision. The judgment was made a few days after the bill that would become the Land Act 1926 was introduced in the Oireachtas. The decision in *Nadan* appears to have been a direct response to the Irish government's 'constitutional protest' at the decision to grant leave to appeal in *Lynham v. Butler*.[94]

British, Irish and Canadian sources in the 1920s were not convinced that the decision in *Nadan v. The King* really concerned Canada. The Canadian department of external affairs concluded 'It is an open secret that one motive in the Privy Council's action [in *Nadan v. The King*] was the desire to be free to hear Irish Free State appeals'.[95] Comments in Canadian newspapers confirm this impression. For example, the *Manitoba Free Press* concluded 'Canada, in addition to having a Privy Council problem of her own, finds herself drawn into the controversy which is now going on as to the right of the Judicial Committee to hear appeals from the Irish Free State'.[96]

Irish legal advisers scrambled to assure their nervous government that there could be no Irish version of *Nadan v. The King*. In fact, this was a real possibility because Irish legislation made it clear that judgments of the Irish Supreme Court in criminal matters would be 'final and conclusive' and ignored the possibility of appeals to the Privy Council.[97] No Irish government could afford to entirely dismiss the possibility of a criminal appeal from the Irish courts to the Privy Council. Arguments that an Irish criminal appeal would be impossible were based on grounds that were disputed by the British government.[98]

93 It seems unlikely that Cave would have been selected to deliver this judgment if he had dissented from it. Decisive evidence on this point may no longer be accessible as the private records of the voting of judges hearing Privy Council appeals were destroyed by a German bomb in 1940. Howell, *Judicial Committee*, pp 203–4.

94 Krikorian, 'British Imperial Politics', 291 and Thomas Mohr, 'Lord Cave, the British Empire and Irish Independence: A Test of Judicial Integrity', *Oxford University Commonwealth Law Journal*, 12:2 (2013), 229.

95 National Archives of Canada, RG 25, vol. 3418, 1–1926/6, 'Notes on the Imperial conference, 1926'. The decision in *Nadan* is also linked to the Irish Free State in K.C. Wheare, *The Statute of Westminster and Dominion Status* (5th ed. Oxford, Oxford University Press, 1953), p. 120.

96 *Manitoba Free Press*, 5 Apr. 1926. Quoted in Krikorian, 'British Imperial Politics' at 313. See also W.P.M. Kennedy, 'The Imperial Conferences, 1926–1930', *Law Quarterly Review*, 48 (1932), 191 at 207.

97 Section 29, Courts of Justice Act 1924.

98 UCDA, Costello Papers, P190/94, memorandum on *Lynham v. Butler*, undated. These assurances

THE CASES ON TRANSFERRED CIVIL SERVANTS

The hostility of the Irish government to the Privy Council appeal reached further heights in the aftermath of the decision in *Wigg and Cochrane v. The Attorney General of the Irish Free State*.[99] The case concerned the level of compensation payable to transferred civil servants in Ireland under Article 10 of the 1921 Treaty.[100] Many of the transferred civil servants disputed the level of compensation determined by the Irish Supreme Court and finally took an appeal to the Judicial Committee of the Privy Council.[101] The controversial decision that resulted from this appeal was delivered by Lord Cave in 1927. This judgment concluded that the civil servants were entitled to a higher level of compensation than had been calculated by the Irish Supreme Court.

The Irish government responded by sending a despatch to London complaining that a basic error had been made in this decision.[102] It argued that the judgment had mixed up a number of key dates and that this error invalidated the entire decision.[103] The Irish government refused to pay any extra compensation. It feared that the Irish civil service might collapse as a consequence of a rush of civil servants wishing to retire on the favourable terms offered in the Privy Council decision.[104] Many Irish nationalists now added accusations of incompetence to their list of grievances against the Privy Council. John J. Hearne, legal adviser to the department of external affairs, felt entitled to accuse the Judicial Committee of 'criminal ignorance' with respect to Irish law.[105] D.A. Binchy, a leading Irish academic and a future ambassador to Germany, wrote a newspaper article that used the embarrassment caused by the error to challenge those who believed that 'Free

were based on arguments that Imperial statutes, such as the Judicial Committee Act 1844 and the Colonial Laws Validity Act 1865, did not apply to the Irish Free State. British governments did not accept these arguments. See Thomas Mohr, 'The Colonial Laws Validity Act and the Irish Free State', *Irish Jurist*, 43 (2008), 21.

99 [1927] IR 285, 293.

100 Article 10, Articles of Agreement for Treaty between Great Britain and Ireland. See Martin Maguire, *The Civil Service and the Revolution in Ireland, 1912–1938* (Manchester, Manchester University Press, 2008), pp 182–95.

101 [1925] 1 IR 149.

102 R.F.V. Heuston, *Lives of the Lord Chancellors, 1885–1940* (Oxford, Clarendon, 1964), p. 441.

103 The Privy Council had apparently calculated the compensation on the assumption that a minute of the British treasury, which came into effect on 20 March 1922, had not been applicable. Lord Cave and the rest of the Privy Council had been under the impression that the civil servants had already been transferred on 20 March whereas, in fact, they had not been transferred until 1 April. [1927] IR 285 at 291.

104 Maguire, *Civil Service*, p. 190.

105 NAI, dept. of foreign affairs, GR 469, Hearne to Martin Eliasoff, 13 Aug. 1930. In 1926 Kevin O'Higgins made much of Lord Dunedin's admission in the preliminary hearing of *Lynham v. Butler* that he was unfamiliar with the Land Act 1923. *Dáil Debates*, vol. 14, col. 333–4, 3 Feb. 1926 and NAI, dept. of the Taoiseach, S11749, shorthand notes of petition for leave to appeal in *Lynham v. Butler*, 7 Dec. 1925. See also Hector Hughes, *National Sovereignty and Judicial Autonomy in the British Commonwealth of Nations* (London, P.S. King, 1931), p. 97.

State Courts should prostrate themselves perpetually in awe before the majestic presence of the Judicial Committee of the Privy Council'.[106]

Although the error was certainly embarrassing, the actions of the Irish government in refusing to implement the decision of the Privy Council also provoked severe criticism. The *Church of Ireland Gazette* accused the Irish government of violating its own Constitution and 'playing fast and loose with Treaty obligations'.[107] Members of the government of Northern Ireland accused the Free State government of violating the rights of their own citizens and so justifying the continuation of partition.[108]

Some observers who were not normally inclined to defend the Privy Council appeal were nevertheless uncomfortable with the prospect of the Irish government simply ignoring the decision of a court of law because it had not given a desired judgment. The *Irish Independent* condemned the repudiation of a judgment of the Privy Council that the Irish government had agreed to accept as final. The actions of the Irish government were also condemned as setting a poor example for private litigants.[109] Professor William Magennis of University College Dublin publicly criticized the stance advocated by the minister for finance, Ernest Blythe, to ignore the decision:

> [T]he Minister admitted the jurisdiction of the Empire Court, for he briefed lawyers and pleaded his case before it. Had the Privy Council decided in his favour, he would undoubtedly have claimed the victory, and abiding by the decision as final and authoritative, would have enforced it rigorously with costs against the appellants. Because he has lost he refuses to abide by the decision! Is this not on all fours with the despicable trick of the gamester who backs horses on credit with a bookmaker, collects all his winnings when he has winners, until having at last backed the wrong horse, he refuses to pay his 'debt of honour' and pleads the Gaming Act to evade his liabilities?[110]

Lord Cave was on his deathbed when this controversy erupted. It is possible that his declining health and that of some of his colleagues who had heard *Wigg and Cochrane* had contributed to the confusion over dates.[111] Cave soon became

106 *Irish Statesman*, 5 May 1928. Daniel Anthony Binchy (1900–89) was a leading authority on linguistics and early Irish law at the Dublin Institute for Advanced Studies. He served as Irish ambassador to Germany from 1929 to 1932. *Dictionary of Irish Biography*, vol. 1, pp 531–5.

107 *Church of Ireland Gazette*, 29 Nov. 1929.

108 Ibid.

109 Quoted in *Hansard*, House of Lords, vol. 70, col. 819, 25 Apr. 1928. There were many observers, including the *Times*, who admitted that the Irish means of calculating compensation was more equitable than that imposed by the Privy Council but who, nonetheless, condemned the position adopted by the Irish government throughout this controversy. *Times*, 16 Nov. 1928.

110 Quoted in *Hansard*, House of Lords, vol. 70, col. 819–20, 25 Apr. 1928.

111 Ibid., at col. 834–41. Sir Claud Schuster claimed that Cave had been in a state of physical distress during the hearing of *Wigg and Cochrane* which, in all probability, accounted for the mistake. TNA, LCO 2/910, memorandum by Sir Claud Schuster, 6 Nov. 1930. Lord Haldane

entangled in one of the strangest events in British parliamentary and legal history. On the 25 April 1928 Lord Haldane rose in the House of Lords to admit that the Judicial Committee, of which he had been a member, had made a serious error in reaching judgment in *Wigg and Cochrane*. Haldane was not alone in this *mea culpa*. A shocked house looked on as law lord after law lord rose from their seats and admitted that a mistake had been made in relation to the Irish appeal. Lord Dunedin declared that it was no pleasant matter to 'stand in a white sheet and say that you were wrong' but that, on the other hand, he considered it 'cowardly for a man to run away and not accept his share of responsibility'.[112] Lord Finlay, another former lord chancellor who had heard the appeal in *Wigg and Cochrane*, avoided this humiliating exhibition by pleading ill health.[113] However, Lord Cave played a very prominent role in the collective admission of error despite the considerable handicap of having died some weeks earlier.

Lord Birkenhead revealed that the decision in *Wigg and Cochrane* had preyed on Cave's mind at a time when his life was rapidly drawing to a close. Cave dictated a letter to the prime minister on this matter just three days before his death. Lord Birkenhead told the House of Lords that the dying lord chancellor had admitted that aspects of his decision in *Wigg and Cochrane* were 'probably wrong in law' and took full responsibility for the error. Birkenhead told the House of Lords, with great dramatic effect, that Cave had been such a faithful servant of public duty that he could not rest until he had discharged this final act of public service.[114]

It was decided to refer the matter back to the Privy Council using special means that allowed the government to argue that it was not technically a rehearing of *Wigg and Cochrane*.[115] This proved to be extremely unfortunate in terms of the history of the Irish appeal. The second decision exacerbated an already tense situation when it upheld the original decision in *Wigg and Cochrane*.[116] The Irish government had clearly not expected this outcome and refused to accept it. Irish ministers were convinced that the Privy Council had compounded one embarrassing mistake by a second even more ignominious error.[117] Once again, the Irish were not prepared to pay the extra compensation awarded by the Privy Council and a serious political dispute followed. This was only resolved when an

was also unwell and approaching death during the decision in *Wigg and Cochrane*. He finally died on 19 August 1928. Heuston, *Lord Chancellors*, pp 236–7.

112 *Hansard*, House of Lords, vol. 70, col. 832, 25 Apr. 1928.

113 Ibid., at col. 826.

114 Ibid., at col. 838–9.

115 The second case on the transferred civil servants was not an appeal involving private litigants but a special reference made at the behest of the British government under Section 4 of the Judicial Committee Act 1833. This provision allowed the British government to refer any matter for consideration by the Privy Council.

116 *In re Compensation to Civil Servants under Article X of the Treaty* [1929] IR 44. This case was heard by the Marquess of Reading, Lord Phillimore, Lord Hanworth, Lord Alness and Anglin CJ.

117 *Dáil Debates*, vol. 32, col. 665, 31 Oct. 1929; *Irish Independent*, 14 Nov. 1928 and *Irish Times*, 15 Nov. 1928.

exasperated British government agreed to pass special legislation and pay the extra compensation itself.[118]

The debacle of the two decisions on the transferred civil servants removed the last vestiges of Irish tolerance for the Privy Council appeal. In 1926 the Irish government had claimed that it might be satisfied with limiting the Irish appeal in place of complete abolition.[119] By 1930 the total abolition of the appeal became one of the main policy objectives of the Irish government.

DID LORD CAVE KILL THE IRISH APPEAL TO THE PRIVY COUNCIL?

To what extent was Lord Cave responsible for the disastrous history of the Irish appeal? Cave's delivery of the judgment in the Canadian case of *Nadan v. The King* ensured that his name was associated with this controversial decision. In addition, Cave openly admitted responsibility for granting special leave to appeal in *Lynham v. Butler* and for the flawed decision in *Wigg and Cochrane v. Attorney General*.[120] He told the House of Lords that he had granted leave to appeal in *Lynham v. Butler* because he believed that the case 'was of importance' and that it 'affected a considerable number of people in the Free State'.[121]

Lord Cave had very different ideas as to the nature of the Irish appeal to the Privy Council than those held by the Lloyd George government that had first insisted upon its recognition by the Irish Constitution of 1922. The Lloyd George government saw the appeal as a vital symbol of Dominion status but also as a means of safeguarding the terms of the 1921 Treaty and the rights of the southern Protestant community. These were powers to be held in reserve and, as far as the Irish government was concerned, the Lloyd George government had given definite assurances that Irish appeals would be very exceptional events. This led Kevin O'Higgins to predict in 1922 that there would be two or three appeals at most in the forthcoming century.[122] By contrast, Lord Cave did not see the appeal to the Privy Council from the Irish courts as a power to be held in reserve for cases concerning the 1921 Treaty or the rights of southern Protestants. Instead of two or three appeals in a century, the Privy Council heard four cases from the Irish Free State in just over three years.[123]

118 Civil Service (Transferred Officers) Compensation Act 1929 (Dublin) and the Irish Free State (Confirmation of Agreement) Act 1929 (Westminster).

119 TNA, CAB 32/56 E(IR-26) 4th meeting, 2 Nov. 1926.

120 The other two judges who heard the petition for leave to appeal in *Lynham v. Butler* were Lord Dunedin and Lord Shaw of Dunfermline.

121 *Hansard*, House of Lords, vol. 63, col. 403, 3 Mar. 1926. See also TNA, LCO 2/910, lord chancellor to Dominions secretary, 3 Feb. 1926; CAB 24/174 SFC 54 (26), memorandum by the lord chancellor, 25 Feb. 1926 and NAI, dept. of the Taoiseach, S11749, shorthand notes of petition for leave to appeal in *Lynham v. Butler*, 7 Dec. 1925.

122 *Dáil Debates*, vol. 1, col. 1404, 10 Oct. 1922. See also letter of 22 Sept. 1922 from Kevin O'Higgins to Thomas Johnson, *Irish Times*, 23 Sept. 1922. *Dáil Debates*, vol. 1, col. 1413–14, 10 Oct. 1922.

123 *Lynham v. Butler* (1926), NAI, dept. of the Taoiseach, S11749, shorthand notes of petition for

The Irish government was deeply alarmed at the prospect of seeing regular appeals from the Irish Supreme Court to the Judicial Committee of the Privy Council in cases that concerned disputes of purely internal significance. It was not just the number of Irish appeals actually heard by the Privy Council that so disturbed the government. It was also dismayed at the sheer number of cases in which leave to appeal was sought, even though leave was refused in most cases. The appeal was proving increasingly popular with dissatisfied Irish litigants. Kevin O'Higgins complained that all sorts of 'trumpery cases' were being brought to London for consideration as to whether they were worthy of the attention of the Privy Council. O'Higgins saw this development as part of 'a conscious and deliberate effort to widen the appeal and to make it a matter of course'.[124] The Irish government saw appeals dealing with domestic issues as a far greater threat to Irish sovereignty than having the Privy Council act as arbiter of the 1921 Treaty. It feared that the Judicial Committee of the Privy Council was asserting the same position over the self-governing Irish Free State as had been enjoyed by the House of Lords over the island of Ireland as a part of the United Kingdom.[125]

There are a number of points that should be raised in Lord Cave's defence. Cave was not 'anti-Irish' in his personal sentiments. He was certainly opposed to the brutal tactics adopted by the temporary constables of the Royal Irish Constabulary, popularly known as the 'Black and Tans', during the Anglo-Irish conflict of 1919 to 1921.[126] He was on friendly terms with the moderate Irish nationalist T.M. Healy, who would eventually become the first Governor-General of the Irish Free State in 1922.[127] As home secretary he allowed Countess Constance Markievicz, the most prominent female figure within Irish nationalism, to receive a visit from her sister when she was imprisoned under sentence of death for participation in the Irish uprising of 1916.[128] It is open to debate whether these considerations would have affected Cave's reputation in Ireland if they had been common knowledge during his lifetime.

In fact, the fundamental error made by Cave pre-dates all of the aforementioned appeals to the Privy Council. His most serious mistake was getting mixed up in the quagmire of Irish politics while holding high judicial office. Cave was not the only person who found himself in this embarrassing situation. Nevertheless, his interventions were of sufficient force to attract condemnation in Ireland, at Westminster and even within the British cabinet itself.[129] On one

leave to appeal, 7 Dec. 1925; *Wigg and Cochrane v The Attorney General of the Irish Free State* [1927] IR 285; *In the Matter of the Reference as to the Tribunal under Article 12 of the Schedule appended to the Irish Free State Agreement Act 1922*. Cmd. 2214 and *Performing Right Society v. Bray U.D.C.* [1930] IR 509.

124 TNA, CAB 32/56 E(IR-26) 4th meeting, 2 Nov. 1926.

125 Ibid. See also *Dáil Debates*, vol. 14, col. 338, 3 Feb. 1926 and *Seanad Debates*, vol. 6, col. 409, 24 Feb. 1926.

126 Mallet, *Lord Cave*, p. 251. 127 Ibid., at pp 201 and 222. 128 Ibid., at p. 201.

129 For example, see TNA, CAB 23/30, CAB 32(22), conclusions of cabinet meeting, 2 June 1922 and Thomas Jones, *Whitehall Diary*, 3 vols (London, Oxford University Press, 1971), iii, p. 206.

occasion, Cave was criticized for his remarks in the House of Lords concerning the border of Northern Ireland. Cave responded by making a public pledge that he would refrain from sitting on any deliberations by the Privy Council on this matter.[130] He was true to his word. In 1924 Cave was absent from the Judicial Committee when it heard a special reference concerning the Irish Boundary Commission.[131] One biographer of Cave has questioned the wisdom of giving this pledge.[132] Yet, it could be argued that Cave's real error was in failing to expand on this pledge given that his interventions in Irish politics went far beyond the question of the border.

The real error made by Lord Cave in *Lynham v. Butler, Wigg and Cochrane v. Attorney General* and perhaps even in *Nadan v. The King* was the decision to select himself as one of the judges to hear these cases. Cave was aware that Irish nationalists perceived the Privy Council as an alien tribunal and had long anticipated that enforcing unpopular decisions would be extremely difficult.[133] Nevertheless, he seemed unwilling to exclude himself from key appeals that directly or indirectly concerned the interests of the Irish Free State. The decisions made in these cases and the timing of the decision in *Nadan v. The King* suggest that Cave was not above using his judicial position to safeguard and expand the jurisdiction of the Privy Council with respect to the Irish Free State. Yet, these decisions had precisely the opposite effect that Cave appears to have intended. In fact, these decisions damaged the appeal to the Privy Council from the Canadian courts and hastened the demise of the appeal from the Irish courts.

Cave was not the only judge who sat on the Judicial Committee in the 1920s and the existence of the single judgment rule should not be used to suggest that this court was a monolith. Lord Cave's approach to the Irish appeal can be contrasted with that taken by other members of the Judicial Committee. Lord Haldane saw the Irish appeal as an instrument that should be held in reserve for matters of exceptional importance.[134] Would the history of the Irish appeal to the Privy Council have been different if another judge had occupied the office of lord chancellor during the formative years of the Irish Free State?

Irish perceptions of the appeal to the Privy Council as a diminution of national sovereignty ensured that it was never likely to be a permanent feature in the constitutional law of the Irish Free State. It is easy to argue that the abolition of the appeal, the dismantling of the terms of the 1921 Treaty and Irish secession from

130 *Hansard*, House of Lords, vol. 49, col. 689, 21 Mar. 1922 and col. 942–3, 29 Mar. 1922.

131 *In the Matter of the Reference as to the Tribunal under Article 12 of the Schedule appended to the Irish Free State Agreement Act 1922.* Cmd. 2214.

132 Heuston, *Lord Chancellors*, p. 423.

133 Cave had anticipated these realities long before the signing of the 1921 Treaty. See George Cave, 'The Constitutional Question' in S. Rosenbaum (ed.), *Against Home Rule – The Case for the Union* (London, Frederick Warne, 1912), pp 81 at 95.

134 *Hull and Co. v. M'Kenna; 'Freeman's Journal' Limited v. Erik Fernstrom* and *'Freeman's Journal' Limited v. Follum Traesliberi.* [1926] IR 402. The judges who heard this petition for leave to appeal were Viscount Haldane, Lord Buckmaster and Lord Parmoor.

the Commonwealth, would have occurred without the interventions of Lord Cave. Although the circumstances that surrounded the origins of the Irish Free State ensured that the history of the Irish appeal was always likely to be brief this does not mean that all aspects of it were inevitable. This is illustrated by the brief period of limited toleration for the Privy Council appeal that existed between 1923 and 1926. The rapid deterioration in relations that followed was the direct result of a number of unfortunate decisions between 1926 and 1928 that can be attributed to Lord Cave. These judgments converted a spirit of suspicious toleration of the appeal into one of uncompromising opposition. Although eventual abolition of the Irish appeal to the Privy Council was inevitable, the bitter and antagonistic history that preceded it was not. The decisions delivered by Lord Cave ensured that complete abolition of the Irish appeal to the Privy Council had become a prime objective of Irish external policy even though the appeal had only been in existence for a few short years. These decisions also guaranteed that the policy of seeking abolition of the appeal enjoyed cross-party support in the Oireachtas in the early 1930s.

Yet there was a section of the Irish population that supported the maintenance of the Irish appeal to the Privy Council and protested the policy of seeking abolition. It should be remembered that one of the reasons that the British government insisted that their Irish counterparts accept the appeal, apart from establishing a reliable arbiter of the Treaty, was to offer a means of safeguarding the rights of the Protestant community that lived in the Irish Free State. Irish governments would later attack this position by arguing that the great majority of southern Protestants did not value or desire the appeal as a minority safeguard.

The assertion that the Privy Council offered a minority safeguard in the Irish Free State increased perceptions of bias among the majority Catholic community. For example, it was widely believed in Ireland that Lord Cave had granted leave to appeal in *Lynham v. Butler* on the mistaken assumption that the case would affect a considerable number of Anglo-Irish landlords.[135] These rumours reflect how deeply entangled the Privy Council appeal had become with sectarian divisions in the Irish Free State.

135 Hughes, *National Sovereignty*, p. 99.

CHAPTER FIVE

A minority safeguard for southern Protestants?

'[C]ertain people differing from the majority in religion, and perhaps also, and I am not sure of that, even in political outlook, were driven from their homes and from their positions in greater numbers than I was aware of until quite recently'.

Kevin O'Higgins, minister for home affairs, 21 September 1922[1]

EX-UNIONISTS?

THE LARGE NUMBER OF loyal British subjects 'abandoned' in the southern and western parts of Ireland remained an emotive issue at Westminster and in the British press for many years after 1922. The secession of the Irish Free State from the United Kingdom, including Northern Ireland, in 1922 left a large number of Irish Protestants on the southern side of the border. In the 1926 census there were just over 200,000 Protestants in the Irish Free State out of a total population of just under three million.[2] This was a considerable reduction from the 1911 census that recorded over 300,000 Protestants out of a total population of just over three million in the territory that would later become the Irish Free State.[3] It is difficult to attribute this disparity in numbers to anything other than the traumatic birth of the Irish Free State. A reduction of one-third in just fifteen years cannot be explained by high mortality, low fertility, religious conversions or even the withdrawal of British security forces in 1922.

The Protestant population of the Irish Free State were often referred to as 'southern unionists' or 'southern loyalists'. Not all Protestants living in the Irish Free State would have described themselves in these terms. For example, Ernest Blythe, a Presbyterian born in Country Antrim, was an ardent nationalist who held

1 *Dáil Debates*, vol.1, col. 572, 21 Sept. 1922.
2 In this context, the term 'Protestants' includes Episcopalians, Presbyterians, Methodists and Baptists. The decline in the Protestant population of the twenty-six counties that would eventually form the Irish Free State is discussed in Robert E. Kennedy, *The Irish: Emigration, Marriage and Fertility* (Berkeley, University of California Press, 1973), pp 110–38.
3 Kennedy, *The Irish*, pp 110–38.

several Irish ministerial portfolios in the 1920s and 1930s.[4] The term 'southern unionist' would certainly not have been an accurate description of the political views of Mabel FitzGerald (née McConnell) despite her Presbyterian background. Her son Garrett, who would hold the office of Taoiseach for much of the 1980s, later wrote of how his mother, 'in a moment of revolutionary fervour, told her former employer, George Bernard Shaw, that she would bring her eldest son up to hate England'.[5] It should also be noted that many 'southern unionists' were not actually Protestants.[6]

Despite the dramatic drop in their numbers, a significant number of southern Protestants remained in the new Irish Free State. Many of these continued to identify with unionist traditions despite being commonly referred to as 'ex-unionists' or 'former unionists'.[7] Even those who lacked unionist sentiment risked discrimination on sectarian grounds. Consequently, the minority community as a whole were given a number of purported safeguards of their religious and political rights during the birth of the Irish Free State.

MINORITY SAFEGUARDS

Soon after the signing of the 1921 Treaty the British and Irish governments agreed on a number of measures designed to reassure southern Protestants. Article 8 of the Constitution of the Irish Free State provided guarantees of freedom of conscience and free profession and practice of religion that were derived from earlier British legislation designed to grant Irish home rule.[8] The new Irish parliament, known as the Oireachtas, included an upper house of parliament, or Seanad, that was to be elected from a single electoral area that spanned the entire Irish Free State.[9] The lower house, or Dáil, was to be elected on a proportional

4 (1889–1975) minister for trade and commerce, first and second Dáil 1919–22; minister for local government 1922–3; minister for finance 1923–32 and vice-president of the executive council 1927–32.

5 Garret FitzGerald, *Ireland in the World* (Dublin, Liberties, 2005), p. 189.

6 A detailed account of the Catholic unionist tradition is provided in John Biggs-Davison and George Chowdharay-Best, *The Cross of Saint Patrick: The Catholic Unionist Tradition in Ireland* (Buckinghamshire, Kensal, 1984).

7 For example, TNA, CAB 32/56 E(I.R.26) 4th meeting, 2 Nov. 1926, UCDA, McGilligan Papers, P35B/108 and NAI, dept. of the Taoiseach, S4285B, transcript of radio broadcast of 9 Nov. 1930. These terms were sometimes used by southern Protestant sources, e.g., *Irish Times*, 13 Feb. 1932. They are still occasionally used today, e.g., L. Weeks, 'We Don't Like (to) Party – A Typology of Independents in Irish Political Life, 1922–2007', *Irish Political Studies*, 24:1 (2009), 1 at 14.

8 These provisions were based on Section 3 of the Government of Ireland Act 1914 and Section 5(1) of the Government of Ireland Act 1920. Similar provisions had, in turn, been replicated in Article 16 of the 1921 Treaty. The sensitivity of religious matters resulted in a reluctance to depart from this established formula in 1922. In the 1930s de Valera also seems to have recognized the need to tread carefully in this area. Almost identical provisions to those that appeared in the 1922 Constitution now appear in Article 44 of the current Constitution of 1937.

9 Article 32, Constitution of the Irish Free State.

representation voting system. Both measures were designed to ensure that the minority Protestant population, scattered throughout the territory of the new state, would be able to elect some representatives to the Oireachtas. In addition, eleventh-hour amendments provided that three representatives from Trinity College Dublin and three from the National University of Ireland would sit in the Dáil.[10] The guarantee of three representatives from Trinity College Dublin, at this time a bastion of the minority community, was often perceived as a concession to southern Protestants.[11]

The first Seanad, which as a transitional measure had half of its members elected by the Dáil and the other half nominated by the president of the executive council,[12] included many prominent southern Protestants. These included W.B. Yeats, Oliver St John Gogarty, Sir Horace Plunkett, the earl of Dunraven, James Douglas, the earl of Granard, Andrew Jameson, the earl of Kerry, Alice Stopford Green, the earl of Mayo, the marquess of Headfort, the earl of Wicklow and Douglas Hyde, who would go on to serve as president of Ireland between 1938 and 1945. The first chairman or Cathaoirleach of the Seanad was Lord Glenavy.[13] This list, which is not exhaustive, is notable for the large number of titled gentry and for its mixture of Protestants of nationalist and unionist sympathies. The composition of the Seanad between 1922 and 1936 does reflect a perceived need to reconcile an insecure minority community to the new state and its institutions.

THE PRIVY COUNCIL APPEAL AS A MINORITY SAFEGUARD

Not all southern Protestants were convinced that the limited powers of the Seanad offered them a real minority safeguard.[14] Nevertheless, there was an additional institution that was intended to act as a final safeguard in the event that an oppressive Irish government should ever come to power. British ministers

10 Article 27, Constitution of the Irish Free State.

11 University representation was originally intended for the Seanad and not the Dáil. The original initiative to move university representation from the upper to the lower house was not based on arguments relating to safeguards for southern Protestants. *Dáil Debates*, vol.1, col. 1106–33, 4 Oct. 1922. However, this initiative was soon perceived in this light. This factor certainly influenced the success of the relevant amendment. *Dáil Debates*, vol.1, col. 1151–7, 4 Oct. 1922; col. 1725, 18 Oct. 1922 and col. 1916–17, 25 Oct. 1922. University representation in the Dáil was removed alongside abolition of the institution of the Seanad in 1936. Constitution (Amendment No. 23) Act 1936 and Constitution (Amendment No. 24) Act 1936.

12 Article 82, Constitution of the Irish Free State.

13 James Henry Mussen Campbell, first Baron Glenavy (1851–1931), was a barrister and unionist MP. He served as solicitor general for Ireland (1901–5), attorney general for Ireland (1905 and 1916), lord chief justice of Ireland (1916–18) and lord chancellor of Ireland (1918–21). On his retirement from the office of lord chancellor he was created Baron Glenavy of Milltown, Co. Dublin. In 1923 he was appointed as chairman of the Judiciary Committee that advised the Irish government on the creation of a new judicial system. He held the office of Cathaoirleach of Seanad Éireann from 1922 to 1928.

14 *Irish Times*, 16 June 1922.

promoted the Privy Council appeal as a safeguard of the Protestant minority immediately after the signing of the 1921 Treaty.[15] There were definite precedents for the appeal as a minority safeguard. The Privy Council appeal was seen as safeguarding the rights of other minority groups throughout the British Empire, such as the French-speaking community in Canada and the Maoris of New Zealand.[16] In later years the appeal would be promoted as a safeguard for the European and Asian minorities in post-independence Kenya.[17]

The controversial origins of the Irish appeal and the perceived diminution of sovereignty ensured that Irish governments already had ample reasons to dislike this institution. However, the suggestion that the rights of southern Protestants required protection by means of recourse to an external court was often perceived as an insult to the honour of the infant Irish Free State.[18] Irish government ministers asserted with total confidence that the great majority of southern Protestants did not actually want this purported safeguard. Patrick McGilligan, minister for external affairs, insisted 'The religious minority numbers one in nine of the entire population, of these, not an infinitesimal proportion desires the retention of the appeal'.[19] W.T. Cosgrave, first president of the executive council, wrote 'As a Court there is no support for it here outside of a small section of the minority'.[20] McGilligan dismissed those who did support the appeal as a 'small clique', 'a handful of extremists' and even 'a small group … who wish to perpetuate religious strife'.[21] Some of these contentions have received the support of historians writing in recent decades who have been content to repeat these claims and insist that the appeal enjoyed the support of 'a tiny vociferous, proportion of former Unionists'.[22]

In 1930, the Irish government ordered an extensive search of its files on the negotiations that led to the signing of the 1921 Treaty in order to discover any discussions on the appeal to the Privy Council as a minority safeguard.[23] The

15 TNA, CAB 43/1 SFB 21, meeting between representatives of the southern unionists and the British representatives on the conference on Ireland, 7 Dec. 1921.
16 For example, see David Harkness, *The Restless Dominion* (New York, New York University Press, 1969), pp 93 and 114 and Megan Richardson, 'The Privy Council and New Zealand', *International and Comparative Law Quarterly*, 46 (1997), 908.
17 Bonny Ibhawoh, *Imperial Justice: Africans in Empire's Court* (Oxford, Oxford University Press, 2013), pp 168–71.
18 NAI, dept. of foreign affairs, 3/1, draft speech on abolition of appeals to the Privy Council, undated 1933.
19 UCDA, McGilligan Papers, P35/166, draft article 'Irish Free State and the Judicial Committee of the Privy Council', undated.
20 NAI, unregistered papers, letter from Michael McDunphy to Diarmuid O'Hegarty with enclosure of draft letter from W.T. Cosgrave to Lord Granard, 7 Nov. 1930 in *Documents on Irish Foreign Policy*, vol. 3 (Dublin, Royal Irish Academy, 2002), p. 688.
21 *The Star*, May 1931.
22 David B. Swinfen, *Imperial Appeal* (Manchester, Manchester University Press, 1987), p. 124.
23 NAI, dept. of the Taoiseach, S4285A, Michael McDunphy to W.T. Cosgrave, 8 Nov. 1930 and Michael McDunphy to Diarmuid O'Hegarty, 8 Nov. 1930.

failure to find any bilateral negotiations on this issue buttressed Irish perceptions that this purported safeguard had been invented in the years that followed 1921 as a device for obstructing the desire of Irish governments to abolish the appeal.[24] If Irish officials had examined pre-1921 material they might have found evidence that contradicted their insistence that the use of the Privy Council appeal as a minority safeguard had only been invented after the signature of the Treaty. The bills and Acts relating to Irish home rule made it clear that the Privy Council had been intended to act as the arbiter of these settlements in the event of dispute.[25] In this context, the Privy Council appeal had long been promoted as a safeguard for Irish Protestants living under a home rule parliament.[26]

The potential offered by the Privy Council appeal to safeguard the rights of southern Protestants gained greater importance as the possibility of complete secession of parts of Ireland from the United Kingdom became a real possibility. Southern Protestant representatives discussed this safeguard with the British government before and immediately after the signature of the 1921 Treaty. The day after the Treaty was signed Lloyd George met a delegation of southern Protestants, consisting of Lord Midleton, Lord Desart, John Henry Bernard and Andrew Jameson. The British prime minister used the prospect of the Privy Council appeal to counter Midleton's complaint that the terms of the Treaty offered nothing to southern Protestants.[27] Although this safeguard was not mentioned in the text of the Treaty, Lloyd George revealed the intention of the British government to use the constitutional link with Canada in the Treaty to secure an appeal to the Privy Council from the Irish courts.[28]

Rejection of the minority safeguard argument became more vociferous as the attitude of the Irish government hardened towards the Privy Council in the aftermath of the dispute surrounding *Lynham v Butler* and the appeals concerning transferred civil servants. In 1930 Patrick McGilligan made a radio broadcast to the United States of America that consisted, for the most part, of a denunciation of the Irish appeal to the Privy Council. It was presented as 'the last element of British control in Ireland'. McGilligan was particularly eager to refute the argument that the appeal was of any utility as a minority safeguard. According to McGilligan, 'Irish Catholics have never been guilty of religious intolerance'. This sweeping statement did not prevent McGilligan from describing southern

24 This formed the basis for a line of argument that was used in successive bilateral negotiations and at the Imperial conferences of the 1920s and 1930s. For example, see TNA, CAB 32/79 PM(30)18, Appendix, meeting of prime ministers and heads of delegations, 5 Nov. 1930 and NAI, dept. of the Taoiseach, S4285A, memorandum for the Imperial conference of 1930, undated.

25 See ch. 2, below.

26 For example, see Sir John MacDonell, 'Constitutional Limitations upon the Powers of the Irish Legislature and the Protection of Minorities' in J.H. Morgan (ed.), *The New Irish Constitution* (London, Hodder and Stoughton, 1912), p. 110.

27 TNA, CAB 43/1 SFB 21, meeting between representatives of the southern unionists and the British representatives on the conference on Ireland, 7 Dec. 1921.

28 Ibid.

Protestants as 'people whose ancestors had been responsible for a regime of religious bigotry and intolerance in Ireland'. He also associated them with 'the remnants of a class which had lived on the toil of Irish peasants working on lands which centuries ago had been torn from the Irish people'.[29]

Although the Irish government was deeply hostile to the idea that the Judicial Committee of the Privy Council might act as the champion of the minority community in the Irish Free State, it had to recognize that this contention created a serious obstacle to the abolition of the appeal. Complaints made by Irish ministers that this issue had not been examined in detail during the Anglo-Irish negotiations of 1921 and 1922 were not sufficient to remove this issue from the political agenda in the years that followed. This reality ensured that the Irish government adopted a number of additional approaches in its efforts to undermine the image of the Privy Council as the ultimate safeguard for the rights of southern Protestants.

CONTESTING THE REALITY OF THE APPEAL AS A MINORITY SAFEGUARD

The first approach used by the Irish government was to stress the inefficacy of the appeal to serve as a minority safeguard. The Irish government had blocked or refused to enforce four appeals in the 1920s.[30] The difficulty with this argument was that it rested on assertions of power on the part of the majority community rather than on any overriding moral consideration. If anything, this consideration seemed to bolster, rather than undermine, arguments that minority safeguards were indeed necessary.

More constructive attempts at undermining the image of the Privy Council as the champion of southern Protestants focused on the assertion that there was no real necessity for minority safeguards in the Irish Free State.[31] The southern Protestant community experienced nothing like the level of discrimination endured by the Catholic community in Northern Ireland in the inter-war years and beyond. Yet this did not mean that sectarian tensions were absent from the twenty-six counties. Protestant members of the Oireachtas had to endure jibes from Fianna Fáil TDs and the *Irish Press* that identified them with freemasonry, British imperialism and as the British garrison in Ireland. Sectarian attacks had occurred

29 NAI, dept. of the Taoiseach, S4285B, transcript of radio broadcast of 9 Nov. 1930.

30 *Lynham v. Butler* [1925] 2 IR 82 (High Court), [1925] 2 IR 82 (Supreme Court); *Wigg and Cochrane v. The Attorney General of the Irish Free State* [1927] IR 285, 293 and *In re Compensation to Civil Servants under Article X of the Treaty* [1929] IR 44. See ch. 4, above. The fourth case was *Performing Right Society v. Bray Urban District Council* [1930] IR 509. See ch. 6, below. The Irish government would also take measures to block the appeal in *Moore v. Attorney General for the Irish Free State* [1935] IR 472 and [1935] AC 484. See ch. 8, below.

31 For example, see TNA, CAB 32/56 E (I.R.26) 4th meeting, 2 Nov. 1926 and NAI, dept. of the Taoiseach, S4285A, memorandum for the Imperial conference of 1930, undated.

during the Anglo-Irish conflict of 1919 to 1921.[32] Throughout the 1920s and 1930s it became clear that Protestants often had different ethical positions on matters such as censorship, divorce and contraception to those of their Catholic neighbours. Protests that the new state should not impose Catholic principles on the population as a whole failed to evoke a sympathetic response.[33] The *Ne Temere* decree, which required non-Catholics in a mixed marriage to agree to raise and educate their children as Catholics, remained a source of contention for much of the twentieth century.[34] A dispute triggered by the appointment of a Protestant librarian to serve an overwhelmingly Catholic population in Co. Mayo gained international attention.[35] The burning of Protestant churches in the 1930s as reprisals for attacks against Catholics in Northern Ireland and the Fethard-on-Sea boycott in the late 1950s illustrate that the creation of the self-governing Irish state had not eliminated sectarian tensions.[36]

Irish politicians also attacked the need for the Privy Council appeal, as a minority safeguard, by arguing that none of the Irish cases heard by the Privy Council had ever involved any question of religion.[37] Some Protestants did argue that official efforts to prevent the availability of divorce constituted religious discrimination and violated Article 8 of the Constitution, but these complaints never crystallized into legal challenges.[38] Nevertheless, those who emphasized the lack of religious content in any of the Irish appeals to the Privy Council failed to consider that perceived attacks on the rights of the minority community need not have been directly concerned with matters of religion. The transferred civil servants involved in *Wigg and Cochrane v Attorney General* and the special reference that followed were, accurately or otherwise, perceived to be Protestants

32 See R.B. McDowell, *Crisis and Decline – The Fate of the Southern Unionists* (Dublin, Lilliput, 1997), pp 78–136; Peter Hart, 'The Protestant Experience of Revolution in Southern Ireland' in Richard English and Graham Walker (eds), *Unionism in Modern Ireland: New Perspectives on Politics and Culture* (Basingstoke, Macmillan, 1996), pp 81–98 and Ian d'Alton, '"A Vestigial Population"? Perspectives on Southern Irish Protestants in the Twentieth Century', *Eire-Ireland*, 44:3&4 (2009), 9 at 25–6.

33 See John Henry Whyte, *Church and State in Modern Ireland, 1923–1979* (Dublin, Gill and Macmillan, 1984), pp 57–60.

34 See *In re Tilson, Infants* [1951] IR 1 and Gerard Hogan, 'A Fresh Look at *Tilson's Case*', *Irish Jurist*, 32 (1998), 311. It has been suggested that the Irish courts may have been guilty of bias in the past with respect to child custody disputes between Catholic and non-Catholic spouses. Paul C. Bartholomew, *The Irish Judiciary* (Dublin, University of Notre Dame, 1971), pp 17–18.

35 Thomas Mohr, 'The Privy Council Appeal as a MinoritySafeguard for the Protestant Community of the Irish Free State, 1922–1935', *Northern Ireland Legal Quarterly*, 63:3 (2012), 365 at 377–8.

36 Kurt Bowen, *Protestants in a Catholic State – Ireland's Privileged Minority* (Kingston and Montreal, McGill-Queen's University Press, 1983), p. 64 and Tim Fanning, *The Fethard-on-Sea Boycott* (Cork, Collins, 2010). See also Heather K. Crawford, *Outside the Glow: Protestants and Irishness in Independent Ireland* (Dublin, UCD Press, 2010) and Marianne Elliott, *When God Took Sides: Religion and Identity in Ireland – Unfinished History* (Oxford, Oxford University Press, 2009).

37 For example, Hector Hughes, *National Sovereignty and Judicial Autonomy in the British Commonwealth of Nations* (London, P.S. King, 1931), pp 107–9.

38 *Irish Times*, 23 Feb. 1925 and *Dáil Debates*, vol. 10, col. 158–82, 11 Feb. 1925.

and unionists by their supporters.[39] The appellants in a later appeal, *Moore v Attorney General*, were Protestants from Donegal and Derry. This case involved a challenge to exclusive fishing rights on the tidal estuary of the river Erne by a number of fishermen. The description of the owners of these property rights as 'foreigners' by those who instigated the legal action reflects an unpleasant sectarian aspect to this dispute.[40]

Another approach, in challenging the claim that the Privy Council appeal provided a minority safeguard, focused on claims that southern Protestants did not value or desire the appeal. Patrick McGilligan believed that only a small clique of southern Protestants supported the appeal and that this was based on a desire to retain class privileges.[41] Irish governments in the 1920s and 1930s were convinced that the whole minority safeguard argument was a convenient ruse employed by unionists in London to ensure the retention of the Privy Council appeal.[42]

The final means by which Irish governments attacked the claim that the Privy Council appeal acted as a minority safeguard was to question its objectivity as a court of law. Irish ministers argued that a court subject to external influence was ill-equipped to act as the final arbiter of relations between the Irish state and religious minorities. Nationalist suspicions as to the objectivity of the Judicial Committee of the Privy Council were ostensibly based on the absence of clear separation of powers in key British institutions. The lord chancellor heard Privy Council appeals but also sat in the House of Lords and had a seat in the British cabinet.[43] Irish commentators, including members of the Irish government itself, openly questioned the independence of the Judicial Committee of the Privy Council vis-à-vis the British government. John A. Costello, a future Irish prime minister or 'Taoiseach', wrote that the Judicial Committee had a 'political tinge' and added that it was 'formed of people who are at one and the same time judges and politicians'.[44] Patrick McGilligan asked his radio audience in 1930:

> Are not the British government and parliament still in a position to interfere in Irish affairs through this purely British Court, the majority of whose judges have most violently opposed the liberation of the Irish people?[45]

39 For example, see *Hansard*, House of Lords, vol. 83, col. 232–3, 1 Dec. 1931. Members of the Dáil condemned the 'disloyal, unpatriotic and rapacious civil servants'. *Dáil Debates*, vol. 18, col. 385, 8 Feb. 1927. The *Clare Champion* condemned the 'lickspittle British-backed civil servants'. *Clare Champion*, 15 Mar. 1930. See Martin Maguire, *The Civil Service and the Revolution in Ireland, 1912–1938* (Manchester, Manchester University Press, 2008), pp 187–8 and 190–1 and 194.

40 *Donegal Democrat*, 12 Aug. 1933.

41 *The Star*, May 1931 and UCDA, McGilligan Papers, P35/166, draft article 'Who wants the Privy Council?'

42 TNA, CAB 32/88 E(I.R.)(30) 8th meeting, 21 Oct. 1930.

43 The office of lord chancellor was finally reformed by the Constitutional Reform Act 2005.

44 UCDA, Costello Papers, P190/94, notes on the memorandum prepared for the Imperial conference of 1926 on appeals to the Privy Council, undated. See also Hughes, *National Sovereignty*, pp 104–5.

45 UCDA, McGilligan Papers, P35B/108, radio broadcast, 9 Nov. 1930.

The controversial origins of the Irish appeal ensured that it was dogged by conspiracy theories throughout its lifetime.[46] McGilligan went on to warn his listeners in his 1930 radio message of sinister elements who wished to use the Privy Council appeal 'as a means of keeping Ireland a pawn in British party politics and of preventing Irish ex-Unionists from becoming an inseparable element of the Irish nation'. He added that attempts were being made through 'a well-subsidised Press and other means to maintain a feeling of discontent amongst the small ex-Unionist population of the Irish Free State'. Behind it all were 'enemies of the Irish people' who were 'violently opposed to the Treaty, and if they were strong enough to-day they would reduce them to subjection once more'.[47] In a subsequent newspaper article McGilligan characterized support for the retention of the appeal as a 'sinister and disloyal campaign'. He asked his readers 'Is it the desire of the Protestant population of our country to become part of the warp and woof of the Irish nation?'[48]

GAUGING PROTESTANT SUPPORT FOR THE PRIVY COUNCIL APPEAL

Between 1926 and 1930 the Irish sought to secure agreement to limit or abolish the appeal through multilateral negotiations. By 1930 the Irish government seemed set on a policy of unilateral abolition of the appeal.[49] The British government feared that the opposition at Westminster would insist that abolition of the appeal threatened the rights of Irish Protestants. Abolition of the Irish appeal was soon seen as a threat to the passage of the Statute of Westminster that was going to be introduced in parliament in 1931. This important legislation was designed to give enhanced autonomy demanded by several of the Dominions. Any defeat or delay in enacting this historic measure would cause a crisis in Imperial relations. In these circumstances the British government became convinced that a potential crisis might be avoided if the Irish government could produce some evidence to support its claims that the Protestant community of the Irish Free State did not value the Privy Council appeal and would not raise serious opposition to its abolition.[50] If

46 For example, see Hughes, *National Sovereignty*, p. 99 and Donal McEgan, 'John Bull's Privy Council' *The Catholic Bulletin*, 23 (1933) 739. Darrell Figgis wrote that 'where a Court exists from which a people presumes injustice in advance, the wells of security and good order are at once poisoned'. Darrell Figgis, *The Irish Constitution* (Dublin, Mellifont, 1922), p. 55.

47 UCDA, McGilligan Papers, P35B/108 and NAI, dept. of the Taoiseach, S4285B, transcript of radio broadcast of 9 Nov. 1930.

48 *The Star*, May 1931, p. 207 and UCD Archives, McGilligan Papers, P35/166, draft article 'Who wants the Privy Council?'

49 *Dáil Debates*, vol. 37, col. 1620–1, 18 Mar. 1931.

50 For example, see UCDA, McGilligan Papers, P35B/115, Walshe to McGilligan, undated, NAI, dept. of the Taoiseach, S6164, report on meeting between Dulanty and Batterbee, 6 Mar. 1931 and TNA, LCO 2/910, Dominions secretary to attorney general, 2 Mar. 1931 and note by Sir H. Batterbee and Mr Machtig, 27 Feb. 1931.

such evidence could be presented at Westminster the abolition of the Irish appeal might form part of a wider settlement on outstanding legal difficulties between the United Kingdom and the Irish Free State.[51] The Irish government agreed to postpone abolition of the appeal in order to explore the feasibility of this solution.[52] This signalled the beginning of negotiations for a draft settlement that soon acquired the strange, but charming, soubriquet of the 'cleaning of the slate' agreement. This attempt to secure a wider settlement in Anglo-Irish relations will be examined in a later chapter.[53]

There were formidable obstacles in gauging Protestant support for the appeal in the early 1930s. The minority community was thinly scattered over the entire territory of the Irish Free State. The political views of its members were and remain difficult to pin down. Many could be accurately described as 'southern unionists' while this term was inappropriate and even offensive to others. Southern Protestants were understandably reticent to speak freely to strangers on sensitive political questions. A referendum confined to the Protestant community of the Irish Free State was obviously out of the question. Yet the British government was never so unrealistic as to ask for evidence of this nature. It suggested to the Irish government that 'the position that the Southern Unionists no longer desire the retention of the appeal' might be illustrated by means of 'a resolution in the Dáil or otherwise'.[54] The British only wanted some indication that there would be no 'active opposition' from southern Protestants in the Irish parliament.[55] This assumed that the attitudes of Protestant members of the Dáil, or more accurately the Protestant members of the Oireachtas given the large representation in the Seanad, reflected those of the wider Protestant community in the Irish Free State. Nevertheless, the task of discovering the attitudes of the Protestant members of the Oireachtas involved asking no more than two dozen individuals. This was hardly an unrealistic undertaking and the Irish government already had a head start. The government had actually anticipated the need to provide some form of evidence that there was no significant support for the Privy Council appeal among the southern Protestant community. In late 1930 or early 1931 the Irish government initiated a quiet process of consulting the Protestant members of the Oireachtas to learn their views on the Privy Council appeal and to search for a means of making these views clear to the British.

51 TNA, LCO 2/910, CP 120(31), The Irish Free State and Appeals to the Judicial Committee of the Privy Council and LCO 2/1231, undated memorandum attached to a letter from Sir Henry Batterbee to Sir Claud Schuster, 21 Mar. 1931 and UCDA, McGilligan Papers, P35/167, undated British communiqué marked 'Secret'.

52 TNA, LCO 2/910, CP 120(31), The Irish Free State and Appeals to the Judicial Committee of the Privy Council.

53 See ch. 6, below.

54 TNA, LCO 2/1231, undated memorandum attached to a letter from Sir Henry Batterbee to Sir Claud Schuster, 21 Mar. 1931 and UCDA, McGilligan Papers, P35/167, undated British communiqué marked 'Secret'.

1 The Privy Council Chamber as it appeared between 1824 and 1845. Sir John Soane, the celebrated architect, designed the room and created this painting of it. By courtesy of the Trustees of Sir John Soane's Museum.

2a&b The Privy Council Chamber, Downing Street, London, as remodelled by Sir Charles Barry. The Judicial Committee of the Privy Council sat in this redesigned chamber between 1845 and 2009. © June Buck.

3 The Irish plenipotentiaries in London during the negotiations that preceded the signing of the 1921 Anglo-Irish Treaty. *Seated from left to right*: Arthur Griffith, Eamonn Duggan, Michael Collins and Robert Barton. *Standing from left to right*: Erskine Childers, George Gavan Duffy and John Chartres. Reproduced by courtesy of the National Library of Ireland.

in Southern Ireland since the passing of the Government of Ireland Act, 1920, and for constituting a provisional Government, and the British Government shall take the steps necessary to transfer to such provisional Government the powers and machinery requisite for the discharge of its duties, provided that every member of such provisional Government shall have signified in writing his or her acceptance of this instrument. But this arrangement shall not continue in force beyond the expiration of twelve months from the date hereof.

18. This instrument shall be submitted forthwith by His Majesty's Government for the approval of Parliament and by the Irish signatories to a meeting summoned for the purpose of the members elected to sit in the House of Commons of Southern Ireland, and if approved shall be ratified by the necessary legislation.

On behalf of the Irish Delegation

Art Ó Gríobhtha (Arthur Griffith)

Mícheál Ó Coileáin

Riobárd Bartún

Eudhmonn S. Ó Dúgáin

Seórsa Ghabháin Uí Dhubhthaigh

On behalf of the British Delegation

D. Lloyd George

Austen Chamberlain

Birkenhead

Winston S. Churchill

December 6, 1921.

5 The committee responsible for drafting the 1922 Constitution of the Irish Free State. *From left to right*: R.J.P Mortished (Secretary), John O'Byrne, C.J. France, Darrell Figgis, E.M. Stephens (Secretary), P.A. O'Toole (Secretary), James McNeill, Hugh Kennedy, James Murnaghan and James Douglas. Michael Collins, Alfred O'Rahilly and Kevin O'Shiel were also members of the committee but are absent from this picture. Reproduced by courtesy of the National Library of Ireland.

4 (*opposite*) Signature page of the Irish government's copy of the 'Articles of Agreement for a Treaty between Great Britain and Ireland' signed in London on 6 December 1921. Reproduced by courtesy of the National Archives of Ireland.

6 Lionel Curtis (1872–1955), author and public servant who played an important role in implementing the 1921 Treaty. Curtis insisted that the Judicial Committee of the Privy Council 'must be the supreme arbiter in interpreting the Treaty'. © National Portrait Gallery, London

7 Hugh Kennedy (1879–1936). Portrait painted in 1925 by Leo Whelan. Reproduced by courtesy of The Honorable Society of King's Inns.

8 Gordon Hewart, 1st Viscount Hewart (1870–1943). Portait painted in 1935 by Sir Oswald Birley. © National Portrait Gallery, London.

9 *(opposite)* Richard Burdon Haldane, 1st Viscount Haldane (1856–1928). Portrait painted in 1914 by Sir Arthur Stockdale Cope. This portrait hung for many years in the Privy Council Chamber, Downing Street, London. It now hangs in Courtroom No. 3, used by the Judicial Committee of the Privy Council, at Middlesex Guildhall, London. © Crown copyright: UK Government Art Collection

10 Kevin O'Higgins, Arthur Griffith and W.T. Cosgrave in 1922. Photograph by W.D. Hogan. Reproduced by courtesy of the National Library of Ireland.

11 Kevin O'Higgins (1892–1927), first minister for justice of the Irish Free State. In 1926 O'Higgins described the Judicial Committee of the Privy Council as 'a bad court, a useless court, an unnecessary court'. Reproduced by courtesy of the National Library of Ireland.

12 Frederick Edwin Smith, 1st Earl of Birkenhead (1872–1930). Pen and ink drawing created in 1929 by Robert Stewart Sherriffs. © National Portrait Gallery, London

13 George Cave, 1st Viscount Cave (1856–1928). Photograph taken in 1921.

14a&b The Erne Fishery Case memorial at the Mall Quay, Ballyshannon, Co. Donegal. Photographs taken by Marta Stokłosa.

THE ERNE FISHERY (KILDONEY MEN'S) CASE, 1925 - 1933

The bountiful salmon fisheries of the river Erne were seized as crown property, in 1603, following the surrender of Tír Chonaill to the English.

By 1620 all royal grants of fishing on the Erne estuary were gathered into a single private ownership. The natural harvest of the estuary was withheld from townland and town alike.

Thereafter, this valuable salmon fishery was operated with complete public exclusion from the Falls of assaroe to the Bar of Ballyshannon.

A local challenge to this exclusion began, in 1925, when a volunteer crew of six young men publicly entered the fishing grounds.

The monumental task of proving that a private fishery on the tidal river Erne could not, and should not, be legally binding had begun.

The legal challenge was brought by the following fishermen;-

John Cleary, Francis Coughlin, Patrick Coughlin, John Daly, Michael Daly, Richard Davis Jnr., Alex Duncan, Charles Furey, James Furey Charles Gallogley, James Gallogley, Hugh Gavigan, John Gavigan Snr., Gerard Gillespie, James Gillespie, John Gillespie, Patrick Gillespie, John Goan, Patrick Goan, Willie Goan Snr., Joe Grimes, Patrick Haughey, William Hilley, Bernard Holland, James Keenan, Joseph Keenan, Michael Kennedy, William Kennedy, Alex McCafferty, John McCafferty, Patrick McCafferty, Red John McCafferty, John McCarthy, Michael McCarthy, Darby McGroarty, Frank McNeely, Tom McNeely, Michael McPhelim Hugh Mooney, William Morrow (Legs), William Morrow, William Phillips, James Scanlon.

It was Kildoney fireside tradition which kept alive the belief that there should be a right of public fishing on the Erne estuary.

Master Martin Keegan, Creevy National School, aware of the Kildoney tradition, resolved to test this belief before the law should a suitable and willing advocate be found.

Frank Gallagher, Donegal Town, an able and daring young solicitor, was willing to espouse this seemingly hopeless case on behalf of the excluded fishermen.

Frank Gettins, respected local merchant, undertook the task of gathering funds, in lean times, from local, national and American supporters.

Frank Gallagher achieved victory for the local fishermen in 1933. The salmon rich waters of the Erne estuary were now open to public fishing.

In memory of the Erne Salmon Fishermen 1925 - 1933.

15a,b&c (*above, below and facing page*) The Judicial Committee of the Privy Council today. The new Courtroom No. 3 at Middlesex Guildhall, London. Photographs taken by the author.

16 The Judicial Committee of the Privy Council as a twenty-first-century tourist attraction. Over half a million people have visited between 2009 and 2015. Photograph taken by Marta Stokłosa.

17 Ptolemy Dean's drawing of the Privy Council Chamber at Downing Street, London, as used by the Judicial Committee of the Privy Council until 2009. © Ptolemy Dean. Reproduced by kind permission.

The consultation process was entrusted to Protestant senators who had come to support the policies of the Irish government with respect to the Privy Council. These were senators James Douglas, Samuel L. Brown and Andrew Jameson. James Douglas had earned the respect of members of the Irish government through his work with the White Cross during the Anglo-Irish conflict (1919–21). He had been on close terms with Michael Collins and had assisted in drafting the 1922 Constitution.[56] Douglas had never been a supporter of the Privy Council appeal. By contrast his colleagues Samuel L. Brown and Andrew Jameson had initially been strong supporters of the appeal but by 1930 had changed their position. Jameson had been a member of the delegations that had spoken on behalf of the southern Protestant community during the negotiations that preceded the signing of the 1921 Treaty and the enactment of the 1922 Constitution. In 1929 Jameson and Brown had formed part of a delegation that delivered a formal protest to W.T. Cosgrave on the government's policy with respect to the Privy Council appeal.[57] It is not easy to trace how and why these men had come to change their minds in 1930. The final conclusion of the fiasco surrounding the transferred civil servants[58] and the success of the Irish government in blocking and undermining appeals are likely to have influenced their conversion.[59] The Irish government's argument that the minority community was not in need of external safeguards was greatly enhanced by the support of men like Brown and Jameson. Yet, as all three senators were to discover, not all of their co-religionists agreed with their conclusions as to the value of the Privy Council appeal.

In January 1931 Douglas and Brown gave preliminary reports on their assessment of Protestant opinion in the Oireachtas. Douglas reported 'Most of the people, to whom we are likely to appeal would favour an appeal to the Privy Council in important cases if this were practical politics'. He added 'there is no doubt that in a general way they mostly disapprove of the government's policy with regard to [blocking] appeals'. This was not an encouraging start but the Irish government persisted. In spring 1931 the Irish government entrusted Brown with the task of carrying out a wider consultation with Protestant members of the Oireachtas. His task was to assess whether they might be prepared to support a

55 TNA, CJ 1/6, corrections by J.H. Thomas to draft letter to be sent by earl of Granard to W.T. Cosgrave, 17 June 1931.

56 James G. Douglas, *Memoirs of Senator James G. Douglas (1887–1954): Concerned Citizen*, ed. J. Anthony Gaughan (Dublin, UCD Press, 1998).

57 TNA, LCO 2/910, statement of 10 Dec. 1929 attached to letter from archbishop of Dublin to prime minister, 27 Sept. 1930.

58 *Wigg and Cochrane v The Attorney General of the Irish Free State* [1927] IR 293 (High Court), [1925] 1 IR 149 (Supreme Court) and [1927] IR 285 (Privy Council) and *In re Compensation to Civil Servants under Article X of the Treaty* [1929] IR 44 . See also *Performing Right Society v Bray Urban District Council* [1928] IR 506 and [1930] IR 509.

59 [1928] IR 506 and [1930] IR 509. Senator Brown was broadly supportive of the enactment of the Copyright (Preservation) Act 1929, which was passed to prevent the appeal in this case. *Seanad Debates*, vol. 12, col. 988, 3 July 1929.

special resolution on the question of Privy Council appeals. In June 1931 a group of Protestant representatives from both Houses of the Oireachtas held an informal conference to draft a report that would reflect their views on the Privy Council appeal.[60]

The draft report began by recognizing that 'The majority of those present at this conference are opposed to the abolition of the right of appeal to the Privy Council, and desire that if possible it should be preserved.' Having made this clear, the participants at the meeting recognized that the appeal had already been made ineffectual in practice and that they were powerless to prevent abolition in the future. The report recognized the inevitability of change and, in these circumstances, urged that abolition be brought about through agreement with the British government in order to avoid the dangers resulting from an alleged breach of the 1921 Treaty. It proposed that Protestant representatives should approach the Irish minister for external affairs to urge him to attempt to bring about the proposed change by agreement with Great Britain. The report also proposed that Protestant representatives in the Oireachtas should support an informal resolution that would reiterate that a majority of their members remained opposed to the abolition of the Privy Council appeal in principle and would oppose any unilateral legislation seeking abolition. Nevertheless, the draft resolution made it clear that Protestant representatives were prepared to accept abolition as a *fait accompli* if an Anglo-Irish agreement could be secured on this matter. If this proved possible, the Protestant representatives would limit their criticism in the Oireachtas to 'an expression of regret that, in spite of the wishes of a large section of the Minority on the subject, the Government had not been willing to continue the right of Appeal to the Privy Council'.[61]

As events transpired, the proposals enshrined in this proposed resolution were never adopted. It seems likely that the Irish government was uncomfortable with many aspects of it. The strong expression of support in principle for the continuation of the Privy Council appeal was at total variance with the government's contention that southern Protestants placed no value on the appeal. Moreover, the proposed resolution made it clear that the position of its adherents was based on their recognition that the appeal had already been rendered ineffective by the Irish government and also on the basis of their own powerlessness to prevent abolition by unilateral means. These admissions gave a definite impression of acquiescence under duress, an impression that would not have been lost on unionists at Westminster. In addition, the strong expression of opposition to unilateral abolition could not have been comfortable reading to a government that was determined to follow this course if bilateral negotiations failed. The Irish government had already drawn up the draft legislation required to bring abolition into effect.[62] However, the final nail in the coffin of the proposal does not seem to

60 UCDA, McGilligan Papers, P35/166, memorandum re Privy Council appeals, 17 June 1931.
61 Ibid.
62 NAI, dept. of foreign affairs, 3/1, draft bills.

have come from the Irish government but from the southern Protestants themselves.

A list of the senators who were consulted by Brown on the Privy Council appeal has survived. The list includes his own name along with those of Douglas and Jameson. It also shows that Brown consulted Sir John Griffith, Henry Guinness, The McGillicuddy, John Bagwell, Arthur Vincent, Sir Edward Biggar and the Countess of Desart.[63] The addition of the last name is interesting because the Countess of Desart was not a Protestant but belonged to the Jewish faith. However, the list does expressly mention that Brown had not consulted two senators, Sir John Keane and William Barrington. No reason is given for ignoring these two senators but subsequent events illustrate that Keane was certainly a supporter of the appeal to the Privy Council. Keane was one of those who objected most strenuously to abolition when de Valera finally put it into practice in 1933.[64] His omission from the consultation process suggests that he and perhaps Barrington were not seen as likely supporters of the intended resolution.

There was certainly strong opposition to the draft resolution among Protestant members of the Dáil. No list of the TDs who were consulted appears to have survived. Nevertheless, W.T. Cosgrave wrote that three 'northern deputies were violently opposed to the proposal'.[65] It is difficult to identify these persons with total certainty, but it is likely that these were Major James Sproule Myles, John James Cole and Alexander Haslett. These southern Protestants were, respectively, TDs for Donegal, Cavan and Monaghan. Myles was a retired officer from the Royal Inniskilling Fusiliers and had served as a unionist MP at Westminster, Cole came from a Protestant farming background while Haslett, another farmer, had been endorsed by the Orange Order in the first election of 1927.[66] It is possible that opposition to the abolition of the appeal extended beyond these three 'northern deputies'. When de Valera sought to abolish the appeal in 1933 his most vocal opponents in the Dáil were southern Protestants from Dublin.[67]

It is uncertain whether a majority of Protestant members of the Oireachtas would have supported the draft resolution on the Privy Council appeal. Even if they had, the presence of a vocal minority who, in Cosgrave's own words, were

63 This list has survived in two sources. It was written on the back of the document entitled 'memorandum re Privy Council appeals', 17 June 1931 and on an envelope containing a letter from Cosgrave to McGilligan, dated 26 June 1931. The author found both of these when the original documents were still accessible to members of the public at UCD Archives (at this time they were archived under McGilligan Papers, P35/196). These files have since been re-organized under the new reference of McGilligan Papers, P35/166. Public access is now limited to microfilm copies that do not reproduce these important lists.

64 *Seanad Debates*, vol. 17, col. 1681, 31 Oct. 1933.

65 UCDA, McGilligan Papers, P35/166, Cosgrave to McGilligan, 26 June 1931.

66 Bowen, *Protestants in a Catholic State*, pp 52–3. See also the database of Oireachtas members at http://www.oireachtas.ie/members-hist/default.asp?housetype=0 (accessed 21 Oct. 2015).

67 These were Professor William Edward Thrift and John Good. Thrift had grown up in England and represented Trinity College Dublin while Good was TD for Dublin County. See ch. 8, below.

'violently opposed' to even a limited form of acquiescence is indicative of the strength of feeling on the Privy Council appeal among certain sections of the Protestant community. It was a situation that was completely at variance with claims made by Irish officials to their British counterparts that none of the southern Protestants in the Dáil would oppose abolition.[68] Even if the proposed resolution had been acceptable to the Irish government and even if a majority of Protestant members of the Oireachtas had given it their support, it is possible that the opposition of a determined minority might have been enough to rally unionist sympathy at Westminster.

The failure of the proposed resolution did not mean that the Irish government had given up on the search for a negotiated settlement on the Privy Council appeal. It explored other means of indicating Protestant acquiescence to abolition. The preferred alternative was to offer the British the testimony of notable southern Protestants as to the feelings of their co-religionists in the Irish Free State as a whole. This task fell to Senators Brown and Jameson who travelled to London in September 1931 and secured an interview with the Dominions secretary, J.H. Thomas.[69]

The two Irishmen met the Dominions secretary on 17 September 1931. Brown and Jameson were keen to stress the fair treatment of the minority by the Irish government. The two senators declared that they had no complaints and went as far as to claim that there was no longer any 'religious question' in the Irish Free State.[70] Brown and Jameson stated that southern Protestants could be divided into three classes on the specific question of the Privy Council appeal:

(1) those who regarded the appeal as futile and an irritant to good relations between the Protestant minority and the rest of the population of the Free State, and who, on these grounds, were in favour of its immediate abolition;

(2) those who, while regretting the disappearance of the appeal, recognized that the Free State government was committed to securing its abolition. Southern Protestants who fell into this class believed that abolition should come by means of agreement with the British government;

(3) those who were opposed to abolition in any shape or form.

Brown and Jameson admitted the difficulties in gauging the opinions of Protestants throughout the Irish Free State. Nevertheless, they were prepared to offer their own estimations of Protestant opinion on the Privy Council appeal. They began by noting that among 'the thinking and educated people' the majority belonged to the first class. Senator Brown added that this category included members of the governing body of Trinity College Dublin. Nevertheless, Brown and Jameson were

68 TNA, LCO 2/910, CP 120(31), The Irish Free State and Appeals to the Judicial Committee of the Privy Council.

69 TNA, DO 35/127/7 file 4431/20, note of interview between J.H. Thomas and Senator Brown and Senator Jameson, Sept. 1931.

70 Ibid.

prepared to concede that a larger proportion of the southern Protestants probably belonged to the second class. In their opinion the number belonging to the third class in the Irish Free State was small and largely confined to the border counties. This claim may have reflected the position of the three 'northern deputies' in the Dáil mentioned by Cosgrave. Brown and Jameson did note that a controversy in the near future might arouse old prejudices and have the effect of driving some of the southern Protestants out of the second class of opinion and into the third.[71]

As for opinions within the Oireachtas, the senators stated that of the eleven or twelve representatives of the minority in the Seanad all belonged to the first class. They added that of the eleven representatives of the minority in the Dáil, three belonged to the first class and eight to the second class. Although the two senators might be expected to be on firmer ground with respect to Protestant opinion in the Oireachtas than with respect to the Irish Free State as a whole, these figures are open to serious question. Their claim that Protestant senators were all of the opinion that the Privy Council appeal was an irritant and should be abolished immediately is particularly dubious. These views do not reflect the conclusions of the informal consultations with Protestant members of the Seanad and Dáil in June 1931 that had made it clear that a majority favoured the retention of the appeal in ideal circumstances. The lack of consultation with Senators Keane and Barrington has already been noted. The figures given with respect to the Dáil are even more questionable. It should be recalled that the proposed resolution, which would have expressed support for the appeal while acquiescing in a position of bilateral abolition, was 'violently opposed' by at least three unidentified 'northern deputies'.[72] The staunch opposition of these persons surely placed them in the third class of southern Protestants.

The testimony offered by Brown and Jameson did not result in the anticipated bilateral agreement that would have paved the way for the abolition of the Privy Council appeal. The opinions offered by the two senators were not sufficient to satisfy the criteria suggested by the original British proposal.[73] First, the opinions of the two senators did not constitute evidence that could be shown to those in the United Kingdom who professed to sympathize with the Protestants of the Irish Free State. Second, the British government had good reasons not to be convinced by their testimony. Senators Brown and Jameson were among those who saw the appeal as 'futile and an irritant' and as such were, by the admission of their own evidence, unrepresentative of the majority of southern Protestants.

The British government stressed the 'immense importance' of providing evidence that southern Protestants would not actively oppose the abolition of the

71 TNA, DO 35/127/7 file 4431/20, note of interview between J.H. Thomas and Senator Brown and Senator Jameson, Sept. 1931.

72 UCDA, McGilligan Paper, P35/166, memorandum re Privy Council appeals, 17 June 1931.

73 See TNA, LCO 2/1231, undated memorandum attached to letter from Sir Henry Batterbee to Sir Claud Schuster, 21 Mar. 1931 and UCDA, McGilligan Papers, P35/166, undated British communiqué marked 'Secret'.

Irish appeal to the Privy Council.[74] J.H. Thomas was convinced that the Irish government had failed to provide any such evidence.[75] The Irish government declined repeated offers by Thomas to come to Dublin in order to break the negotiating deadlock.[76]

SOUTHERN PROTESTANT INSTITUTIONS THAT SUPPORTED THE APPEAL

There are definite indicators that suggest that southern Protestant support for the Privy Council appeal outside the Oireachtas was far more substantial than the Irish government was prepared to admit. Two major Protestant institutions gave unwavering support to the Privy Council appeal throughout the 1920s and 1930s. The first was the *Irish Times*, the main newspaper read by the minority community, which repeatedly stressed the importance of the appeal as 'a very precious guarantee of their personal liberties, and has helped to reconcile them to the revolutionary changes of recent years'.[77] The *Irish Times* condemned the policy of the Irish government to dilute the effectiveness of the appeal as one of 'sap and mine'.[78] In particular, the *Irish Times* condemned the practice of blocking Privy Council appeals as a 'standing protest against the Free State's membership of the British Empire, and a warning to the English people that the Saorstát will secede at the earliest opportunity'.[79] This newspaper also challenged nationalist claims that the appeal lacked democratic legitimacy by noting that it was sanctioned by the law of the Irish Free State and was the 'highest Court under its own Constitution'.[80] The *Irish Times* even raised the possibility that the Privy Council appeal could facilitate eventual unification of Northern Ireland with the Irish Free State. After unification the Privy Council could act as an external arbiter in a federal settlement.[81]

The second institution that supported the appeal was the Church of Ireland itself. Its official publication, the *Church of Ireland Gazette*, insisted immediately after the signing of the 1921 Anglo-Irish Treaty that southern Protestants did need constitutional safeguards.[82] This publication proved a staunch supporter of the Privy Council appeal as a safeguard for the minority community and as an integral part of the Irish Free State's identity as a Dominion.[83] The views of the *Gazette* also reflected the attitude of the church hierarchy. In late 1929 the standing

74 TNA, CAB 24/221/20, Thomas to McGilligan, 1 May 1931.
75 TNA, CJ1/6, Thomas to Granard, 5 June 1931.
76 TNA, CAB 24/221/20, notes on discussion between Thomas and McGilligan, 19 Mar. 1931; Thomas to McGilligan, 1 May 1931 and McGilligan to Thomas, 6 May 1931.
77 *Irish Times*, 4 Feb. 1926.
78 Ibid.
79 Ibid., 11 Apr. 1930.
80 Ibid., 5 Dec. 1929.
81 Ibid., 19 Feb. 1929.
82 *Church of Ireland Gazette*, 9 Dec. 1921.
83 For example, *Church of Ireland Gazette*, 5 Mar. 1926, 10 Aug. 1928, 29 Nov. 1929 and 14 Nov. 1930.

committee of the general synod of the Church of Ireland decided to send a delegation to interview President Cosgrave on the Irish government's declaration that it intended to seek the abolition of the appeal at the Imperial conference of 1930.[84] This delegation included representation from a third southern Protestant institution, Trinity College Dublin.

On 10 December 1929 the southern Protestant delegation met with Cosgrave and delivered a prepared statement of protest on behalf of the minority community at the policy of the Irish government towards the Privy Council appeal.[85] The statement 'most respectfully' protested the policy of the Irish government and made clear that 'the minority which we represent must not be taken as acquiescing therein'.[86] Indeed, the deputation sought to 'impress on the president of the executive council the fact that there is a feeling of grave disappointment – we might even say of alarm, on the part of those whom we represent'.[87] The efforts of the delegation to impress the strength of their objections on Cosgrave were not successful. Cosgrave recounted, almost two years after the meeting, that the delegation had been resigned to the position that the Privy Council appeal was bound to be abolished and, consequently, had focused on securing an enlargement of the Supreme Court as an alternative safeguard.[88]

The failure to impress the seriousness of objections to government policy on Cosgrave's mind at the meeting of 10 December 1929, either through poor communication or lapse of memory, had serious consequences. It had a profound influence on the Irish government's reaction to a letter to the *Times* written by the Church of Ireland archbishops of Armagh and Dublin at the time of the Imperial conference of 1930.[89] Although the letter did little more than repeat the concerns raised with Cosgrave the previous year, the Irish government seemed to regard it as a bolt from the blue. The government refused to consider the letter as a genuine protest and preferred to regard the archbishops as proxies in the hands of the British government.[90] This is yet another example of the conspiracy theories that emerged from the breakdown in relations between the Irish government and the Judicial Committee of the Privy Council. In fact, the initiative behind this intervention came from the archbishops themselves.[91] The British government had

84 *Church of Ireland Gazette*, 23 May 1930.

85 The delegation consisted of the Church of Ireland archbishop of Dublin, the provost of Trinity College Dublin, Edward John Gwynn, together with Senators John Bagwell, Samuel L. Brown and Andrew Jameson.

86 TNA, LCO 2/910, statement of 10 Dec. 1929 attached to letter from archbishop of Dublin to prime minister, 27 Sept. 1930.

87 Ibid.

88 NAI, dept. of the Taoiseach, S4285A, Michael McDunphy to Diarmuid O'Hegarty, 8 Nov. 1930.

89 *Times*, 7 Nov. 1930.

90 See NAI, dept. of the Taoiseach, S4285B, Diarmuid O'Hegarty to Michael McDunphy, 7 Nov. 1930 and W.T. Cosgrave to Lord Granard, 8 Nov. 1930.

91 The archbishops wrote to the Dominions secretary, J.H. Thomas, on 27 Sept. 1930 outlining the arguments that were later used in their letter to the *Times*. The letter ended with an appeal to Thomas to resist any proposal to limit what they saw as a constitutional right granted by the

actually considered the archbishops' letter to be an unhelpful intervention and had opposed its publication in the press.[92]

CONCLUSION

It has already been noted that the political views of the southern Protestant community in the 1920s and 1930s remain notoriously difficult to pin down. Even persons living in that time who were themselves members of that community admitted the difficulties of gauging the overall opinion of their co-religionists.[93] As late as 1956 the *Church of Ireland Gazette* admitted that there was an understandable attitude among many southern Protestants that maintained 'we should keep ourselves to ourselves and, if we speak, confine our remarks to platitudinous exhortations on non-controversial subjects …, lest such attention should result in material or social disadvantages'.[94] Nevertheless, it is clear that most Protestant members of the Oireachtas in the 1920s and 1930s disapproved of the Irish government's actions in blocking Privy Council appeals. This is evident from the informal consultations that took place in 1931. Senators Douglas and Brown even warned the Irish government of the danger of radicalizing Protestant opinion if this policy was maintained.[95]

It is clear that the extent and depth of southern Protestant support for the appeal to the Privy Council from the Irish courts was consistently underestimated throughout the lifetime of that appeal. This is evident in the flawed analysis of the opinions of Protestant members of the Oireachtas that was presented to the British government by Senators Brown and Jameson in 1931. The views of the delegation that visited W.T. Cosgrave in 1929 to protest the policy of his government towards the appeal proved to be words written on water. The letter written to the press by the Church of Ireland archbishops in 1930 was written off as a ploy by proxies of a devious British government. The consistent stance of the *Irish Times* seems to have made little impact outside the readership of that newspaper.

The constant underestimation of support for the Privy Council appeal among the southern Protestant community came at a heavy price. It guaranteed the failure of the resolution that was intended to show that Protestant members of the Oireachtas did not value the appeal, which, in turn, doomed the proposed 'cleaning

Treaty. TNA, DO 35/88, 4002/3 and LCO 2/910, archbishop of Dublin to prime minister, 27 Sept. 1930. The British government was given the text of their letter to the *Times* three days before publication. TNA, DO 35/88, 4002/5.

92 TNA, LCO 2/910, C. Schuster to N.M. Butler, 7 Nov. 1930.

93 Senators Brown and Jameson admitted this in their interview with J.H. Thomas on 17 Sept. 1931. TNA, DO 35/127/7 file 4431/20, note of interview between J.H. Thomas and Senator Brown and Senator Jameson, Sept. 1931.

94 *Church of Ireland Gazette*, 30 Nov. 1956 and Ian d'Alton, '"A Vestigial Population"' at 38.

95 UCDA, McGilligan Papers, P35/166, undated memoranda by Senators James Douglas and Samuel L. Brown.

of the slate' agreement of 1931. This evidence should cause the historian to hesitate before echoing the position asserted by representatives of Irish governments, who were by no means disinterested parties, and concluding that opposition to the abolition of the Privy Council appeal in the 1930s only came from 'a tiny vociferous, proportion of former Unionists'.[96] Nor is it safe to dismiss a position that was supported by the majority of southern Protestants who sat at Westminster, by a significant number of Protestant members of the Oireachtas, by the *Irish Times* as the major newspaper of the minority community, by three successive Provosts of Trinity College Dublin[97] and by the leaders of the Church of Ireland as the viewpoint of 'cranks' or 'a handful of extremists'.[98]

The image of the Privy Council offering a minority safeguard to southern Protestants was a constant theme in the history of the Irish appeal. It was raised whenever the Irish government proposed to limit or abolish the appeal and proved an important consideration during the enactment of the historic Statute of Westminster in 1931. The surviving evidence on Protestant attitudes towards the appeal provides a new perspective on inter-denominational relations in the early years of the self-governing Irish state. It suggests that a substantial portion of the population of the Irish Free State did feel uneasy and vulnerable in this new and untested entity. This reality ensured that a considerable number, perhaps even a majority, of southern Protestants did value an appeal to an external tribunal in order to uphold their rights in the last resort. It is uncertain how much longer these sentiments were maintained beyond the 1930s. Nevertheless, these considerations suggest that the gradual easing of sectarian divisions in the twenty-six counties was not as swift or as inevitable as contemporary Irish governments cared to admit.

96 Swinfen, *Imperial Appeal*, p. 124.

97 John Henry Bernard (1919–27), Edward John Gwynn (1927–37) and William Edward Thrift (1937–42).

98 TNA, DO 35/127/7, Granard to Thomas, 20 Aug. 1931 and *The Star*, May 1931.

CHAPTER SIX

Failed attempts to reform or abolish the Irish appeal

HISTORICAL AND LEGAL ANALYSES OF THE IRISH APPEAL IN THE 1920S AND 1930S

THOSE WHO OPPOSED the Irish appeal to the Judicial Committee of the Privy Council never tired of drawing on unflattering analogies from Irish legal history. Comparisons were made with the eighteenth century case of *Annesley v. Sherlock*[1] as part of the battle between the Irish House of Lords and its equivalent in London over final appellate jurisdiction in Ireland. This battle lasted until the Act of Union came into force in 1801. The origins of the jurisdiction of the Judicial Committee of the Privy Council as a crown prerogative were also used to draw analogies with the infamous Court of Star Chamber together with occasional references to its Irish equivalent, the Court of Castle Chamber.[2] Although it was always possible to dispute the accuracy of these historical analogies they remained stubbornly popular among Irish commentators and academics in the inter-war years.[3]

Irish legal commentators often argued that Ireland had never been subject to the appeal to the Judicial Committee of the Privy Council before the creation of the Irish Free State. As seen earlier, this was not actually true.[4] This did not prevent Darrell Figgis, an important figure in drafting the 1922 Constitution, from gaining considerable attention in the British press when he wrote that the proviso in Article 66 of the Irish Constitution was ineffective as it assumed a pre-existing right of appeal before the creation of the Irish Free State.[5] Figgis was convinced that no

1 *Annesley v. Sherlock* 21 Journals of the House of Lords [Great Britain] 755 (1718) on appeal from *Sherlock v. Annesley* 2 Journals of the House of Lords [Ireland] 541 (1716).

2 See J.G. Swift MacNeill letter to the *Irish Independent*, 16 Feb. 1926.

3 For example, see UCDA, Kennedy Papers, P4/340, memorandum by Henry Harrison on 'The Draft Constitution of the Irish Free State', 18 Sept. 1922; UCDA, Costello Papers, P190/97, J.J. Hearne to John A. Costello, 22 Oct. 1931; J.G. Swift MacNeill, *Studies in the Constitution of the Irish Free State* (Dublin, Talbot, 1925), pp 56–9; Henry Harrison, *Ireland and the British Empire, 1937* (London, R. Hale, 1937), p. 181; *Dáil Debates*, vol. 1, col. 1406 and 1414, 10 Oct. 1922; *Dáil Debates*, vol. 14, col. 348, 3 Feb. 1926 and *Irish Independent,* 10 Oct. 1922.

4 See Ch. 2, below.

5 *Daily Mail*, 13 Sept. 1923. For a response to Figgis see A.B. Keith, 'Notes on Imperial Constitutional Law', *Journal of Comparative Legislation and International Law*, 6 (1924), 204 at 205. See also *Hansard*, House of Commons, vol. 159, col. 368–79, 27 Nov. 1922 and Hector

right of appeal to the Privy Council in London had ever existed in Ireland before 1922. Although Figgis was mistaken he was not the only legal commentator who stressed this argument. For example, professor J.G. Swift MacNeill of University College Dublin raised a similar argument supported by detailed references to Irish legal history. MacNeill added that the reference to 'His Majesty in Council' mentioned in the text of the Irish Constitution must be interpreted as a reference to the Irish Privy Council that had once sat in Dublin Castle.[6] These convoluted arguments were taken very seriously in certain quarters, attracted some international attention[7] and were even raised in the pleadings of one Irish appeal to the Privy Council.[8]

Commentators on Irish constitutional law in the 1920s and 1930s were predictably hostile to the Privy Council appeal. A short explanation of the 1922 Irish Constitution by Darrell Figgis, one of its principal drafters, attacked the appeal as hostile to the spirit of the Constitution.[9] Barra Ó Briain's *The Irish Constitution* (1929) concluded that the Privy Council appeal was 'humiliating and offensive'.[10] Leo Kohn's better-known work on the 1922 Constitution was no more restrained and declared that the appeal was 'the most obnoxious feature of the Constitution'.[11]

One of the most colourful commentators on the appeal was Irish barrister and politician Hector Hughes.[12] Hughes was born in Dublin, practiced law in Ireland and England and was a firm advocate of the need to establish full Irish judicial sovereignty. He raised arguments based on the alleged expense and delay caused by Privy Council appeals that were common to all parts of the Empire but also stressed considerations that were unique to the Irish Free State. Hughes was convinced that Irish public opinion perceived the Privy Council as politically biased against the Irish Free State 'where it is not fully believed that the Treaty of 1921 has dissipated the former antagonism towards that country of some who became members of the Judicial Committee'.[13] Yet Hughes was not content to challenge the Irish appeal in isolation and wrote a book in 1931 that advocated complete abolition of the Privy Council appeal for all the self-governing

Hughes, *National Sovereignty and Judicial Autonomy in the British Commonwealth of Nations* (London, P.S. King, 1931), pp 36–8.

6 See letter to the *Times*, 15 Mar. 1926. See also *Dáil Debates*, vol. 1, col. 1404–5, 10 Oct. 1922 and *Seanad Debates*, vol. 6, col. 422, 24 Feb. 1926. Leo Kohn described this argument as 'untenable'. Leo Kohn, *The Constitution of the Irish Free State* (Dublin, Allen and Unwin, 1932), p. 361.

7 For example, see *Manitoba Free Press*, 5 Apr. 1926 and the *Daily Colonist* (Victoria, British Columbia), 6 Apr. 1926. UCDA, McGilligan Papers, P35/161.

8 *Performing Right Society v. Bray Urban District Council* [1930] IR 509.

9 Darrell Figgis, *The Irish Constitution* (Dublin, Mellifont, 1922), p. 51.

10 Barra Ó Briain, *The Irish Constitution* (Dublin, Talbot, 1929), p. 124.

11 Leo Kohn, *The Constitution of the Irish Free State* (Dublin, 1932), pp 355–6.

12 (1887–1970) *Dictionary of Irish Biography*, vol. 4, pp 829–30.

13 Hector Hughes, *National Sovereignty and Judicial Autonomy in the British Commonwealth of Nations* (London, P.S. King, 1931).

Dominions.[14] Although Hughes was an Irish nationalist he later entered the British House of Commons as a Labour MP for North Aberdeen in 1945. Hughes caused some surprise in his later years when he became one of the leading exponents of creating a new and stronger Commonwealth court.[15]

THE IMPERIAL CONFERENCE OF 1926

In 1926, an Irish delegation travelled to London to participate in an Imperial conference attended by the governments of the United Kingdom and all the self-governing Dominions of the Empire. The Irish delegation to this conference carried a long list of desired constitutional reforms aimed at augmenting the autonomy of the Dominions, including the Irish Free State.[16] Top of the list was a demand for reform of the Irish appeal to the Privy Council. The decision to allow an appeal in *Lynham v. Butler*, which many considered a blatant attempt to interfere in Irish domestic affairs, remained fresh in the memory of the Irish delegates. Yet when they tried to complain about the debacle in *Lynham v. Butler* they ended up facing Lord Cave, the man who bore primary responsibility for the decision, across the negotiating table. In addition, the Irish faced the formidable obstacle of overcoming British convictions that the appeal was a vital safeguard for the Protestant minority in the Irish Free State. It soon became clear that the Irish would only gain concessions if they first won support from the other Dominions attending the conference.

The Imperial conferences were occasions held approximately every three or four years in the late nineteenth and early twentieth centuries in which the self-governing entities of the British Empire met to discuss matters of common interest. In 1923, the Irish Free State took its seat for the first time alongside government delegations from the United Kingdom, Canada, Australia, New Zealand, South Africa, Newfoundland and India.[17] The Imperial conferences provided important opportunities to advance the status of the Irish Free State by means of negotiated agreement. The Imperial conference of 1926 saw the adoption of the 'Balfour declaration' that recognized the equality of the Dominions with the

14 Hughes, *National Sovereignty*, p. 98. One Irish review of this book praised it as being 'free from bias or political prejudice'. The *Law Journal: Irish Free State Section*, 19 Dec. 1931. In fact, Sir John Simon and Sir William Jowitt refused requests to write a foreword to this book on the basis of Hughes' opinions, in particular his assertions that the Irish appeal to the Privy Council was not required by the Treaty. TNA, DO 35/108 4171/12.

15 David Swinfen, *Imperial Appeal: The Debate on the Appeal to the Privy Council, 1833–1986* (Manchester, Manchester University Press, 1987), pp 180–91.

16 UCDA, Costello Papers, P190/106, untitled memorandum, 2 Nov. 1926.

17 India was not a self-governing Dominion at this date but its particular importance to the British Empire ensured that it sent delegations to the Imperial conferences of the early twentieth century. H. Duncan Hall, *Commonwealth – A History of the British Commonwealth of Nations* (London, Hutchinson, 1971), p. 26.

United Kingdom, the mother country of the Empire.[18] This Balfour declaration, not to be confused with the 1917 declaration of the same name concerning a future Jewish homeland in Palestine, is seen as an important milestone in the evolution of Dominion autonomy.[19] The next constitutional milestone to emerge from the Imperial conferences of 1926 and 1930 was far more important to the history of the Irish Free State. The 1931 Statute of Westminster, a measure designed to considerably advance the autonomy of the Dominions, will be considered in a later chapter.[20]

The Imperial conferences were important social occasions and discussed a wide range of subject matter, including foreign affairs, economic matters and defence. Constitutional reform in the direction of greater autonomy for the Dominions had not been a major feature of the early Imperial conferences. A determined effort to secure constitutional reform had actually been defeated at the Imperial conference of 1921. This initiative, led by General Jan Smuts, prime minister of South Africa, failed as a result of indifference and hostility from the other Dominions.[21] The other participants in the conference even declined proposals to hold a future conference to explore possible constitutional reforms.[22]

In these circumstances the Irish government could be forgiven for not aggressively seeking reforms at its first Imperial conference in 1923.[23] By 1926 the Irish had learned that they could rely on support from South Africa and Canada for limited measures of constitutional change. The Irish were sufficiently encouraged to send their shopping list of proposed constitutional reforms to the other participants in advance of the conference. The exceptional importance of the issue of the Irish appeal to the Privy Council was underscored by its appearance in a separate document from the rest of the list of proposed reforms.[24] By 1926, the Privy Council appeal had become the most pressing issue in Irish constitutional affairs.

18 'They are autonomous Communities within the British Empire, equal in status, in no way subordinate one to another in any aspect of their domestic or external affairs, though united by a common allegiance to the Crown, and freely associated as members of the British Commonwealth of Nations.' Cmd. 2768, p. 14. This sentence was italicized and thus distinguished from the other paragraphs on 'Status of Great Britain and the Dominions' as a consequence of a printer's error. L.S. Amery, *My Political Life*, 3 vols (London, Hutchinson, 1953), ii, p. 392.

19 For example, Hall, *Commonwealth*, p. 628.

20 See ch. 7, below.

21 Hall, *Commonwealth*, p. 962. TNA, CAB 32/4, meeting of prime ministers, 27 July 1921, Appendix 1.

22 Cmd. 1474.

23 For a contrasting opinion see Ged Martin, 'The Irish Free State and the Evolution of the Commonwealth, 1921–49' in Ronald Hyam and Ged Martin (eds), *Reappraisals in British Imperial History* (London, Macmillan, 1975), p. 210.

24 UCDA, Blythe Papers, P24/217, memorandum on the Judicial Committee of the Privy Council and UCDA, Costello Papers, P190/106, untitled memorandum, 2 Nov. 1926.

The Irish had some hopes that Boer-dominated South Africa might prove sympathetic to their position on the Privy Council appeal. However, the South African prime minister, General Hertzog, did not believe that the appeal was a serious threat to the autonomy of his own Dominion and did not support abolition of the South African appeal in the 1920s.[25] The most likely ally was Canada, the eldest Dominion of the Empire. The shock and outrage in Canada caused by the case of *Nadan v. The King*, which had seen the Privy Council strike down provisions of the Canadian Criminal Code, gave the Irish some cause for optimism that they might win support from Ottawa.[26] The Australian position was a little more difficult to predict. Australia was staunch in its loyalty to the Empire but tended to be less supportive of the particular institution of the Privy Council appeal.[27] Enthusiasm for the appeal in Australia had not been improved by a number of unpopular decisions.[28] The United Kingdom, New Zealand and Newfoundland were certain to oppose any initiative to limit the Privy Council appeal. The Indian delegation was made up of British officials and Indian princes and could be relied on to support the British position on constitutional matters. The Irish could also rely on opposition from one very determined individual, lord chancellor Cave, who prioritized the maintenance of the Irish appeal.

Many histories of the Imperial conference of 1926 make reference to an unflattering account provided by the Canadian journalist D.B. MacRae of the *Manitoba Free Press* in which Lord Cave 'stamped out of the conference, saying he was not going to be a party to the breaking up of the British Empire'. 'With him gone', concluded MacRae 'the conference made better progress'.[29] This anecdote reflects Cave's reputation as a strong supporter of the principles of Imperial unity. Yet it has also created a distorted impression of events in 1926. Journalists did not have direct access to the closed sessions of the conference. Cave certainly did not 'stamp out' of the discussions concerning the Irish appeal to the Privy Council. In fact, British delegates to the Imperial conference were instructed that Lord Cave was to be summoned on every occasion that the subject of the Irish appeal was raised in any of the sessions.[30]

25 TNA, LCO 2/3465, extract from a report on General Hertzog's visit to Frankfort, 12 Oct. 1928.
26 [1926] AC 482. NAI, dept. of foreign affairs, EA1/26, memorandum by J.P. Walsh, 21 Apr. 1926.
27 For example, see H. Duncan Hall, *The British Commonwealth of Nations* (London, Methuen, 1920), pp 263–70.
28 For example, *Deakin v. Webb* (1904) 1 CLR 585, *Webb v. Outrim* [1907] AC 81 and *Baxter v. Commissioners of Taxation, New South Wales* (1907) 4 CLR 1087.
29 Letter from D.B. MacRae, journalist with the *Manitoba Free Press* to his editor J.W. Dafoe, 21 Nov. 1926. See Ramsay Cook (ed.), 'A Canadian Account of the 1926 Imperial Conference', *Journal of Commonwealth Political Studies*, 3:1 (1965), 50 at 60–1. MacRae's account is also repeated in D.W. Harkness, *The Restless Dominion* (New York, New University Press, 1969), p. 114 and Jacqueline D. Krikorian, 'British Imperial Politics and Judicial Independence: The Judicial Committee's Decision in the Canadian Case *Nadan v. The King*', *Canadian Journal of Political Science*, 33:2 (2000), 291 at 326.
30 TNA, LCO 2/3465, memorandum on Imperial conference, 1926, 13 Oct. 1926.

The Irish delegates soon discovered that Cave was not prepared to apologize for his actions in *Lynham v. Butler*. Cave stoutly denied that the Irish Free State had been treated differently from the other Dominions and dismissed Irish accusations that the Judicial Committee was trying to broaden the appeal so as to occupy the position formerly enjoyed by the House of Lords in Ireland. Cave noted that leave to appeal had only been given in two cases out of about ten arising from the Irish Free State and that the Irish government had only objected to one of these.[31] He had already rejected claims of discrimination against the Irish Free State and insisted that the Judicial Committee would have given leave to appeal if a case like *Lynham v. Butler* had come from any the other Dominions.[32]

The Irish delegates now revealed their strategy of appealing to the self-interest of the other Dominions, in particular Canada. They insisted that Canada would be permitted to abolish the appeal if she were inclined to do so. Next, they argued that a challenge to the right of the Irish Free State to abolish the appeal was a challenge to the rights of every other Dominion.[33] Lord Cave responded by pointing out that, from a strict legal perspective, none of the Dominions had the right to abolish the Privy Council appeal. This point lay at the heart of the judgment that he had delivered in *Nadan v. The King*.[34] Cave insisted that the institution of the Privy Council appeal was an important link that bound the Empire together. The consent of all the Dominions would be required before a change could be made to this pillar of Imperial unity.[35]

When the Irish delegates looked around the negotiating table it soon became clear that their hopes of winning Dominion support were misplaced. Prime minister William Lyon Mackenzie King of Canada, who had taken a strong line on Dominion autonomy at the previous Imperial conference, rebuffed Irish efforts to involve him in discussions concerning the Privy Council appeal.[36] The recent case of *Nadan v. The King* had certainly raised some hackles in Canada, but the Privy Council appeal touched on sensitive issues of national unity. The provincial parliaments and the French Canadian community were seen as strong supporters of the appeal as a safeguard of their rights against the government in Ottawa.[37]

The Irish government had tried to involve South Africa in their campaign against the Privy Council appeal before the Imperial conference had even begun. It claimed that the Privy Council's actions in granting leave to appeal in *Lynham v. Butler* had broken undertakings given by the Lloyd George government in 1922 that the Irish appeal would follow the restrictive practice used with respect to appeals from South Africa.[38] Lord Cave immediately ordered an investigation of

31 TNA, CAB 32/56 E(IR-26) 4th meeting, 2 Nov. 1926.
32 *Hansard*, House of Lords, vol. 63, col. 405, 3 Mar. 1926.
33 TNA, CAB 32/56 E(IR-26) 4th meeting, 2 Nov. 1926. 34 [1926] AC 482.
35 TNA, CAB 32/56 E(IR-26) 4th meeting, 2 Nov. 1926.
36 NAI, dept. of foreign affairs, EA1/26, memorandum by J.P. Walsh, 21 Apr. 1926.
37 For example, see Harkness, *Restless Dominion*, p. 114.
38 *Dáil Debates*, vol. 14, col. 117, 27 Jan. 1926.

British government files to check the accuracy of these claims. Cave insisted that he found no evidence to support the assertion that the Irish Free State had been promised precisely the same treatment as South Africa.[39] In any case, the practice followed by the Privy Council in dealing with South African appeals was not actually as restrictive as the Irish seemed to believe.[40] This allowed Cave to conclude 'I have no doubt that if a similar application [to that in *Lynham v. Butler*] had been made in a South African case, leave would have been granted'.[41]

The South Africans did not get involved in this dispute despite the references to their own appeal to the Privy Council. They had little interest in what precisely the British and Irish delegates had agreed in 1922 during the negotiations on the Free State Constitution. As for the remaining Dominions, the issue of reforming or abolishing the Privy Council appeal was not a priority for the Australian delegation in 1926. New Zealand and Newfoundland were predictably hostile to the Irish position.[42]

The second strand of the Irish negotiating stance in 1926 was to stress that they were only seeking the *right* to abolish the Privy Council appeal. The Irish delegates said that if this right were admitted, the Irish Free State might be satisfied with limiting the appeal in place of outright abolition.[43] It is open to speculation how far this reflected the true position of the Irish government and how far it represented tactical considerations. At one point O'Higgins even suggested a solution of requiring that all appellants receive a certificate from the Irish Supreme Court before an appeal could be taken before the Privy Council.[44] This suggestion seems to have been inspired by the provisions of the Australian Constitution.[45] It would have effectively abolished the Irish appeal to the Privy Council and, for this reason, was unacceptable to the British.

Lord Cave admitted that a Dominion request to modify the appeal would merit serious consideration but repeated that any such request would concern the Empire as a whole. He admitted that if, for example, the Commonwealth of Australia demanded the abolition of the appeal the British government would probably try to persuade Australia to retain it, but that if abolition was insisted upon they would probably give the Australians what they wanted. Nevertheless, Cave added that although the other Dominions might be permitted to abolish the appeal 'The position of the Irish Free State was singular'.[46] The Irish appeal was seen as having its basis in the settlement imposed by the Anglo-Irish Treaty of 1921 and Cave was convinced that it was too early for the Irish government to seek to modify it.[47] He suggested that the best course would be to

39 See ch. 2, above. 40 See ch. 2, above.
41 CAB 24/174 SFC 54 (26), memorandum by the lord chancellor, 25 Feb. 1926.
42 TNA, CAB 32/56 E(IR-26) 4th meeting, 2 Nov. 1926. 43 Ibid.
44 TNA, LCO 2/3465, Whiskard to Schuster, 9 Sept. 1926.
45 Section 74 of the Commonwealth of Australia Constitution Act 1900.
46 TNA, CAB 32/56 E(IR-26) 4th meeting, 2 Nov. 1926.
47 TNA, LCO 2/3465, Imperial conference 1926, Appeals to the King in Council, 1 Nov. 1926.

postpone further consideration of this matter until the next Imperial conference.[48]

The Irish attempt to secure recognition of their right to abolish the Irish appeal to the Privy Council was doomed by the absence of Dominion support. On the other hand, some members of the British delegation, in particular Lords Balfour and Birkenhead, were receptive to the idea of negotiating a limitation of the Irish appeal. Balfour was a former chief secretary of Ireland (1887–91) while Birkenhead was a signatory of the 1921 Treaty. It is possible that their knowledge of Ireland and Irish nationalism caused them to seek a viable compromise on the appeal. Balfour concluded 'By all means limit the right of appeal in trivial cases, but keep it as a "bulwark of great principles".'[49] Lord Birkenhead agreed that the Irish appeal should be 'rigidly delimited' and proposed that a special sub-committee within the Imperial conference could be set up to discuss how this might be achieved.[50] The limitation of the Irish appeal would minimize the chances of any repetition of cases like *Lynham v. Butler* and so preserve the role of the Judicial Committee of the Privy Council as arbiter of the Treaty settlement.

Lord Cave was horrified by these proposals. He argued that the Judicial Committee was an independent body and that, since the rules affected all the Dominions, it was not possible for the British government to negotiate a change of rules with just one Dominion.[51] Cave's resistance and the absence of Dominion support defeated the Irish initiative on the Privy Council appeal in 1926.

Lord Cave proved remarkably successful in thwarting initiatives to limit or abolish the Irish appeal. He also succeeded in securing formal recognition of the principle that changes should not be made with respect to the appeal without prior consultation and discussion with other members of the Commonwealth.[52] Dominion support for limiting or abolishing the Privy Council appeal was considered unlikely as long as French Canadians and other influential minority communities supported it.[53] The Irish delegation had come to the Imperial conference seeking Dominion support for their position on the Privy Council appeal. Lord Cave helped to ensure that the Irish left the Imperial conference with a Dominion veto over their attempts at reform.

48 TNA, CAB 32/56 E(IR-26) 4th meeting, 2 Nov. 1926 and TNA, LCO 2/3465, Imperial conference 1926, Appeals to the King in Council, 1 Nov. 1926.

49 TNA, CAB 32/56 E(IR-26) 4th meeting, 2 Nov. 1926.

50 Ibid.

51 TNA, LCO 2/3465, Imperial conference 1926, Appeals to the King in Council, 1 Nov. 1926 and CAB 32/56 E(IR-26) 4th meeting, 2 Nov. 1926.

52 Cmd. 2768, pp 19–20. Similar restrictions were placed on Dominion acceptance of the compulsory arbitration of the Permanent Court of International Justice, a court that was often seen as a potential competitor in terms of jurisdiction with the Judicial Committee of the Privy Council. Cmd. 2768, p. 28.

53 Keith, *Responsible Government* (1928), ii, p. 1230. William Lyon Mackenzie King was prime minister of Canada 1921–6, 1926–30 and 1935–48.

The lack of any progress in abolishing the appeal forced the Irish to make the most of a statement in the conference report that 'it is no part of the policy of His Majesty's Government in Great Britain that questions affecting judicial appeals should be determined otherwise than in accordance with the part of the Empire primarily affected'.[54] In reality this provided nothing that had not been said to the Irish by British politicians during the 1922 negotiations on the Free State Constitution or by the Privy Council itself when dealing with Irish appeals.[55] Arthur Berriedale Keith dismissed it as 'the usual, it must be feared insincere, declaration'.[56]

The Irish attempt to secure the abolition of the appeal during the formal sessions of the Imperial conference had failed. The negotiations retreated to an informal meeting between Kevin O'Higgins and Lord Birkenhead, with John A. Costello, Patrick McGilligan and Lord Hailsham also in attendance. According to Irish reports of this meeting, Birkenhead recognized the justice of the Irish position on the Privy Council appeal but urged that they not press the matter to a conclusion. Birkenhead noted that he had already taken great political risks in supporting other Irish initiatives and that sections of the Conservative party were suspicious of every action taken by the Irish. Not enough time had elapsed to overcome these suspicions and many would argue that the Irish were moving ahead too rapidly. Birkenhead urged the Irish to leave the matter until the next Imperial conference when he would give them the full weight of his support.[57]

The Irish delegation agreed to drop the matter for the time being, but inserted a statement in the final conference report that they reserved the right to bring up the Privy Council appeal again at the next Imperial conference.[58] In spite of the assurances given to the Irish delegation, it was well known that this was an issue on which the British would be reluctant to compromise. O'Higgins speculated 'I wonder will they keep their promise'.[59]

O'Higgins would never learn if his British counterparts were sincere or otherwise. He was assassinated while walking to church on 10 July 1927, just a few months after the conclusion of the Imperial conference. His assassination set in

54 Cmd. 2768, p. 19.

55 For example, see the comments made by Viscount Haldane when hearing the three petitions, *Alexander E. Hull and Co. v. Mary A.E. M'Kenna, The 'Freeman's Journal' Limited v. Erik Fernstrom* and *The 'Freeman's Journal' Limited v. Follum Traesliberi* [1926] IR 402 at 404.

56 Keith, *Responsible Government* (1928), ii, p. 1230. See also the comments of the *Times* on this declaration. *Times*, 22 Nov. 1926. The British government would argue at the Imperial conference of 1930 that this proviso could not be considered a commitment to remove the Privy Council appeal. NAI, dept. of the Taoiseach, S4285B, memorandum by Michael McDunphy, 7 Nov. 1930.

57 NAI, dept. of the Taoiseach, S4285B, Patrick McGilligan to Ramsay MacDonald, 4 Nov. 1930. Prime minister Bruce of Australia also recalled O'Higgins agreeing to a postponement of the Privy Council question at a private dinner attended by Bruce, O'Higgins and Birkenhead. Hall, *Commonwealth*, p. 631.

58 Cmd. 2768, p. 20.

59 UCDA, Costello Papers, P190/56, draft article, and NAI, dept. of the Taoiseach, S4285B, W.T. Cosgrave to Lord Granard, 8 Nov. 1930.

train a series of events that saw Eamon de Valera and his supporters end their policy of refusing to take their seats in the Oireachtas. De Valera had been president of the underground government during the Anglo-Irish conflict of 1919–21 but his subsequent opposition to the 1921 Treaty had left him in a political wilderness. In 1926 he founded a new political party, Fianna Fáil, and committed it to a programme of extensive constitutional reforms that would radically alter the settlement enshrined in the 1921 Treaty and in the Constitution of the Irish Free State. W.T. Cosgrave's Cumann na nGaedheal party had been in government since 1922 and faced challenges on many fronts that far outranked the issue of the Privy Council appeal, including the economy, public order and unemployment. By late 1931 it had become clear that de Valera had a good chance of winning the approaching general election.

O'Higgins' death in 1927 saw him replaced by Patrick McGilligan as minister for external affairs, who now inherited the initiative to abolish the Irish appeal to the Privy Council. The transition saw little change in policy although McGilligan, a native of county Derry, was prone to use less temperate language in refuting claims that the appeal offered a safeguard for southern Protestants.[60] While these important political events were unfolding Irish appeals continued to go to London and the Irish government continued to do everything in its power to block them.

PERFORMING RIGHT SOCIETY v. BRAY URBAN DISTRICT COUNCIL

Although this 1930 appeal from the Irish Supreme Court was primarily concerned with issues of infringement on copyright it also raised a number of important constitutional questions.[61] As with *Lynham v. Butler*, the Irish government responded by enacting special legislation designed to block the appeal. Once again it was argued that the Privy Council was interfering in Irish domestic affairs and that the Irish government was justified in blocking its decision in this case.[62] The Irish persisted in this argument even though British governments had long regarded copyright as an Imperial matter[63] and international copyright associations regarded the rights of authors as an international concern.[64] In truth the Irish

60 See NAI, dept. of the Taoiseach, S4285B, transcript of radio broadcast of 9 Nov. 1930.

61 [1930] IR 509. This case raised questions as to the applicability of Imperial statutes in the Irish Free State. It also raised the difficult question as to the date on which the Irish Free State came into existence. On a more immediate level, the case raised the question of what, if any, copyright law extended to the Irish Free State in the 1920s. See Thomas Mohr, 'British Imperial Statutes and Irish Law: Statutes Passed Before the Creation of the Irish Free State', *Journal of Legal History*, 31:2 (2010), 299.

62 *Seanad Debates*, vol. 12, col. 1216–20, 10 July 1929.

63 See the Copyright Acts of 1842 and 1911. See also A.B. Keith, *Responsible Government in the Dominions*, 3 vols (Oxford, Clarendon, 1912), iii, pp 1216–37.

64 The actions of the Irish government in response to this case attracted censure at an international conference of the *Confédération Internationale des Sociétés des Auteurs et Compositeurs Dramatiques*

government was less interested in the finer points of copyright law and far more concerned about winning another round in its duel with the Privy Council. The contents of the final decision delivered by the Privy Council in this case were actually preferable to the Irish government on purely legal grounds than the judgment delivered by the Irish Supreme Court.[65] This scarcely mattered. The Privy Council was treated as a usurper that was, in the words of Patrick McGilligan, 'operating as if superior to our Supreme Court'.[66]

The Oireachtas passed a special provision in the Copyright (Preservation) Act 1929 designed to nullify any decision made by the Privy Council in this case.[67] This measure placed another nail in the coffin of the previous policy of limited tolerance of the appeal. The Irish government was reminded that it had once considered international or Commonwealth concerns, as raised in *Wigg and Cochrane*, as acceptable for consideration by the Privy Council. Ernest Blythe, minister for finance, answered 'We have learned since then'.[68] By the end of the 1920s the Irish government had largely abandoned arguments that they were entitled to South African practice or that the Privy Council was breaching assurances and understandings given by the Lloyd George government in 1922. Patrick McGilligan was content to issue a warning that 'people who look for leave to appeal to the Privy Council do so at their own risk'.[69]

ALTERNATIVES TO THE JUDICIAL COMMITTEE OF THE PRIVY COUNCIL

If an arbiter of the 1921 Treaty was required, the Irish government had a definite preference for other tribunals in place of the Judicial Committee of the Privy Council. Irish governments always had a great deal of enthusiasm for the League of Nations as a counterweight to the Imperial connection. The Irish Free State

held in Madrid that same year. A resolution was passed condemning Section 4 Copyright (Preservation) Act 1929 as being 'contrary to the universally accepted principles of justice and the spirit and tenor of the Berne Convention'. Members of the Confederation were advised to protest to their respective governments against the proposed legislation as being 'contrary to natural justice and a direct confiscation of the rights of authors'. *Hansard*, House of Lords, vol. 75, col. 490, 13 Nov. 1929.

65 The decision of the Privy Council mirrored many of the conclusions put forward by counsel for the attorney general of the Irish Free State when this case appeared before the Supreme Court. *Performing Right Society v Bray U.D.C.* [1928] IR 506 at 515.

66 *Seanad Debates*, vol. 12, col. 1219, 10 July 1929.

67 Section 4 of the Copyright (Preservation) Act 1929 made an exception to the retrospective provisions of the Act by prohibiting remedies for all past infringements of copyright. Since there was no other pending litigation in the Irish Free State concerning breach of copyright this measure was an obvious attempt to block the pending appeal to the Privy Council in the case of *Performing Right Society v. Bray U.D.C.*

68 *Seanad Debates*, vol. 12, col. 1221, 10 July 1929.

69 *Dáil Debates*, vol. 22, col. 109, 22 Feb. 1928 and *Seanad Debates*, vol. 12, col. 1221, 10 July 1929.

finally joined the League in 1923, and this opened the possibility of the Permanent Court of International Justice adjudicating on Anglo-Irish disputes.

The Irish government insisted that the 'Articles of Agreement for a Treaty between Great Britain and Ireland' signed in London on 6 December 1921 was an international treaty, a position contested by British authorities.[70] If the 1921 agreement was an international treaty disputes over its interpretation could be brought to the Permanent Court of International Justice in The Hague. Irish ministers such as Kevin O'Higgins, Ernest Blythe and Patrick McGilligan made clear their preference for a League of Nations arbiter over any Imperial body, including the Privy Council.[71] Irish officials who wanted their government to register the 1921 Treaty with the League of Nations emphasized the advantages of an international arbiter of that agreement.[72] The Irish Free State finally registered the Treaty on 11 July 1924.

In the mid-1920s the Irish government made clear its desire to sign the 'optional clause' of the Permanent Court of International Justice. This was widely perceived as an attempt to replace the Privy Council as arbiter of the Treaty.[73] The 'optional clause' made it possible for the Permanent Court of International Justice to exercise compulsory jurisdiction in disputes between states. The United Kingdom and the Dominions had declined to accept this in the early 1920s. The Irish Free State proved to be an enthusiastic supporter of the optional clause and raised the possibility of signing it at the 1926 Imperial conference. The British insisted that disputes between members of the Empire/Commonwealth should be entirely removed from the jurisdiction of the Permanent Court of International Justice.[74] The Irish eventually lost patience and signed the optional clause on 14 September 1929. Although the British signed some months later they did so subject to an explicit reservation that excluded disputes between members of the Commonwealth.[75] The Irish made no such reservation.

In 1928 Arthur Berriedale Keith asked whether the time had come for 'the abandonment of the claim that the Judicial Committee shall be the arbiter in

70 *Dáil Debates*, vol. 1, col. 1486–7, 11 Oct. 1922.

71 *Dáil Debates*, vol. 1, col. 1486–8, 11 Oct. 1922 and vol. 33, col. 836, 893–4 and 897–8, 26 Feb. 1930.

72 NAI, dept. of foreign affairs, 417/105, Michael MacWhite to Joseph P. Walshe, 6 Dec. 1924. The British government protested against the actions of the Irish Free State in registering the Anglo-Irish Treaty with the League of Nations. NAI, dept. of foreign affairs, 417/105, memorandum by Joseph P. Walshe for minister for external affairs on 'The Registration of the Treaty', 1 Dec. 1924. Not all Irish nationalists were convinced that having the League of Nations act as arbiter of the 1921 Treaty was necessarily a good idea, based on suspicions that the organs of the League were heavily influenced by the British. *Seanad Debates*, vol. 6, col. 423, 24 Feb. 1926 and Dáil Debates, vol. 33, col. 903, 26 Feb. 1930.

73 Article 36 of the Statute of the Permanent Court of International Justice, 16 Dec. 1920. See *Dáil Debates*, vol. 33, col. 911–14, 26 Feb. 1930, Harkness, *Restless Dominion*, pp 120, 143 and 166 and Michael Kennedy, *Ireland and the League of Nations, 1919–1946* (Dublin, Irish Academic Press, 1996), p. 121.

74 Cmd. 2768, p. 22.

75 *Dáil Debates*, vol. 33, col. 887–8, 26 Feb. 1930. See also Swinfen, *Imperial Appeal*, p. 199.

disputes as to the meaning of the [Anglo-Irish] treaty?' Keith, writing in the middle of the fiasco caused by *Wigg and Cochrane*, proposed that a new Commonwealth tribunal should take over this role.[76] Proposals for creating a reformed Imperial court became a regular feature of Imperial gatherings in the early twentieth century. Examples include the Colonial conferences of 1901 and 1907, the Imperial conference of 1911 and the Imperial war conference of 1918. Australia tended to be the most enthusiastic originator and supporter of these proposals, an obvious reflection of dissatisfaction with the current form of the Privy Council appeal.[77] There was much less support for these proposals within the other Dominions and the United Kingdom. The need for unanimity on these proposals guaranteed their ultimate failure.[78]

Supporters of a new Imperial court were divided between those who valued the role of the Privy Council as a pillar of legal unity but believed that it should be improved and modernized. This was the position that Hector Hughes came to support in his later years.[79] There were other statesmen and commentaters who supported the idea of reform as a pretext to replace the Privy Council appeal with a weak institution that would, in reality, give the final say to national appellate courts. The Irish delegations that attended the Imperial conferences of the 1920s and early 1930s fell into this category.

The Irish did support creating a new form of appeal when the matter was raised at the Imperial conference of 1930. However, Irish statesmen were convinced that 'Anything in the shape of a permanent Court would be dangerous for us' because 'The British could hardly fail to use it for the purpose of maintaining control or enforcing their views on constitutional matters'.[80] Consequently they supported proposals for a new 'Commonwealth tribunal' with voluntary jurisdiction that would not be a permanent court but would simply convene when the need arose.[81] The Irish were adamant that questions concerning the interpretation of the 1921 Treaty be excluded from the jurisdiction of any new court and received solid support from South Africa on this point.[82] Although the 1930 Imperial conference approved the idea for a new Commonwealth tribunal it never functioned in practice.[83] In truth, the Irish never had any genuine enthusiasm for any new or

76 A.B. Keith, *The Scotsman*, 26 Apr. 1928 and *Letters on Imperial Relations, Indian Reform, Constitutional and International Law, 1916–1935* (Oxford, Oxford University Press, 1935), p. 79 and 'Notes on Imperial Constitutional Law', *Journal of Comparative Legislation and International Law*, 4 (1922) 104 at 105.

77 TNA, LCO 2/179.

78 Ibid.

79 ISwinfen, *Imperial Appeal*, pp 180–91.

80 UCDA, Costello Papers, P190/141, preliminary note for the Imperial conference of 1930, undated.

81 Cmd. 3717, pp 22–4.

82 TNA, CAB 32/88 E(I.R.)(30) 1st meeting, 7 Oct. 1930.

83 Proposals for using this proposed tribunal did occasionally surface in the years that followed. For example, it was proposed that the tribunal be used to settle Anglo-Irish disputes concerning the parliamentary oath and the land annuities. TNA, DO 35/137/7 file 4431/1, note of a discussion with regard to the various outstanding questions with the Irish Free State, 31 Mar. 1931; TNA, LCO 2/910, CP 120(31), The Irish Free State and Appeals to the Judicial Committee of the Privy

reformed Commonwealth tribunal. An Irish memorandum on the establishment of a new tribunal written in 1930 openly admitted that 'for the moment we must regard it as a purely political expedient for getting rid of the Privy Council'.[84]

BACKGROUND TO THE IMPERIAL CONFERENCE OF 1930

The Irish had made clear their intention to seek the abolition of the Privy Council appeal in the official report of the Imperial conference of 1926.[85] By doing so the Irish government had placed considerable pressure on its own shoulders to deliver on this commitment. Preparations for the 1930 Imperial conference began with the convening of a special sub-conference in 1929.[86] The main purpose of this sub-conference was to put in place the foundations of legal reforms designed to give the Dominions more autonomy. These reforms would later become law in the Statute of Westminster in 1931. The Irish government had to face criticism in the Dáil for failing to secure the abolition of the Privy Council appeal at this 1929 sub-conference. The Irish government argued, not unreasonably, that the Privy Council appeal had not been on the conference agenda.[87] Nevertheless, the matter was raised during the discussions and many of the remarks that were made could only have boosted Irish confidence in securing their objective at the forthcoming Imperial conference.

A Canadian report on the 1929 conference indicated that private discussions 'had indicated a rapidly growing feeling that the Privy Council was losing prestige'.[88] Sir Claud Schuster, permanent secretary in the Lord Chancellor's Office, had noted that the Privy Council was evolving into little more than a 'Supreme Court for India' since, with the exception of Canada, relatively few appeals now came from the Dominions.[89] The attorney general, Sir William Jowitt, went even further by remarking that it was not possible to continue the Privy Council appeal in its current form. He even declared his intention to prepare a memorandum for the next Imperial conference that would pave the way for the abolition of the appeal if this were demanded by one of the Dominions.[90] Shrewd

Council; TNA, LCO 2/910, Sir Henry Batterbee, Agreed note on Lough Foyle, 26 Feb. 1931 and CP 120(31). De Valera refused to submit disputes to this proposed tribunal on the basis of objections to the rule that membership of the tribunal was limited to citizens of the British Commonwealth. *Times*, 18 June 1932 and *Seanad Debates*, vol. 15, col. 1376–82, 20 July 1932.

84 Harkness, *Restless Dominion*, p. 178. See also *Irish Times*, 28 Sept. 1929.

85 Cmd. 2768, p. 20.

86 This was known as the Operation of Dominion Legislation (ODL) conference. See Harkness, *Restless Dominion*, p. 141.

87 *Dáil Debates*, vol. 33, col. 2202, 20 Mar. 1930.

88 NAC (National Archives of Canada), Oscar Skelton Fonds, MG30 D33, vol. 4, 4–1.

89 Ibid. Indian cases had not always dominated the Privy Council appeal and the number of Indian appeals in the early twentieth century was below average when its large population is taken into account. See ch. 1, above.

90 NAC (National Archives of Canada), Oscar Skelton Fonds, MG30 D33, vol. 4, 4–1.

Canadian diplomats noted that it was not clear that Jowitt actually spoke for the British government in saying this.[91] The Irish would have done well to share this caution. Instead, the Irish government made no secret of its intention to seek abolition at the 1930 Imperial conference. This guaranteed that the government would face serious recriminations from domestic opponents, including de Valera's Fianna Fáil party, if this objective were not achieved.[92] Unfortunately, the Irish government was seeking concessions from a minority Labour government in London that felt vulnerable to charges of surrendering the Empire from its own opposition in parliament.

The minority Labour government had a number of reasons to be worried. First, it was concerned that the inclusion of a provision abolishing the Irish appeal to the Privy Council in the proposed Statute of Westminster would delay or even endanger this important measure designed to augment Dominion autonomy.[93] This, in turn, would cause difficulties with the Dominions that had pushed for this reforming legislation including South Africa, Canada and the Irish Free State itself. Second, the appeal was widely seen as a safeguard for the Protestant community of the Irish Free State who still retained considerable influence and sympathy at Westminster. Finally, Labour ministers proved correct in surmising that the leaders of the opposition Conservative party strongly opposed conceding the abolition of the Irish appeal to the Privy Council.[94] In short, the vulnerable Labour government saw the Privy Council appeal as an issue that could undermine its continued survival. Prime minister Ramsay MacDonald warned his cabinet 'no United Kingdom Government could survive which attempted to reverse the provisions of the Irish Treaty and the Free State Constitution in this respect'.[95] For this reason the Labour government denied that its Conservative predecessor had made any definite commitment in 1926 to secure the abolition of the Irish appeal at the next Imperial conference.

In 1926, the Irish had relied on unwritten undertakings and assurances on the Privy Council appeal, as they had done during the negotiations on the Irish constitution in 1922. By the time the 1930 conference convened Birkenhead and O'Higgins were both dead and the only surviving British witness to their discussions, Lord Hailsham, claimed that both parties had retained complete freedom of action on the Privy Council appeal.[96] Once again unwritten promises proved unenforceable and the Irish could do nothing about it.[97]

91 Ibid. 92 Cmd. 2768, p. 20. 93 TNA, CAB 32/70, meeting of 23 Sept. 1930.

94 TNA, CAB 32/79 PM(30)18, meeting of 5 Nov. 1930.

95 TNA, CAB 32/70, meeting of 23 Sept. 1930.

96 Hailsham was under the impression that the Irish government could not change the Treaty for eight years and that this had been one of the reasons why the Irish had agreed to postpone consideration of the Privy Council appeal in 1926. As McGilligan pointed out, this position was based on a serious misinterpretation of Article 50 of the Irish Constitution. TNA, CAB 32/79 PM(30)18. See also NAI, dept. of the Taoiseach, S4285B, Diarmuid O'Hegarty to Michael McDunphy of 7 Nov. 1930 and memorandum by Michael McDunphy of 7 Nov. 1930.

97 TNA, CAB 32/79 PM(30)18.

THE IRISH CASE FOR ABOLITION

The Irish delegation to the 1930 Imperial conference justified their case for abolishing the Privy Council appeal on the basis that its retention was contrary to the wishes of the majority of the Irish people and that it undermined the principle of Dominion equality with the United Kingdom declared in 1926.[98] They added that the appeal was a 'menace to our sovereignty', that it was one of the greatest obstacles to closer Anglo-Irish relations and that it prevented many Irish people from accepting the Irish Free State's position in the Commonwealth.[99] The Irish delegation even complained that the existence of the appeal was detrimental to popular respect for the law and undermined loyalty to the institutions of the state.[100]

The Irish government denied all claims that the appeal constituted a safeguard for the southern Protestants.[101] McGilligan took a hard line on this issue stating that even if there were an active movement on the part of southern Protestants to keep the appeal, it would not alter his view that it should be abolished.[102] He also stressed that his government had successfully blocked Irish appeals in the past and that, therefore, any safeguard would be ineffective.[103]

Above all else, the Irish delegation was anxious to refute the contention that the Privy Council appeal constituted a commitment derived from the 1921 Treaty. They added that, even assuming that this were true, the numerous constitutional advances in Dominion status since 1922 gave their parliament the power to abolish the appeal.[104] The Irish delegation emphasized that the Irish people considered the removal of the appeal as the acid test of the sincerity of the principle of Dominion equality.[105]

THE 1921 TREATY AS A CONTRACT

The British government was concerned that the enhanced autonomy promised to the Dominions in the proposed Statute of Westminster might be seen as giving the Irish Free State new powers to abolish the appeal notwithstanding the provisions of the 1921 Treaty. It felt obliged to argue at the 1930 Imperial conference that the settlement contained in the 1921 Treaty and the Irish Constitution of 1922 represented a binding contract between the United Kingdom and the Irish Free State. This contractual relationship differentiated the Irish Free State from the all the other Dominions. Although the Balfour declaration of 1926 confirmed the equal status of the Irish Free State in the Commonwealth, it was argued that this

98 TNA, CAB 32/79 PM(30)5.
99 TNA, CAB 32/83 E(B)(30)27, McGilligan to Thomas, 12 Sept. 1930.
100 UCDA, FitzGerald Papers, P80/970, J.P. Walsh to D. O'Hegarty, 16 Apr. 1930.
101 TNA, CAB 32/79 PM(30)18.
102 TNA, CAB 32/88 E(I.R.)(30) 8th meeting, 21 Oct. 1930.
103 Ibid.
104 TNA, CAB 32/79 PM(30)5.
105 TNA, CAB 32/79 PM(30)18.

declaration had to be read in light of this contract. The British concluded that this binding contract would be breached by any unilateral abolition of the Privy Council appeal by the Irish Free State.[106] They added that the Irish were also constrained from breaking the Treaty on moral grounds that were no less binding than legal ones.[107]

The British never went into any detail as to the precise nature of this binding 'contract'. Instead, they made repeated offers that the dispute be placed in the hands of a reformed Commonwealth tribunal or some other body for the purposes of arbitration.[108] McGilligan did his best to involve the other Dominions in refuting the idea that the Irish Free State was bound by a legal or moral contract.[109] However, these issues were rapidly overshadowed by a legal argument that shattered all Irish hopes of success.

WAS THE AUTONOMY OF THE IRISH FREE STATE DYNAMIC OR STATIC?

The British knew that the best chance the Irish had of rallying Dominion support at the 1930 conference was to argue that a threat to the autonomy of one Dominion was a threat to all. This meant that they had to find some means of separating the status of the Irish Free State from the other Dominions. This could be done, as mentioned earlier, by arguing that the Irish Free State was subject to a binding contract in the form of the 1921 Treaty but there was also a more extreme and far-reaching method. This was the argument that the Anglo-Irish Treaty had only given the Irish Free State the status of Canada as it had existed in 1921 without the benefit of subsequent constitutional advances achieved by the other Dominions.[110] In short, the Irish Free State was bound in perpetuity to the precise conditions offered by Treaty in 1921.

British legal experts had concluded that the autonomy of the Irish Free State was static rather than dynamic since at least 1923.[111] Nevertheless, this 'static theory' had never been raised in any official context until now.[112] In 1930, the British government knew that this radical position would outrage their Irish counterparts. Consequently, they were careful not to endorse it themselves but to claim that their opposition in parliament, in particular the Conservative party, was likely to raise this argument if the Irish tried to abolish the appeal. The Irish refused to accept these tactics and demanded to know the position of the current British government on whether or not the Irish Free State could advance with the other Dominions or must remain frozen to the position held by them in 1921.

106 TNA, CAB 32/79 PM(30)5. 107 TNA, CAB 32/79 PM(30)18.
108 TNA, CAB 32/79 PM(30)18 and 21.
109 TNA, CAB 32/79 PM(30)21 and CAB 32/79 PM(30)27. 110 TNA, CAB 32/79 PM(30)5.
111 TNA, CO 532/257, law officers to colonial secretary, 31 Dec. 1923.
112 For example, see NAI, dept. of the Taoiseach, S4285B, Cosgrave to Lord Granard, 8 Nov. 1930.

After attempts at evading the question proved unsuccessful the attorney general Sir William Jowitt and prime minister Ramsay MacDonald revealed that they believed that the Irish Free State was frozen to the position granted in 1921 as a strict matter of law.[113] McGilligan was appalled and threatened to repeat their conclusions in the Oireachtas.[114]

Eight years had passed since the negotiations that had established the Treaty and the 1922 Constitution. Nevertheless, the scale of progress achieved since that time made it appear that the Labour government were attempting to set the clock back to a remote antediluvian era. For example, the Irish Free State had reformed the office of the Governor-General, set up their own diplomatic representation abroad and had been included in a declaration of the principle of Dominion equality with the United Kingdom in 1926. The Irish Free State was also on the verge of gaining recognition of additional autonomy in the forthcoming Statute of Westminster.[115] To advance the idea that all this was in jeopardy was a move of unparalleled recklessness that forced Irish ministers to re-examine their entire policy of achieving constitutional reforms by means of negotiation, to doubt their endeavours to create a Commonwealth association that could be accepted by the Irish people and even to question their deep-seated belief in the sanctity of the 1921 Treaty.

The remainder of the discussions were taken up with a series of bitter recriminations that illustrate how low the British government had brought relations with even the most enthusiastic advocates of the Treaty and the Commonwealth in Ireland. Desmond FitzGerald, who had had some involvement in the 1921 negotiations, told the other delegations at the Imperial conference that it had been generally assumed that the Treaty had offered a dynamic status. FitzGerald and McGilligan noted that if this were not so, the Irish had signed the Treaty on the basis of a misunderstanding and had recommended it to the Irish people under false pretences.[116] McGilligan pointed out that if the Irish Free State could not advance with the other Dominions it seemed illogical that she had even been invited to this or any of the previous Imperial conferences.[117] If all this were true it was doubtful that the Irish Free State could really be considered a Dominion and a member of the Commonwealth. As for the British offers of arbitration, these were adamantly rejected. McGilligan made it clear that if the result of such arbitration was to establish that the Treaty gave the Irish Free State something less than Dominion status the Irish would have little choice but to denounce the Treaty.[118] At a stroke, the history of Irish participation at the Imperial conferences had been brought to its nadir.

113 TNA, CAB 32/79 PM(30)27. 114 Ibid.
115 See Harkness, *Restless Dominion*, pp 63–7, 96–104 and 106–9.
116 TNA, CAB 32/79 PM(30)16.
117 NAI, dept. of the Taoiseach, S4285B, memorandum by on Privy Council appeal by Michael McDunphy, 7 Nov. 1930 and TNA, CAB 32/79 PM(30)5.
118 TNA, CAB 32/79 PM(30)21.

THE POSITION OF THE OTHER DOMINIONS

The Irish government was not without friends among the other Dominions at the 1930 conference. It had, however, suffered a setback when the Liberal Canadian government that had campaigned for expanded Dominion autonomy at previous Imperial conferences lost power. Nevertheless, the new Conservative administration in Ottawa led by R.B. Bennett was not unfriendly to the Irish Free State. The Canadians were sceptical of claims that although their Dominion was free to abolish the Privy Council appeal the same could not be said of the Dominion with whom they shared a constitutional link.[119] Nevertheless, prime minister Bennett was impatient with the entire dispute. He took the position that the Treaty was essentially an Anglo-Irish concern and was not a matter for the Imperial conference.[120]

The Irish received more proactive support from South Africa and, more unusually, from Australia. Although Australia was seldom at the forefront of campaigns to push for more Dominion autonomy, the Privy Council appeal was not always popular in Canberra. In any case, the Australians now had a cabinet that included several members of Irish Catholic descent, including prime minister James Scullin. The Australian delegation joined with General Hertzog, prime minister of South Africa, to emphatically reject the idea that the Irish Free State's status was in any way frozen to the position of 1921.[121] Scullin and Hertzog were in no doubt that the Irish did indeed have a right to abolish the appeal to the Privy Council.[122] The Irish delegation later paid tribute to the support that they received from both prime ministers on these vital matters.[123] Scullin even tried to mediate between the British and Irish governments to prevent this dispute from escalating. Matters had gone too far and the Australian efforts proved unsuccessful.[124]

Although the British government felt unable to openly agree to the abolition of the Irish appeal at the 1930 Imperial conference it was prepared to facilitate this objective by less official means. Lord Sankey, the Labour government's lord chancellor, made a secret proposal that was communicated to W.T. Cosgrave while the Imperial conference was still in session. The matter was considered so sensitive that Sankey did not write directly to Cosgrave but used the earl of Granard, a southern Protestant who sat in the Irish senate, as an intermediary. Sankey's proposal sought to find a way to allow the Irish to abolish the Privy Council appeal without implicating the British government or endangering the passage of the Statute of Westminster through parliament. He suggested that the Irish government should make use of unilateral legislation to prevent further appeals.

119 TNA, CAB 32/79 PM(30)5. 120 TNA, CAB 32/79 PM(30)18
121 TNA, CAB 32/79 PM(30)5 and 18. UCDA, Costello Papers, P190/144, transcript of meeting of 17 Oct. 1930.
122 TNA, CAB 32/79 PM(30)5 and 18
123 UCDA, FitzGerald Papers, P80/1411, Desmond FitzGerald to Mabel FitzGerald, 10 Oct. 1930 and NAI, dept. of the Taoiseach, S4285B, Diarmuid O'Hegarty to Michael McDunphy of 7 Nov. 1930. 124 TNA, CAB 32/79 PM(30)25 and 27.

Sankey was even prepared to provide an understanding that the British government would not take any steps to oppose such a course of action.[125] The Irish delegation at the Imperial conference saw Sankey's initiative as a dishonest effort to sidetrack their efforts to achieve official abolition in London and recommended that Cosgrave refuse it.[126] Cosgrave did so in a letter that condemned the British contention that the status of the Irish Free State had been frozen in 1921 without the benefit of subsequent advances in Dominion autonomy.[127]

REASONS FOR FAILURE IN 1930

The escalating dispute caused by the Privy Council appeal was largely the result of the weakness of the administrations in Dublin and in London. Members of the Irish government had painted themselves into a corner by publicizing their intention to seek abolition of the appeal before the 1930 Imperial conference. They now feared that failure would leave them vulnerable to their domestic opponents, in particular Eamon de Valera's Fianna Fáil party, at the forthcoming Irish election. This ensured that the Irish delegation to the 1930 Imperial conference had no choice but to insist on nothing less than recognition of their right to completely abolish the appeal. One historian of the British Empire/Commonwealth, H. Duncan Hall, concludes 'No pending election in the history of the Commonwealth had led to such an uncompromising and persistent effort on the part of a government to get its own way at an Imperial Conference'.[128]

The minority Labour government in London also felt vulnerable and took an equally uncompromising position at the 1930 Imperial conference. Its insecurity was reflected when prime minister Ramsay MacDonald felt obliged to consult opposition leaders on the future of the Irish appeal to the Privy Council during the course of the 1930 conference. Stanley Baldwin, leader of the Conservative party and Lord Hailsham, a former lord chancellor, proved hostile to any proposal that permitted the Irish to abolish the appeal without the consent of the minority southern Protestant community.[129] Yet, there was little real conviction behind the firm stance adopted by the Labour administration. British ministers privately acknowledged that the Irish appeal to the Privy Council could no longer be salvaged.[130] The offer to put the legality of abolition out to arbitration was nothing more than an effort to buy time. Lord Sankey's effort to encourage the Irish to

125 NAI, dept. of the Taoiseach, S4285B, memorandum by Michael McDunphy, 7 Nov. 1930.
126 Ibid. and W.T. Cosgrave to Lord Granard, 8 Nov. 1930.
127 NAI, dept. of the Taoiseach, S4285B, W.T. Cosgrave to Lord Granard, 8 Nov. 1930.
128 Hall, *Commonwealth*, 694.
129 TNA, CAB 32/79 PM(30)18, meeting of 5 Nov. 1930. See also letter from Diarmuid O'Hegarty to Michael McDunphy of 7 Nov. 1930 and memorandum by Michael McDunphy of 7 Nov. 1930. NAI, dept. of the Taoiseach, S4285B. Lord Hailsham was lord chancellor 1928–9 and 1935–8.
130 TNA, CAB 32/83 E(B)(30)27, memorandum by the Dominions secretary, Sept. 1930.

discontinue the appeal without involving the British government was a blatant effort to deflect blame away from itself. There was very little real enthusiasm for the contention that the status of the Irish Free State had been frozen in 1921 and even influential figures within the British government felt that it was unsustainable.[131] It was little more than a clumsy negotiating tactic that had immediately backfired.

The failed negotiations on the Privy Council appeal mark the end of efforts to advance the autonomy of the Irish Free State through negotiations at the Imperial conferences.[132] Members of the Irish delegation certainly believed, in the aftermath of the 1930 conference, that they had advanced as far as they could by this route. The secretary of the Irish department of external affairs wrote to his Canadian counterpart that he was convinced of 'the complete futility of [attending] further Imperial Conferences'.[133] Patrick McGilligan wrote a newspaper article revealing that he agreed with the view that the Imperial conferences had 'served their purpose'.[134]

THE 'CLEANING OF THE SLATE' NEGOTIATIONS

One final effort was made to secure Anglo-Irish agreement on the abolition of the Irish appeal in the aftermath of the Imperial conference. In 1931 the two governments negotiated a proposed settlement that was provisionally called the 'cleaning of the slate' agreement.[135] This draft agreement covered a wide range of issues of varying degrees of importance. These included the settlement of a maritime dispute between Northern Ireland and the Irish Free State over Lough Foyle, the *inter se* operation of international conventions between the United Kingdom and the Irish Free State, the surrender of fugitive offenders, mutual enforcement of judgments and court orders, the use of the Great Seal, the sealing

131 TNA, LCO 2/910, Thomas to Granard, 5 June 1931 and TNA, LCO 2/910, memorandum by Sir Claud Schuster, 6 Nov. 1930.

132 An Irish delegation did attend the Imperial economic conference of 1932 in Ottawa. The Irish returned from this conference with little more than two minor trade agreements with their traditional Commonwealth allies, Canada and South Africa. NAC (National Archives of Canada), RG, External Affairs, vol. 1593, file 1931–159AT-C. The Irish Free State did not send a delegation the Imperial conference of 1937. *Dáil Debates*, vol. 66, col. 2–3, 31 Mar. 1937 and col. 1635–6, 27 Apr. 1937.

133 Joseph P. Walsh to Oscar Skelton, NAC (National Archives of Canada), RG25 D1, vol. 804, file 566.

134 *The Star*, Dec. 1930.

135 See UCD Archives, McGilligan Papers, P35/196, John J. Hearne, draft agreement between Great Britain, the Irish Free State and Northern Ireland; and between the Irish Free State and Northern Ireland; TNA, LCO 2/1231, drafts of 'cleaning of the slate' agreement and TNA, DO 35/127/7 file 4431/9, negotiations with the Irish Free State, 30 Apr. 1931. A detailed treatment of the proposed 'cleaning of the slate' agreement can be found in Thomas Mohr, 'The Irish Free State and the Legal Implications of Dominion Status' (PhD, UCD, 2007), pp 99–149.

of probates, Irish maritime lights, estates of persons of unsound mind, execution of criminal warrants, maintenance and bastardy orders, repatriation of paupers and cable and wireless facilities.[136] However, the dominant issue in the entire 'cleaning of the slate' agreement was always the search for a bilateral agreement on the appeal to the Privy Council.

The Irish government had now committed itself to drafting legislation that would unilaterally abolish the Irish appeal to the Privy Council. The proposed 'cleaning of the slate' agreement was a last ditch effort to prevent this legislation from creating a crisis in Anglo-Irish relations. The Irish were now determined to abolish the appeal themselves but were prepared to seek a formula that would avoid charges of having broken the Treaty.

In early 1931, the Irish showed every sign that they were not going to be delayed or deflected from reaching their goal of abolishing the appeal to the Privy Council. On 26 February 1931, Joseph P. Walshe, secretary of the Irish department of external affairs, arrived at the Dominions office in London to discuss matters that included the appeal to the Privy Council. Walshe told the British that the Irish delegation had been 'outrageously treated' at the Imperial conference of 1930. He insisted that the immediate abolition of the Privy Council appeal was now a political and a constitutional necessity and added that 'failure to legislate would be a tacit admission of the static theory'. Walshe told his British counterparts that the Irish were no longer willing to negotiate on the basis of Dominion analogies or provisions within the reports of the Imperial conferences. He even attempted to convince the British that the Irish government intended 'wiping out the Privy Council at once (within 14 days)'. This threat was a bluff as the drafting of the anticipated legislation was far from complete at this stage. Nevertheless, the British were left in no doubt that the Irish government's position had hardened and that they seemed determined to unilaterally abolish appeals to the Privy Council from the Irish courts.[137]

The British government wanted to avoid a controversy that might endanger the enactment of the forthcoming Statute of Westminster and so damage relations with the Dominions. It was afraid that unilateral abolition of the Irish appeal would result in calls to amend the final text of the proposed Statute of Westminster that had been agreed after long negotiations with the Dominions. The argument that the Privy Council appeal constituted a vital safeguard for Protestants in the Irish Free State was a source of particular concern as this was an emotive cause capable of garnering widespread support if properly harnessed. Such sympathies might lead to powerful calls for the amendment of the agreed text of the Statute of Westminster in order to limit recognition of the autonomous powers of the Irish Free State. It was doubtful whether the agreed text of the Statute of Westminster

136 Ibid.

137 UCDA, McGilligan Papers, P35B/115, Walshe to McGilligan, undated and TNA, LCO 2/910, Dominions secretary to attorney general, 2 Mar. 1931 and note by Sir H. Batterbee and Mr Machtig, 27 Feb. 1931.

could be amended without the consent of all parties and therefore the very survival of the minority Labour government might be endangered if this challenge proved successful. However, the British government was presented with repeated claims from their Irish counterparts that the Protestant community of the Irish Free State did not value the Privy Council appeal and would not raise serious opposition to its abolition.[138] If these claims could be verified, an agreed settlement might become a real possibility.

As seen in the previous chapter, the Irish government proved unable to provide evidence of Protestant acquiescence that could be presented in parliament by the British government. The evidence that the Irish government did collect suggested that retention of the appeal was actually supported by a substantial number of southern Protestants.[139] However, the negotiations broke down before the position of the Protestant community could come under close scrutiny in the negotiations. The British finally revealed that, in return for evidence of Protestant acquiescence, they were prepared to make a statement clarifying that the constitutional status and autonomy of the Irish Free State had not been frozen to the status held by the Dominions at the time of the signing of the 1921 Treaty but could grow in tandem with developments in the other Dominions. This statement would be issued once the Statute of Westminster had been safely enacted and so remove all legal obstacles to allowing the Irish Free State to abolish the Privy Council appeal.[140]

The Irish delegation to the 1930 Imperial conference had been infuriated at the suggestion that the status of the Irish Free State had been frozen in time. Their counterparts at the 1931 'cleaning of the slate' negotiations reacted with the same fury when this theory was resurrected once again. John J. Hearne, an important legal advisor to the Irish government, noted that if this theory was accurate the Irish people had been 'misinformed' when they accepted the Treaty in 1921.[141] Other delegates declared that, if this theory was accurate, the Irish government 'had engaged in a civil war on a false issue'.[142] Hearne would later report to Dublin that the British proposal 'was a joke' and added that, in his opinion, the British were 'merely wasting time'.[143]

As far as the Irish were concerned the British offer gave them nothing that they had not already possessed for the past decade. It would certainly have been difficult

138 For example, see UCDA, McGilligan Papers, P35B/115, Walshe to McGilligan, undated, NAI, dept. of the Taoiseach, S6164, report on meeting between Dulanty and Batterbee, 6 Mar. 1931 and TNA, LCO 2/910, Dominions secretary to attorney general, 2 Mar. 1931 and note by Sir H. Batterbee and Mr Machtig, 27 Feb. 1931. 139 See ch. 5, above.

140 TNA, LCO 2/910, memorandum dated 16 Apr. 1931 attached to letter from Batterbee to Schuster, 16 Apr. 1931.

141 UCDA, McGilligan Papers, P35/196, report on London discussions, 1 May 1931. John Joseph Hearne (1893–1969) would become one of the major architects of the Irish Constitution of 1937. *Dictionary of Irish Biography*, vol. 4, pp 582–3.

142 NAI, dept. of the Taoiseach, S4285B, memorandum by on Privy Council appeal by Michael McDunphy, 7 Nov. 1930.

143 UCDA, McGilligan Papers, P35/196, report on London discussions, 1 May 1931.

to explain such an agreement to the opposition in the Oireachtas and to the general public in the Irish Free State. Seán Murphy, assistant secretary at the Irish department of external affairs, pointed to the progress that had been achieved by the Irish Free State since 1921 in appointing its own diplomatic representatives, in becoming a member of the League of Nations and in having been elected to a seat on the Council of the League of Nations. Murphy concluded 'and now *in 1931* the Minister for External Affairs was to come down to the Dáil and say "Look what an achievement I've scored, we have the same status as Canada has"'.[144] The Irish felt that open recognition of the static theory would give it an element of legitimacy. There was also reason to fear that such recognition would imply that the status of the Irish Free State had been static before the conclusion of the agreement.

The Irish really wanted a legislative provision passed through Westminster that clarified that the Irish Free State had the right to abolish the Privy Council appeal.[145] This would spare the Irish Free State from accusations of having breached the legal and moral foundations of the 1921 Treaty and avoid charges of having unilaterally removed a safeguard for the Protestant minority. The British government were convinced that they would have serious difficulties getting such a measure through parliament.[146] The 'cleaning of the slate' negotiations collapsed once this became clear.

The Cosgrave administration now seemed determined to abolish the appeal by unilateral means without British acquiescence. Its determination was now augmented by the need to bury the argument that the constitutional status of the Irish Free State was frozen to the position fixed in 1921.[147] An Irish government that had built its identity around adherence to the 1921 Treaty now prepared to face accusations of breaking it.

144 Ibid. The words in italics are underlined in the original.

145 Irish drafts of the proposed 'cleaning of the slate' agreement contained the following provision: 'No appeal to petition for special leave to appeal whether statutory or prerogative shall lie to His Majesty in Council from any judgment, order or decree pronounced or made by any court in the Irish Free State.' UCDA, McGilligan Papers, P35/196, draft agreement between Great Britain, the Irish Free State and Northern Ireland; and between the Irish Free State and Northern Ireland, John J. Hearne, undated.

146 TNA, LCO 2/910, memorandum attached to letter from Batterbee to Schuster, 16 Apr. 1931.

147 For example, see UCDA, McGilligan Papers, P35/196, Privy Council – Reasons for Immediate Action, undated and P35B/115, Walshe to McGilligan, undated.

CHAPTER SEVEN

The Statute of Westminster

DRAFT LEGISLATION TO ABOLISH THE APPEAL

THE IRISH GOVERNMENT could not hide its failure at the 1930 Imperial conference to secure abolition of the Privy Council appeal from the Irish public. In these circumstances, the Irish government concluded that the abolition of the appeal was vital in avoiding a fatal loss of prestige in the run up to the forthcoming general election in which it faced a serious challenge from Fianna Fáil.[1] Internal government documents made clear that 'The people here expect us to act at once' and that hesitation would be regarded as 'sheer funk or the result of some secret bargain'.[2] The government had already been forced to face difficult questions in the Dáil as to when the proposed legislation on the Privy Council appeal would be introduced.[3] Patrick McGilligan could only answer that the Privy Council appeal required 'difficult legislation' and that its drafting might take considerable time.[4]

Government memoranda focused on the loss of prestige vis-à-vis the British government if the Irish delayed abolishing the Privy Council appeal. One unnamed Irish official admitted in a memorandum 'The Privy Council has probably been given an exaggerated place in our home policy'. Nevertheless, the memorandum admitted that the future of the appeal had now become a 'test' in Anglo-Irish relations that left no alternative but immediate action. This unnamed Irish official seemed convinced that the British would regard an Irish delay as a form of 'surrender' that would make Anglo-Irish negotiations much more difficult in the future.[5] The Irish government was faced with the challenge of completing a difficult balancing act in dealing with the British in 1931. It wanted to abolish the Privy Council appeal while simultaneously ensuring that the Irish Free State received the full benefit of the enhanced autonomy offered by the proposed Statute of Westminster.

1 UCDA, McGilligan Papers, P35/196, Privy Council – Reasons for Immediate Action, undated.
2 Ibid.
3 *Dáil Debates*, vol. 37, col. 1620–1, 18 Mar. 1931. TNA, LCO 2/1231, McGilligan to Thomas, 6 May 1931.
4 *Dáil Debates*, vol. 39, col. 2360, 17 July 1931.
5 UCDA, McGilligan Papers, P35/196, memorandum on the Privy Council, undated.
6 NAI, dept. of the Taoiseach, S6164, Arthur V. Matheson to Michael McDunphy, 12 Nov. 1930.

The task of drafting the legislation aimed at ending the appeal to the Privy Council from the Irish courts was well advanced even before the final conclusions of the Imperial conference of 1930.[6] By the middle of 1931 no less than five draft bills, each presenting different options, had been submitted to the Irish government.[7] The most important question facing the government was how far it was prepared to go in its attempt to abolish the Privy Council appeal.

One of the draft bills considered by the Irish government would have removed the provision known as the 'repugnancy clause' that placed all Irish law in a subservient position to the provisions of the 1921 Treaty. It would also have removed the jurisdiction of the Irish High Court and Supreme Court to determine the validity of laws by reference to their compatibility with the terms of the Treaty.[8] These provisions illustrate that the Irish were no longer prepared to allow any court, even an Irish one, to act as guardian and arbiter of the Treaty settlement.[9] After some consideration the Irish government rejected these proposals. It should be recalled that the Irish often denied that the Privy Council appeal could really be considered a requirement of the Treaty. Any alteration of the relationship between the Constitution and the Treaty would have suggested that the Irish *did* consider the Privy Council appeal to constitute a requirement of the Treaty whose terms they were now renouncing.[10] Nevertheless, this draft legislation would provide guidance for de Valera's removal of the repugnancy clause in 1933, a measure that marked the beginning of the end of the entire legal settlement established in 1922.[11]

In 1931 the Cumann na nGaedheal government finally decided to abolish the appeal by means of a measure that would have been called the Constitution (Amendment No. 18) Bill.[12] The government decided not to place a new provision in the Constitution expressly prohibiting Privy Council appeals.[13] Instead the proposed Constitution (Amendment No. 18) Bill 1931 did little more than remove all reference to the appeal from the text of the Constitution.[14] It is likely an explicit ban on the appeal was considered unnecessarily provocative.

7 NAI, dept. of foreign affairs 3/1 and dept. of the Taoiseach, S6164.

8 NAI, dept. of foreign affairs 3/1, Constitution (Amendment No. 18) Bill 1931. Irish legal advisers also prepared a draft Constitution (Amendment No. 19) Bill 1931 that would have removed the words from Article 50 of the Constitution that ensured that all constitutional amendments had to be 'within the terms of the Scheduled Treaty'. NAI, dept. of foreign affairs, 3/1, Constitution (Amendment No. 19) Bill 1931.

9 See also NAI, dept. of foreign affairs, 3/1, John J. Hearne to Seán Murphy, 27 May 1931.

10 *Dáil Debates*, vol. 41, col. 2115–16, 19 May 1932.

11 In 1931 John J. Hearne concluded 'the Oireachtas has the undoubted power to pass a law repugnant to the Treaty and that such a law is valid and unavoidable notwithstanding such repugnancy'. NAI, dept. of foreign affairs, 3/1, John J. Hearne to Seán Murphy, 27 May 1931.

12 NAI, dept. of foreign affairs 3/1.

13 This option was considered in an early draft bill. See NAI, dept. of the Taoiseach, S6164, Arthur V. Matheson to Michael McDunphy with drafts bills, 12 Nov. 1930.

14 This would have altered Article 66 of the Constitution to provide the following wording: 'The decision of the Supreme Court shall in all cases be final and conclusive, and shall not be reviewed

It was virtually certain that British legal experts would dispute the legality of any unilateral abolition of the appeal by the Irish Free State. Moreover, the Irish government could not actually prevent Irish litigants from travelling to London to have petitions and appeals heard by the Judicial Committee. In these circumstances it was considered necessary to put in place some form of mechanism that would limit the ability of the Privy Council to defy the wishes of the Irish government. The Supreme Court (Confirmation of Judgment) Bill 1931 was heavily influenced by the blocking measures taken by the government in relation to Irish appeals between 1926 and 1930.[15] The draft bill would have included a provision allowing the government to make an order declaring that a particular judgment, order or decree of the Supreme Court should have statutory effect from the date on which it was made.[16] This would render rendundant any Privy Council appeal that attempted to overturn a judgment of the Irish Supreme Court. It was a provision that was drafted by politicians and not by lawyers which might explain its unconventional approach in allowing the government to issue an order giving statutory effect to a court judgment.[17] The Irish government's intention to make use of such an extraordinary legislative device is testament to its determination to put an end to appeals to the Privy Council and also to the constraints of the legal straitjacket in which it was forced to operate.[18]

By the latter half of 1931 the Irish government had settled on abolishing the appeal to the Judicial Committee of the Privy Council by means of the draft Constitution (Amendment No. 18) Bill 1931 and the Supreme Court (Confirmation of Judgment) Bill 1931. Both draft bills were considered necessary to effectively abolish the appeal.[19] The British learned the general scheme of both bills during

or capable of being reviewed by any other Court, Tribunal or Authority whatsoever *whether judicial or prerogative*.' (New words in italics.) NAI, dept. of the Taoiseach, S6164, Arthur V. Matheson to Michael McDunphy with drafts bills, 12 Nov. 1930.

15 The Irish government also considered another draft bill aimed at blocking Privy Council appeals that reflected a number of suggestions made by the attorney general, John A. Costello. NAI, dept. of foreign affairs, 3/1, The Judicial Committee Bill 1931.

16 NAI, dept. of foreign affairs 3/1, Section 1, draft Supreme Court (Confirmation of Judgment) Bill 1931.

17 NAI, cabinet minutes, Cab 1/3, 8 Jan. 1931 and NAI, dept. of the Taoiseach, S6164, Michael McDunphy to John A. Costello, 8 Jan. 1931.

18 This draft bill allowed the Governor-General, acting on the advice of the executive council, to make an order declaring that a particular judgment, order, or decree of the Supreme Court should have statutory effect from the date on which it was made. The draft bill, in its original form, had provided that orders granting statutory effect to decisions of the Supreme Court could not be of any effect until they had been laid before each House of the Oireachtas and approved by resolutions passed by the Dáil and the Seanad. NAI, dept. of foreign affairs 3/1, Section 1(2), Supreme Court (Confirmation of Judgment) Bill 1931. Under the revised bill the power to make an order giving statutory effect to a judgment, order, or decree was placed entirely in the hands of the executive council. The function of the houses of the Oireachtas was limited to annulling an order after it had been made effective. NAI, dept. of the Taoiseach, S6164, Section 1(2), draft Supreme Court (Confirmation of Judgment) Bill 1931, version of 4 Mar. 1931.

19 NAI, cabinet minutes, Cab. 1/3, 20 Oct. 1931.

the 'cleaning of the slate' negotiations.[20] They were predictably unimpressed and made it clear that they would regard both measures as violations of the 1921 Treaty.[21]

FAILURE TO ABOLISH THE APPEAL IN 1931

Why did the Cumann na nGaedheal administration fail to introduce these two bills into the Oireachtas after the final collapse of bilateral negotiations with the British in 1931? The British government was so convinced that the Irish Free State would unilaterally abolish the appeal in 1931 that it prepared an official response that would have accused the Irish of breaking the Treaty.[22] The British government even went to the trouble of gaining cross-party support by consulting opposition leaders on the contents of this prepared response.[23] Yet all this proved unnecessary as the promised legislation never appeared.

British officials were grateful for the breathing space that they had been granted and concluded 'Presumably the wiser counsels of Mr Cosgrave have prevailed'.[24] While the British government had every reason to feel relieved, it could not be sure why the Irish government had failed to carry out its oft-repeated threat. One British memorandum speculated whether this failure was based on a desire not to prejudice Irish chances of obtaining Imperial trade preferences at some point in the future.[25] While this argument is hardly convincing, it must be admitted that subsequent scholarship, with full benefit of hindsight, has not shed much more light on this mystery. D.W. Harkness, in his influential work *The Restless Dominion*, does no more than suggest that there might have been unforeseen legal difficulties or a change of priorities.[26] David Swinfen, author of an analysis of the decline of the Privy Council appeal, suggests that the Irish government was aware that abolition could be used as a precedent by de Valera to repeal the entire Treaty settlement and that 'this likelihood was a grave probably insuperable obstacle to unilateral legislation'.[27] It should be reiterated that the Cosgrave administration was adamant that the Privy Council appeal was not a Treaty commitment. Even leaving this consideration aside, members of the Cumann na nGaedheal government were well aware that a de Valera administration would need no

20 UCDA, McGilligan Papers, P35B/115, Walshe to McGilligan, undated.

21 TNA, LCO 2/910, Dominions secretary to attorney general, 2 Mar. 1931 and note by Sir H. Batterbee and Mr Machtig, 27 Feb. 1931.

22 TNA, CAB 24/221/20, memorandum by Dominions secretary, May 1931 and CAB 23/67/3, meeting of 13 May 1931.

23 TNA, LCO 2/1190, J.H. Thomas to Viscount Hailsham, 16 Nov. 1931.

24 TNA, DO 35/127/7 file 4431/18, Edward Harding to J.H. Thomas, 18 July 1931.

25 TNA, LCO 2/1190, 'Statute of Westminster', 16 Nov. 1931.

26 D.W. Harkness, *The Restless Dominion* (New York, New York University Press, 1969), p. 239.

27 David Swinfen, *Imperial Appeal: The Debate on the Appeal to the Privy Council, 1833–1986* (Manchester, Manchester University Press, 1987), p. 130.

prompting from them to launch an assault on the Treaty. The search for an explanation must examine other considerations.

Although the Irish government appeared resolved to abolish the appeal in early 1931 it also showed a certain willingness to delay its draft measures to permit the search for a negotiated settlement. On the surface, Irish willingness to unilaterally abolish the appeal remained intact as the search for a bilateral settlement began to unravel. On 6 May 1931, McGilligan wrote to Dominions secretary J.H. Thomas that he could see no other option but to return to 'My own method of dealing with the Privy Council'. He noted that the required legislation was at an advanced state of completion and that he had only postponed the finishing touches because of British requests for an agreed solution. Now McGilligan indicated a sense of urgency, declaring that 'Time is, however, of the essence of this problem for us'. He noted that the fruitless search for an agreement had not merely resulted in the loss of valuable time but had led to embarrassing press articles and parliamentary questions. McGilligan told Thomas that the relevant legislation would have to be on the statute book before the summer recess and declared his intention to place it before the Oireachtas in the second week of June.[28] On 9 May McGilligan declined Thomas' offer of further meetings on the Privy Council appeal.[29]

McGilligan's emphasis on the need for haste might be seen as little more than a last ditch effort to wrest some form of agreement from the British. The Irish suspected that the British were playing for time in delaying yet another controversy over Ireland. Yet, it is clear that McGilligan's indications of urgency in his negotiations with the British hid serious doubts within the Irish government as to the wisdom of introducing the proposed legislation at that particular time. These doubts seem to have been motivated by tactical rather than by legal considerations. A number of unsigned and undated memoranda weighing up the advantages and disadvantages of immediate abolition point to a vigorous internal debate within the Irish government on this matter. It is not entirely clear which members of the Irish government supported immediate action and which favoured a tactical delay. The evidence suggests that the department of external affairs, including its minister Patrick McGilligan and secretary Joseph P. Walshe, inclined towards immediate action[30] while W.T. Cosgrave and attorney general John A. Costello were exponents of delay.[31]

The Irish government considered the option of immediate abolition throughout the summer of 1931 but seemed unable to decide on any definite course of action. In June Patrick McGilligan attempted to get the executive council to make a decision on the matter. However, W.T. Cosgrave revealed in a letter 'I don't think

28 TNA, LCO 2/910, CP 120(31), The Irish Free State and Appeals to the Judicial Committee of the Privy Council, Appendix VI, McGilligan to Thomas, 6 May 1931.
29 Ibid., at Appendix VIII, McGilligan to Thomas, 9 May 1931.
30 NAI, dept. of the Taoiseach, S6164, extract from cabinet minutes, 20 Oct. 1931 and UCDA, McGilligan Papers, P35B/115, Walshe to McGilligan, undated.
31 NAI, dept. of foreign affairs, 3/1, John J. Hearne to Seán Murphy, 27 May 1931.

we are likely to bring in the Bill concerning Appeals to the Privy Council on June 2nd'.[32] W.T. Cosgrave certainly favoured continuing the search for a negotiated settlement with the British long after McGilligan had given up his efforts and threatened the British with unilateral action. Cosgrave and Thomas continued to make efforts to achieve a bilateral settlement by means of an indirect correspondence through Lord Granard.[33] This correspondence continued until August 1931 when Cosgrave's initiative ran into the same brick wall that McGilligan had met some months earlier. The British still required evidence that southern Protestants did not favour retention of the appeal. Assuming that such evidence was forthcoming, the most that the British were prepared to offer was an agreement indicating that the status of the Irish Free State under the 1921 Treaty was not static but was capable of development with that of Canada. Thomas reiterated his earlier insistence that the British government could not contemplate any agreement in which they would openly agree to abolish the appeal.[34]

The Irish were back at square one and the passage of time had greatly reduced the possibility of any unilateral abolition of the Privy Council appeal. By the time Cosgrave's efforts had run their course, the Dáil was in its summer recess until the middle of October. The more time that passed the less advantage there was in seeking immediate abolition. No formal decision was made on the proposed legislation until 20 October 1931. By this time it was expected that the Statute of Westminster would be introduced in the British parliament within a matter of weeks. In these circumstances, there can be little surprise at the decision of the Irish government to suspend consideration of their proposed legislation for a period of two months.[35] The main advantages of waiting until after the enactment of the Statute of Westminster was that the enhanced autonomy offered by that legislation would weaken British accusations that the Irish were acting illegally in abolishing the appeal. Restraint would also have the benefit of weakening the strength of a body of opinion within the British parliament that wanted to limit the autonomy offered to the Irish Free State by the proposed Statute of Westminster.

THE PROVISIONS OF THE STATUTE OF WESTMINSTER

The enactment of the Statute of Westminster in 1931 represents one of the most significant events in the history of the British Empire. It recognized significant advances in the evolution of the self-governing Dominions into fully sovereign states. International lawyers had been reluctant to class the Dominions as sovereign

32 TNA, LCO 2/910, Cosgrave to Granard, 26 May 1931.

33 TNA, LCO 2/910.

34 TNA, DO 35/127/7 file 4431/16, Thomas to Granard, 5 June 1931, file 4431/18, Thomas to Granard, 24 July 1931 and file 4431/20, Cosgrave to Granard, undated, Aug. 1931.

35 NAI, dept. of the Taoiseach, S6164, extract from cabinet minutes, 20 Oct. 1931.

states before 1931.[36] These doubts evaporated after the enactment of the Statute of Westminster.[37]

Parliamentary debates reveal that the Statute of Westminster was largely perceived as an incident in Anglo-Irish relations at the expense of wider Imperial concerns at the time of its enactment. The impact of the statute on Australia, Canada, New Zealand and even South Africa never received anything like the level of attention given to the Irish Free State during the debates at Westminster in 1931. The lengthy discussions on the internal politics of the Irish Free State certainly had no parallel with respect to any of the other Dominions.[38] Stanley Baldwin, leader of the Conservative party and former prime minister, expressed a sense of frustration in the House of Commons when he complained 'There is a tendency, in concentrating on Ireland, to lose sight of the fundamental question here, which is the question of Imperial relationship'.[39] These considerations ensure that the debates on the enactment of the Statute of Westminster should be seen as the last in a series of great parliamentary debates on the future of Ireland that was a major feature of British politics in the late nineteenth and early twentieth centuries.

The great advantage of the elevated title of 'Statute of Westminster' was that it made no reference to its contents. This was highly advantageous since the provisions of the statute were often condemned as sounding the death-knell of Imperial unity.[40] The text of the statute gradually crystallized during the negotiations of the 1926 and 1930 Imperial conferences and the 1929 sub-conference. Its creation was largely driven by the Irish Free State, South Africa and Canada. The governments of Australia[41] and New Zealand[42] saw the statute as a dangerous blow to Imperial unity and only adopted the most important provisions in 1942 and 1947 respectively. These provisions never applied to Newfoundland as a separate Dominion. As mentioned earlier, Newfoundland lost its status as a self-governing Dominion as a consequence of a serious financial crisis in 1933.[43]

36 For example, see P.J. Noel Baker, *The Present Juridical Status of the British Dominions in International Law* (London, Longmans, Green, 1929), p. 356 and Pearce Higgins, *Hall's International Law* (Oxford, Clarendon, 1924), p. 34.

37 For example, see H. Lauterpacht (ed.), *Oppenheim's International Law* (8th ed. London, Longmans, 1963), pp 203–5.

38 For example, see *Hansard*, House of Commons, vol. 260, col. 303–55, 24 Nov. 1931, *Hansard*, House of Lords, vol. 83, col. 202–8, 26 Nov. 1931 and vol. 83, col. 231–45, 1 Dec. 1931.

39 *Hansard*, House of Commons, vol. 260, col. 342, 24 Nov. 1931.

40 For example, see J.H. Morgan, 'Secession by Innuendo', *National Review* (1936), 313.

41 Statute of Westminster Adoption Act 1942. The adoption of these provisions of the Statute of Westminster were given retrospective effect from 3 December 1939, the day in which Australia entered the Second World War.

42 Statute of Westminster Adoption Act 1947.

43 See ch. 1, below. Newfoundland did not send delegates to the operation of Dominion legislation conference in 1929 that created the first draft of the Statute of Westminster. It should be noted that Newfoundland was included in Section 1 of the statute, which provided the definition of a Dominion for the purposes of the Act. However, Section 10 named Newfoundland, along with

One of the best known provisions of the Statute of Westminster was to give the Dominions a say in changes to the law concerning succession to the throne.[44] These provisions ensured that the Dominions had to be consulted when King Edward VIII abdicated in 1936.[45] The statute also confirmed that the Dominions had the power to make laws that extended beyond the bounds of their own frontiers.[46] In addition, the statute confirmed that the Imperial parliament at Westminster could only legislate for the Dominions if they had requested and consented to the relevant legislation.[47]

The most important provision of the statute, from an Irish perspective, was that Dominion statutes would no longer occupy a subservient position to statutes passed by the Imperial parliament.[48] Previously, any Dominion law could be declared null and void if it was repugnant to a statute passed by the Imperial parliament that extended to that Dominion.[49] This rule had been put into practice as recently as 1926 in *Nadan v. The King*[50] when Lord Cave and his colleagues delivered a decision that saw a provision of the Canadian Criminal Code struck down because it was seen as inconsistent with a number of Imperial statutes. The Statute of Westminster would guarantee that this could never be done with respect to Irish legisation.

The Statute of Westminster also had the potential to change the position under which all Irish law was subservient to the 1921 Treaty as a consequence of the repugnancy clause contained in the Imperial statute enacting the 1922 Constitution.[51] After the enactment of the Statute of Westminster the British would not be able to challenge the removal of the repugnancy clause and the subsequent removal of provisions reflecting the settlement imposed by the 1921 Treaty. These included the controversial parliamentary oath that had gained such notoriety during the Irish Civil War together with the provisions that demanded the retention of the Irish appeal to the Judicial Committee of the Privy Council.

Australia and New Zealand, as Dominions that would not be affected by key provisions of the statute, Sections 2 to 6, until a statute passed by the parliament of the relevant Dominion adopted any or all of these provisions.

44 Preamble, Statute of Westminster Act 1931.

45 Donal Coffey, 'British Commonwealth and Irish Responses to the Abdication of King Edward VIII', *Irish Jurist*, 44:1 (2009), 95.

46 Section 3, Statute of Westminster Act 1931. See Thomas Mohr, 'The Foundations of Irish Extra-Territorial Legislation', *Irish Jurist*, 40 (2005), 86–110.

47 Section 4, Statute of Westminster Act 1931.

48 Ibid., at Section 2.

49 This position was recognized at common law and regulated by statute in the Colonial Laws Validity Act 1865.

50 [1926] AC 482 and [1926] 2 DLR 177.

51 Preamble, Irish Free State Constitution Act 1922. See also Section 2, Constitution of the Irish Free State (Saorstát Éireann) Act 1922.

THE IRISH FREE STATE AND THE STATUTE OF WESTMINSTER

The particular emphasis on the impact of the Statute of Westminster on Irish affairs in contemporary parliamentary debates is hardly surprising when it is considered that, in contrast to most of the other Dominions, the full provisions of this historic measure would apply without any restriction or qualification to the Irish Free State in 1931. Canada agreed that its Constitution, at that time composed of Imperial legislation, would remain unaffected by the provisions of the statute.[52] Even South Africa passed a parliamentary resolution protecting certain entrenched provisions within its Constitution from the impact of the statute.[53] No equivalent action to exempt the Irish Constitution, or key aspects of it, from the impact of the statute was ever undertaken by the Irish parliament.

The special position of the Irish Free State with respect to the provisions of the statute was an important consideration in ensuring that British parliamentary debates focussed on this particular Dominion more than any other. Those who were hostile to the general scheme of the statute often blamed the Irish Free State for its introduction. J.H. Morgan, a leading authority on British constitutional law with strong unionist sympathies, noted with approval that the Statute of Westminster was often called the 'Statute of Dublin' in loyal New Zealand.[54] In Australia, former prime minister William Hughes condemned the British government for listening 'to men who, in some instances, were newcomers to the table of the Empire'.[55]

Those who held unionist principles were determined that the proposed Statute of Westminster must be amended before it was enacted into law. They believed that this was vital in preventing the Irish Free State from removing the repugnancy clause and abolishing the Privy Council appeal which, it was predicted, would form the first steps in a wholesale revision of the 1921 Treaty settlement. The British government anticipated that the House of Lords was almost certain to introduce an amendment designed to protect the Treaty.[56] Matters were not helped when it became clear that the government's own leader in the House of Lords, Lord

52 Section 7(1) of the Statute of Westminster Act 1931 provided 'Nothing in this Act shall be deemed to apply to the repeal, amendment or alteration of the *British North America Acts, 1867 to 1930*, or any order, rule or regulation made thereunder.'

53 The resolution provided that 'the proposed legislation will in no way derogate from the entrenched provisions of the South Africa Act'. Manley O. Hudson, 'Notes on the Statute of Westminster, 1931', *Harvard Law Review* 46:1 (1932), 261 at 266. The weakness of this constraint did not become entirely apparent for some time after the enactment of the statute. See Denis V. Cowen, 'The Entrenched Sections of the South Africa Act', *South African Law Journal*, 70:3 (1953), 238 and Erwin N. Griswold, 'The "Coloured Vote Case" in South Africa', *Harvard Law Review*, 65:8 (1952), 1361.

54 J.H. Morgan, 'Secession by Innuendo', 313. John Hartman Morgan (1876–1955) was a British general, politician, lawyer and professor of constitutional law at the University of London.

55 Quoted at *Hansard*, House of Lords, vol. 83, col. 201, 26 Nov. 1931.

56 TNA, LCO 2/910, memorandum attached to letter from Batterbee to Schuster, 16 Apr. 1931 and NAI, dept. of foreign affairs, 19/6, Dulanty to Walshe, 23 Nov. 1931.

Hailsham, was opposed to granting legal concessions to the Irish Free State.[57] The British prime minister, Ramsay MacDonald, assured the Irish government in late 1931 that the provisions of the Parliament Act 1911 would be used in the event of an amendment by the House of Lords. He added that this would mean, at worst, a delay of around eighteen months in enacting the Statute of Westminster.[58] This was hardly encouraging news for an Irish government facing an election within the next nine months. Yet, as events transpired, the main challenge took the more serious form of a proposed amendment in the House of Commons.

ATTEMPTS AT AMENDMENT IN THE HOUSE OF COMMONS

On 20 November 1931, Colonel John Gretton MP proposed an amendment to the Statute of Westminster Bill that was specifically aimed at the Irish Free State. Gretton was a strong opponent of concessions to Irish nationalists and had resigned the Conservative whip in 1922 in protest at the conciliatory policies of the coalition government led by David Lloyd George. He rejected the political settlement in Ireland that had culminated in the signing of the Anglo-Irish Treaty of 1921. A decade later Gretton joined forces with such figures as Lord Carson, Lord Danesfort, A.A. Somerville and J.H. Morgan to circulate letters and hold public meetings that urged the amendment of the Statute of Westminster Bill with respect to the Irish Free State.[59] Gretton's proposed amendment was intended to guarantee that the Statute of Westminster would not undermine the legal safeguards protecting the settlement imposed by the Anglo-Irish Treaty.[60] It was given additional force when it was endorsed by Winston Churchill, one of the British signatories of the Treaty in 1921.

In the words of the *Times* there was an 'unfriendly atmosphere' in the House of Commons on 20 November 1931 when Colonel Gretton's proposed amendment to the Statute of Westminster was introduced. The House was poorly attended and largely composed of supporters of Gretton's amendment. J.H. Thomas was convinced that there was a real risk of the government suffering an embarrassing defeat on 20 November that would have put the entire statute in jeopardy.[61] He managed to calm the situation by announcing that 'every consideration' would be given to the arguments behind the amendment and 'the Government will be asked

57 TNA, LCO 2/1190, Schuster to Thomas, 18 Nov. 1931.

58 NAI, dept. of foreign affairs, 19/6, Dulanty to Walshe, 23 Nov. 1931.

59 See the *Times*, 16 and 17 Nov. 1931.

60 'Nothing in this Act shall be deemed to authorise the Legislature of the Irish Free State to repeal, amend, or alter the Irish Free State Agreement Act 1922, or the Irish Free State Constitution Act 1922, or so much of the Government of Ireland Act 1920, as continues to be in force in Northern Ireland.' *Hansard*, House of Commons, vol. 260, col. 303, 24 Nov. 1931.

61 NAI, dept. of foreign affairs, 19/6, John Dulanty to Joseph Walshe, 23 Nov. 1931. This is supported by other sources. For example, see dept. of foreign affairs, 19/6, John Dulanty to Joseph Walshe, 23 Nov. 1931 and *Times*, 21 Nov. 1931.

to consider the whole situation in the light of the Debate that has taken place'.[62] These assurances proved sufficient to buy time and stave off the immediate threat to the British government and to the Statute of Westminster itself.

Thomas' apparent willingness to consider the proposed amendment to the Statute of Westminster Bill was based on a need to play for time.[63] This was not obvious to the Irish government, which took the threat of amending the bill very seriously. An Irish memorandum noted that British acceptance of this amendment would 'destroy the whole basis of the Irish Free State as we have conceived it' and negate nine years of Irish government policy.[64]

W.T. Cosgrave responded to the perceived threat by writing a letter to prime minister Ramsay MacDonald on 21 November that demanded resistance to Gretton's proposal.[65] The letter was an attempt to reassure the British that the Irish government had no intention of making use of the Statute of Westminster to break the 1921 Treaty. Cosgrave wrote that the Irish government had reiterated time and again 'that the Treaty is an agreement which can be altered only by consent'.[66] He asserted that the Irish people believed in the solemnity of the Treaty but added that any attempt by the British parliament to alter its terms would undermine Irish faith in the sanctity of this instrument.[67]

Cosgrave's letter was deplored by members of the Fianna Fáil opposition.[68] Yet, Cosgrave's emphasis on the solemnity of the Treaty and the need to maintain a position of good faith at the heart of Anglo-Irish relations had a different impact on a British audience. The British government was sufficiently impressed with the contents of the letter as to actually read out the vital paragraphs to the House of Commons.[69] Ramsay MacDonald declared that he agreed with every word of the letter.[70] Austen Chamberlain, one of the British signatories of the 1921 Treaty, revealed that he had not intended to intervene in the debate until the effect of Cosgrave's letter stirred him into open opposition to Gretton's amendment.[71] Even die-hard unionists seemed touched by Cosgrave's integrity.[72] The *Morning Post*, a unionist newspaper, described Cosgrave's letter as a 'trump card'.[73] One unionist

62 *Hansard*, House of Commons, vol. 259, col. 1253, 20 Nov. 1931.
63 NAI, dept. of foreign affairs, 19/6, John Dulanty to Joseph Walshe, 23 Nov. 1931.
64 UCDA, P35/174 McGilligan Papers, P35/174, Statute of Westminster Bill 1931, the Churchill Amendment and the Irish Free State, undated.
65 NAI, dept. of the Taoiseach, S5340/19, Cosgrave to MacDonald, 21 Nov. 1931.
66 Ibid.
67 TNA, LCO 2/1190, extract from a speech by President Cosgrave on Sunday, Nov. 22nd at Charleville Co. Cork and NAI, dept. of the Taoiseach, S5340/19, Cosgrave to MacDonald, 21 Nov. 1931. Patrick McGilligan, minister for external affairs, wrote a similar letter to J.H. Thomas, Dominions secretary. NAI, dept. of the Taoiseach, S5340/19, McGilligan to Thomas, 21 Nov. 1931.
68 *Dáil Debates*, vol. 41, col. 595, 27 Apr. 1932.
69 *Hansard*, House of Commons, vol. 260, col. 311, 24 Nov. 1931.
70 NAI, dept. of foreign affairs, 19/6, Dulanty to Walshe, 23 Nov. 1931.
71 Ibid., at Dulanty to Walshe, 25 Nov.1931.
72 Ibid., at Dulanty to Walshe, 27 Nov. 1931 and 5 Dec. 1931 and *Times*, 26 Nov. 1931.
73 Ibid., at Dulanty to Walshe, 25 Nov. 1931.

MP, Arthur Shirley Benn, claimed that he had actually torn up his speech supporting Colonel Gretton's amendment on hearing Cosgrave's letter.[74]

Cosgrave was not without his admirers at Westminster. His government had received considerable praise for restoring stability to the Irish Free State. The Cosgrave administration and, perhaps more importantly, Cosgrave himself enjoyed a certain amount of esteem even among die-hard unionists. Most of those who supported Gretton's amendment made sure to praise Cosgrave's record of adherence to the terms of the Treaty.[75] The Cosgrave administration has often been accused, from the 1920s to the present, of displaying a post-colonial psyche that craved the approval of former masters.[76] Yet, the positive reputation that had been cultivated by the Cosgrave government was vital to the process of advancing the status of the Irish Free State at the Imperial conferences of the 1920s and early 1930s. This positive image also proved its worth during the enactment of the Statute of Westminster.

The British government could never accept the proposed amendment to the Statute of Westminster notwithstanding the strength of unionist opinion that lay behind the efforts of Gretton and Churchill. This was made clear in internal memoranda drafted for the benefit of the British government.[77] Acceptance of the amendment would have forced the British to violate established constitutional practice by enacting Imperial legislation for a Dominion that no longer consented to the measure.[78] Breaking this practice with respect to the Irish Free State was seen as threatening wider Imperial consequences. British officials argued that it was difficult to see how their government could justify placing legal safeguards in the statute relating to the Anglo-Irish Treaty without making similar demands with respect to certain 'entrenched clauses' in the South African Constitution that were designed to protect the rights of the English-speaking minority and the black majority.[79] It was obvious to British officials that the latter course 'would arouse the most violent opposition from General Hertzog, and cannot be contemplated for one moment'.[80]

The British government would have faced serious opposition from the Dominions even if attempts to amend the Statute of Westminster were limited to the Irish Free State. In early 1931 Irish ministers went to the trouble of trying to

74 Ibid., at Dulanty to Walshe, 26 Nov. 1931.
75 For example, see *Hansard*, House of Commons, vol. 260, col. 320 and 328–9, 24 Nov. 1931.
76 For example, see J.J. Lee, *Ireland 1912–1985* (Cambridge, 1989), p. 173.
77 TNA, LCO 2/1190, 'Reasons why it is impossible to accept the amendment standing in the name of Colonel Gretton and others', undated.
78 K.C. Wheare argues that if the proposed amendments with respect to the Irish Free State had taken a different form they would have had a better chance of satisfying constitutional convention. K.C. Wheare, *The Statute of Westminster and Dominion Status* (5th ed. Oxford, Oxford University Press, 1953), pp 256–7.
79 Ibid., at p. 256.
80 TNA, LCO 2/1190, 'Reasons why it is impossible to accept the amendment standing in the name of Colonel Gretton and others', undated. See also *Hansard*, House of Commons, vol. 260, col. 311–12, 24 Nov. 1931.

secure advance support from the other Dominions in resisting a possible amendment to the Statute of Westminster that would limit its impact on the Irish Free State. These efforts achieved some success. Patrick McGilligan was able to tell the Dominions secretary, J.H. Thomas, that prime minister Bennett of Canada had given assurances that 'the Free State would have the support of all members of the Commonwealth if the House of Lords were to attempt to tack on to the Statute of Westminster a provision saving the right of appeal [to the Privy Council] in the Free State'.[81] The British took this threat seriously and concluded that any attempt to limit the effect of the future Statute of Westminster with respect to the Irish Free State would meet opposition from Canada, Australia and South Africa in addition to the Irish Free State itself.[82]

The British government finally mustered its parliamentary strength and the amendment was finally defeated by 360 votes to 50.[83] Constitutional practice and Dominion pressure ensured that the British government could never accept Gretton's amendment. Nevertheless, Cosgrave's intervention made an important contribution to limiting support for Gretton's initiative.

ATTEMPTS AT AMENDMENT IN THE HOUSE OF LORDS

The desire not to undermine the Cosgrave administration on the eve of a general election provided the British government with an additional incentive to defeat Gretton's amendment. British ministers could point to the positive record of the Irish government in adhering to the 1921 Treaty. The great exception to this otherwise positive record was, of course, the attitude of the Cosgrave administration towards the Privy Council appeal. In addition to numerous instances of blocking the appeal, members of the Irish government had made repeated declarations advocating its abolition in the very near future.[84] One British memorandum noted that the Irish had acted as 'very wrong-headed people' and had only themselves to blame for the creation of suspicions on this issue.[85] Yet, British officials were prepared to concede that the Irish position was 'honestly held'.[86]

Gretton's amendment in the House of Commons was designed to protect the entire Treaty settlement, including the Privy Council appeal. A second attempt at amending the Statute of Westminster Bill with respect to the Irish Free State was

81 TNA, LCO 2/910, CP 120(31), 'The Irish Free State and Appeals to the Judicial Committee of the Privy Council'.
82 TNA, LCO 2/910, memorandum attached to letter from Batterbee to Schuster, 16 Apr. 1931 and LCO 2/1190, Schuster to Thomas, 19 Nov. 1931.
83 *Hansard*, House of Commons, vol. 260, col. 354–5, 24 Nov. 1931.
84 For example, see *The Star*, May 1931 and UCDA, McGilligan Papers, P35B/108 and NAI, dept. of the Taoiseach, S4285B, transcript of radio broadcast of 9 Nov. 1930.
85 TNA, LCO 2/1190, 'Statute of Westminster', 16 Nov. 1931.
86 TNA, LCO 2/1190, 'Reasons why it is impossible to accept the amendment standing in the name of Colonel Gretton and others', undated.

made in the House of Lords. This targeted the retention of the Privy Council appeal as guardian of the wider Treaty settlement. The amendment would have ringfenced the Irish appeal to the Privy Council from the effects of the Statute of Westminster. This would mean that, under British law, the Irish Free State would continue to be prohibited from removing this guardian of the 1921 Treaty.[87]

This amendment was moved by Lord Danesfort, one of the most obdurate unionists in the House of Lords who hailed from the territory of the Irish Free State. Danesfort was convinced that the Privy Council was an effective safeguard for southern Protestants and made it clear that his actions were motivated by concern for the position of his co-religionists in the Irish Free State.[88] He seemed prepared to accept Cosgrave's sincerity when the Irish premier wrote in his letter of 21 November 1931 'The Treaty is an agreement which can only be altered by consent'. However, Danesfort noted that this statement was not sufficient to safeguard the appeal to the Privy Council since members of the Irish government had argued that the appeal was not strictly required by the 1921 Treaty.[89] He also pointed to statements made by Cosgrave himself that advocated abolition of the Privy Council appeal.[90]

Despite impassioned argument, this proposed amendment never had any real chance of acceptance. The British government made it clear that amendment of the agreed text of the Statute of Westminster would never be acceptable to the Dominions. Lord Hailsham,[91] leader of the Conservative party in the House of Lords, also stressed that acceptance of the amendment would damage Anglo-Irish relations and would have wider ramifications throughout the Commonwealth.[92] The defeat of the amendment meant that all that Danesfort and his supporters could do was to call upon the leaders of the Irish government to pause before carrying out a measure that would be seen as a 'gross breach of faith'.[93]

87 Danesfort's proposed amendment would have inserted the following provisions into the Statute of Westminster: 'Without prejudice to maintenance of the other provisions of the Treaty of sixth December, nineteen hundred and twenty-one, and of the Irish Free State (Agreement) Act 1922, and of the Irish Free State Constitution Act 1922, it is hereby declared that nothing in this Act shall be deemed to authorise the Parliament of the Irish Free State to alter or repeal Section two of the said Treaty or the provisions contained in the Irish Free State Constitution Act 1922, as to the right of any person to petition His Majesty for leave to appeal from the Supreme Court of Southern Ireland to His Majesty in Council or the right of His Majesty to grant such leave.' *Hansard*, House of Lords, vol. 83, col. 231, 1 Dec. 1931. Danesfort's amendment was, in many respects, a poorly drafted provision. See Thomas Mohr, 'The Statute of Westminster: An Irish Perspective', *Law and History Review*, 31:1 (2013), 749.
88 *Hansard*, House of Lords, vol. 83, col. 232–3, 1 Dec. 1931.
89 TNA, CAB 32/79 PM(30)5 and CAB 32/79 PM(30)27.
90 *Hansard*, House of Lords, vol. 83, col. 232–5, 1 Dec. 1931.
91 Douglas McGarel Hogg, Viscount Hailsham (1872–1950) was lord chancellor (1928–9) and (1935–8).
92 *Hansard*, House of Lords, vol. 83, col. 237–41, 1 Dec. 1931.
93 Ibid., at col. 243.

THE STATUTE OF WESTMINSTER AND THE TREATY

Those who tried to limit the impact of the Statute of Westminster on the Irish Free State were convinced that their efforts were necessary to preserve legal safeguards protecting the 1921 Treaty settlement. The British government argued that legal constraints would continue to prevent the Irish from breaking the Treaty even after the enactment of the Statute of Westminster.[94] Stanley Baldwin, then lord president of the council, claimed that he had received legal advice that concluded 'the binding character of the Articles of Agreement will not be altered by one jot or tittle by the passing of the statute'.[95] It is curious that none of the supporters of Gretton's amendment asked for a detailed explanation of these conclusions. The legal advice mentioned by Baldwin was based on perceptions that the signing of the 1921 Treaty had created a contractual relationship between the United Kingdom and the Irish Free State that was unaffected by the enactment of the statute.[96] This argument was not tested in public in 1931. Instead, Stanley Baldwin was content to provide the blithe conclusion 'That Treaty will be just as binding, so I am advised after the passing of this Statute as before' and added 'this country has every security'.[97] Although Baldwin's assurances had a calming effect in 1931, they would later return to haunt him.

The Statute of Westminster was finally passed on 11 December 1931. The Cosgrave government had played a leading role in the creation of the statute and openly claimed credit for this achievement. A press statement issued by the Irish government boasted 'it must be said that while very valuable help was received from Canada and South Africa the brunt of the task was admittedly borne by our government'.[98] More importantly, the Irish government had ensured that the final form of the statute applied without restriction or qualification to the Irish Free State. The Cosgrave administration trumpeted the final enactmentment as representing 'the end of an epoch' and as marking a 'mile-stone on the onward march of this nation'.[99]

In fact, the fears expressed by Churchill, Gretton and Danesfort were not without foundation. The Cosgrave administration had already drafted its proposed legislation for abolishing the Irish appeal to the Privy Council.[100] As seen earlier,

94 TNA, CAB 23/69/1, meeting of 29 Oct. 1931. See also remarks of Thomas Inskip, solicitor general. Hansard records Inskip referring to 'Article 50 of the Treaty'. However, it is clear from the context that he intended to refer to Article 50 of the Irish Constitution. *Hansard*, House of Commons, vol. 260, col. 328, 24 Nov. 1931.

95 *Hansard*, House of Commons, vol. 260, col. 344, 24 Nov. 1931.

96 This contractual argument had been raised at the Imperial conference of 1930. See TNA, CAB 32/79 PM(30)5.

97 *Hansard*, House of Commons, vol. 260, col. 345, 24 Nov. 1931.

98 NAI, dept. of foreign affairs, 5/3, press statement by Patrick McGilligan on the Statute of Westminster, 11 Dec. 1931.

99 *Dáil Debates*, vol. 39, col. 2290, 16 July 1931 and *Seanad Debates*, vol. 14, col. 1620, 23 July 1931.

100 NAI, dept. of the Taoiseach, S6164, Arthur V. Matheson to Michael McDunphy with drafts bills, 12 Nov. 1930.

the Irish government decided to postpone the publication of this draft legislation in the period preceding the parliamentary debates on the statute. Yet the delay proved disastrous for the Cosgrave administration, which lost power in a general election that occurred within weeks of the enactment of the Statute of Westminster. This ensured that the new Fianna Fáil administration led by Eamon de Valera would be the main beneficiary of the successful initiatives of its predecessor.

CHAPTER EIGHT

De Valera and abolition of the appeal

THE OATH

THE FIANNA FÁIL GOVERNMENT led by Eamon de Valera came to power in early 1932 with different priorities to its predecessor. De Valera was not content with abolition of the Privy Council appeal and aimed to remove all features of the settlement imposed by the 1921 Treaty. Over the next five years he succeeded in dismantling it piece by piece. The Privy Council appeal was not even his first target in this wider programme of constitutional reform. This dubious honour was reserved for the controversial parliamentary oath contained in the Treaty and in the 1922 Constitution. All members of the government and the Oireachtas were required to take the following oath as a condition of taking office:

> I .... do solemnly swear true faith and allegiance to the Constitution of the Irish Free State as by law established, and that I will be faithful to H.M. King George V, his heirs and successors by law in virtue of the common citizenship of Ireland with Great Britain and her adherence to and membership of the group of nations forming the British Commonwealth of Nations.[1]

For many opponents of the Treaty this symbolic gesture was the most objectionable feature of the entire settlement – far outweighing the Privy Council appeal in terms of attention and opprobrium. The symbolism of the oath proved so potent that it can be considered as one of the causes of the bitter Irish Civil War of 1922–3.

Why did a parliamentary oath gain such unfortunate prominence? The wording did refer to the King and certainly offended Irish republican sentiment. Yet, the King was also mentioned throughout the 1922 Constitution – for example, as a constituent part of the Oireachtas and as the source of executive power.[2] Part of the explanation for the disproportionate emphasis that was placed on the oath lies in the reality that other aspects of the settlement put in place by the 1921 Treaty required some knowledge of constitutional law and governance. No such knowledge was required with respect to the oath, which offended deep nationalist sentiment and was seen as symbolic of a monarchical connection associated with

1 Article 4 of the Articles of Agreement for a Treaty between Great Britain and Ireland, 6 December 1921 and Articles 17 and 55 of the Constitution of the Irish Free State, 1922.

2 Articles 12 and 51, Constitution of the Irish Free State, 1922.

centuries of external rule. The religious connotations of taking an oath and a long history in Ireland of using oaths as a means of discrimination against Catholics and Dissenters were also contributory factors. Although known to opponents of the Treaty as the 'oath of allegiance' this term is often disputed on the basis that the wording of the oath indicated allegiance to the Irish Constitution and only fidelity to King George V as head of the Commonwealth.[3]

W.T. Cosgrave's Cumann na nGaedheal government, in power between 1922 and 1932, also had private misgivings on the subject of the oath. Yet, the presence of the oath in the text of the Treaty made it difficult to deny that it was anything other than an integral part of the 1921 settlement. By contrast, the Cosgrave administration disputed the status of the Privy Council appeal as a Treaty requirement in the mid-1920s on the basis that it was not mentioned in the text. In practical terms though, the Privy Council, as the arbiter and guardian of the Treaty, constituted a far greater threat to Irish autonomy than the provisions of the oath. Although this reality rarely entered the consciousness of the wider public, the Cosgrave administration prioritized the issue of removing the Privy Council appeal. Nevertheless, the Cosgrave administration also made efforts to remove the oath by agreement. Seán Murphy, a high-ranking civil servant in the department of external affairs, was sent to London in 1931 to persuade the British government that an agreed removal of the oath would lessen the possibility of de Valera coming to power at the next election.[4] These efforts proved unsuccessful and the oath became an election issue when the Dáil dissolved in 1932.

The abolition of the oath had been included in Fianna Fáil's 1932 election manifesto.[5] The required legislation was drafted and presented to the Oireachtas soon after de Valera's election victory. Although de Valera had little love for the 1921 Treaty he was forced to argue that he was not actually breaking its terms in abolishing the oath.[6] While many Fianna Fáil voters would have welcomed an open declaration of breaching the hated Treaty, the leader of their party had to proceed with greater caution. De Valera had already brought the Irish Free State into a trade war with the United Kingdom over rival interpretations of the 1921 Treaty. The main issue of this trade war was whether the British or Irish governments were entitled to certain 'land annuities' derived from loans given to Irish tenant farmers to purchase land. This led to a dispute popularly known as the 'economic war' that lasted from 1932 to 1938. There was little incentive in providing the British government with additional ammunition in this dispute by declaring an open breach of the Treaty.

De Valera also faced legal constraints in openly declaring that he was breaking the Treaty. The Treaty had been given priority over all Irish law under the

3 For example, see Tom Garvin, *1922: The Birth of Irish Democracy* (Dublin, Gill and Macmillan, 1996), p. 17. See 'note on terminology', below.

4 D.W. Harkness, *The Restless Dominion* (New York, New York University Press, 1969), pp 239–40.

5 *Irish Press*, 12 Feb. 1932.

6 *Irish Independent*, 11 Feb. 1932.

'repugnancy clause'. This provision appeared in Section 2 of the Constitution of the Irish Free State (Saorstát Éireann) Act 1922 and ensured that all Irish law including the Constitution and all constitutional amendments had to be consistent with the Treaty or be rendered null and void.[7] Since the direct road to abolition of the oath was blocked by the repugnancy clause, a more ambiguous route was required. De Valera justified abolition on the grounds of the advances made in the constitutional status of the Irish Free State within the Empire/Commonwealth. By the mid-1920s the Dominions had been recognized as enjoying equal status with the United Kingdom. If Australia, New Zealand and the United Kingdom itself had the right to alter their constitutional positions surely the Irish Free State enjoyed the same right. This was a vague argument because de Valera never specified what specific powers the Irish Free State had not enjoyed in 1922 that had now become available a decade later. De Valera did not attempt to legally justify the abolition of the oath on the basis of the reports of Imperial conferences or on the provisions of the Statute of Westminster; he merely pointed to these measures as examples of British recognition of the co-equal status of the Dominions and of the Irish Free State.[8]

The intended legislation was entitled the Constitution (Removal of Oath) Bill. The title of this measure was set apart from all other amendments of the 1922 Constitution, which were merely given numbers. The name was deceptive as well as exceptional. It disguised the reality that the bill did far more than merely abolish the oath but also quietly abolished the repugnancy clause. The loud political noise generated by the abolition of the oath was actually beneficial to de Valera. It allowed the destruction of the repugnancy clause, a far more significant provision from a legal perspective, to almost slip under the radar. In 1932 and 1933 most of the attention of the press, public and parliament was on the oath while the revolutionary change implicit in the removal of the repugnancy clause was completely overshadowed. Yet it was the removal of the repugnancy clause that was the preliminary to the unraveling of the entire Treaty settlement and, ultimately, for the enactment of the current 1937 Irish Constitution.

Although the issue of the oath dominated debate in the Oireachtas, some members of the opposition did ask why de Valera was so anxious to remove all legal force from the Treaty if the abolition of the oath was really compatible with the Treaty. Did de Valera really believe his own arguments? However, de Valera had some useful cards up his sleeve in combating his opponents. In particular, he now had access to the files of his predecessors in government. De Valera revealed that the possibility of removing the repugnancy clause had been submitted to the Cumann na nGaedheal government by their legal advisers.[9] One of the draft bills produced in 1931 aimed at abolishing the Privy Council appeal had included the

7 The 'repugnancy clause' also appeared in the Preamble of Westminster's Irish Free State Constitution Act 1922.

8 *Dáil Debates*, vol. 41, col. 570, 27 Apr. 1932.

9 *Dáil Debates*, vol. 41, col. 573–4, 27 Apr. 1932 and col. 1018, 29 Apr. 1932.

removal of the repugnancy clause as a preliminary to abolition. After some deliberation, the Cumann na nGaedheal government had finally rejected the need to remove the repugnancy clause. Nevertheless, the legal analyses that accompanied their draft legislation would guide the Fianna Fáil government in removing it.[10] The draft legislation concerning the Privy Council appeal created under the Cosgrave administration was also useful in deflecting opposition arguments that the Fianna Fáil government was breaking the Treaty in abolishing the oath. The Fianna Fáil government used this draft legislation to suggest that there was far more continuity than divergence in the policies of the two administrations. Conor Maguire, the new attorney general, argued that the British had regarded the abolition of the Privy Council appeal as being just as much a breach of the Treaty as the removal of the oath.[11]

Members of the former Cumann na nGaedheal government denied the comparison on repeated occasions by stressing that the Privy Council appeal had never been mentioned in the text of the Treaty whereas an entire article of that instrument was devoted to the oath.[12] They also emphasized that the proposed removal of the repugnancy clause had merely appeared in one of several draft measures and had been firmly rejected by the cabinet.[13] These arguments did not perturb de Valera who claimed that the Cumann na nGaedheal decision not to abolish the repugnancy clause had been based on matters of policy rather than on legal considerations.[14] He continued to vex his predecessors by insisting that the difference between the position of the Privy Council appeal and the position of the oath under the 1921 Treaty was the difference between 'tweedledum and tweedledee'.[15]

Although there were certain undeniable continuities between the Cumann na nGaedheal and the Fianna Fáil governments in their approach to constitutional reform there were also important differences. The proposals put forward in 1931 were limited to the removal of the Privy Council in its roles as arbiter and guardian of the Treaty. They were not intended as a prelude to the dismembering of the entire Treaty settlement. Second, there is a wide gulf between considering a course of action and actually putting it into practice. Patrick McGilligan claimed that the proposal to remove the repugnancy clause was nothing more than 'research work, done at my request, as to what might happen if certain steps were taken'.[16] Third, the Cumann na nGaedheal government as a whole rejected the proposed removal of the repugnancy clause considered by McGilligan. In 1933 McGilligan claimed

10 In 1931 John J. Hearne concluded 'the Oireachtas has the undoubted power to pass a law repugnant to the Treaty and that such a law is valid and unavoidable notwithstanding such repugnancy'. NAI, dept. of foreign affairs, 3/1, John J. Hearne to Seán Murphy, 27 May 1931.

11 *Dáil Debates*, vol. 43, col. 701, 12 July 1932

12 *Dáil Debates*, vol. 41, col. 604, 27 Apr. 1932; col. 998, 29 Apr. 1932; col. 1152, 3 May 1932; col. 2114, 19 May 1932 and vol. 43 col. 713, 12 July 1932.

13 *Dáil Debates*, vol. 41, col. 2055, 19 May 1932.

14 Ibid.

15 *Dáil Debates*, vol. 41, col. 1174–5, 3 May 1932.

16 Ibid. at vol. 43, col. 656–7, 12 July 1932.

that the previous government had rejected the removal of the repugnancy clause on the grounds that it was felt to constitute a breach of the Treaty.[17]

Some members of Fianna Fáil argued that the removal of the repugnancy clause was necessary to prevent members of the opposition from mounting a legal challenge to the abolition of the oath and even taking it to the Judicial Committee of the Privy Council.[18] This was a calculated insult given the long history of Cumann na nGaedheal opposition to this British Imperial court. However, there were also southern Protestants in the Oireachtas who were seen as possible litigants in a legal challenge that could be taken to the Privy Council.[19] This line of reasoning allowed the government to justify the removal of the repugnancy clause in the same statute as the provisions relating to the oath on the basis that it was a 'precautionary measure'.[20] The Fianna Fáil government firmly refused to submit the contents of the Constitution (Removal of Oath) Bill to any tribunal, foreign or domestic.

REMOVING THE IRISH APPEAL TO THE PRIVY COUNCIL

The removal of the repugnancy clause by the Constitution (Removal of Oath) Act 1933 unlocked the potential to unravel the remainder of the Treaty settlement. De Valera encountered little opposition when he stripped the office of Governor-General of its most significant powers.[21] The same could not be said when de Valera challenged the continuation of the Irish appeal to the Privy Council. Nevertheless, the introduction of the Constitution (Amendment No. 22) Bill 1933 was a matter of particular satisfaction for Fianna Fáil. The abolition of the Privy Council appeal was a commitment that had been promised for some years by their predecessors but never delivered. The new administration had an opportunity to show how they could succeed where their predecessors had failed.

The Constitution (Amendment No. 22) Act 1933 removed the reference to the Privy Council appeal in Article 66 of the Constitution:

> Provided that nothing in this Constitution shall impair the right of any person to petition His Majesty for special leave to appeal from the Supreme Court to His Majesty in Council or the right of His Majesty to grant such leave.

The Fianna Fáil government did not enact any equivalent to the previous government's proposed Supreme Court (Confirmation of Judgment) Bill 1931 that

17 Ibid., at col. 655–6 and 707.
18 Ibid., at vol. 41, col. 1203, 3 May 1932. See also de Valera's remarks at Dáil Debates, vol. 41, col. 2024, 19 May 1932.
19 *Dáil Debates*, vol. 41, col. 1203, 3 May 1932.
20 Ibid., at col. 2032 and 2137, 19 May 1932.
21 The Constitution (Amendment No. 20) Act 1933 and Constitution (Amendment No. 21) Act 1933.

had provided special means to block appeals in case the British might not recognize the validity of the abolition of the Irish appeal.[22] The enactment of the Statute of Westminster had enhanced the confidence of the Irish Free State in its ability to abolish the Privy Council appeal.

The enactment of the Constitution (Amendment No. 22) Act 1933 was a bitter pill for the leadership of Cumann na nGaedheal, which had now been incorporated into the new Fine Gael party. The *Irish Press* was unable to resist the opportunity of taking a swipe at the previous government for its failure to abolish the appeal themselves, implying that Cosgrave had meekly bowed to British pressure over the issue.[23] The leadership of Fine Gael, which had stressed the importance of the Privy Council appeal for well over a decade, now dismissed the matter as 'trivial' and a matter that 'should not excite the smallest enthusiasm in anyone'.[24] The *Irish Independent*, which tended to favour Fine Gael in this period, dismissed de Valera's constitutional amendment as a matter of exaggerated importance since the appeal had, in any case, become 'virtually a dead letter under Mr Cosgrave's government'.[25] The *Irish Independent* added that the Cosgrave administration had been on the brink of achieving a bilateral agreement as to the abolition of the Privy Council appeal.[26] In fact, the Cosgrave administration never came close to achieving any such agreement.

THE ERNE FISHERY CASE

The final appeal to the Privy Council, *Moore v. Attorney General*, is often called the 'Erne Fishery Case'. On 3 June 1925 an excited crowd gathered along the tidal estuary of the River Erne's tidal estuary in Co. Donegal. They watched while six local men from the village of Kildoney rowed a tar and canvas fishing boat away from the shore. It soon became clear that their intention was to fish for salmon in waters in which the Erne Fishery Company operated a several fishery, a particular type of private fishery. The exclusive fishing rights owned by the Erne Fishery Company had been in existence since at least the time of the seventeenth-century Plantation of Ulster and were largely owned by Major Robert Lyon Moore, who lived not far from the place where this incident occurred, with smaller shares owned by other members of the Protestant community in the area. The extremely profitable fishing rights on the Erne were resented by many of the local people who, inevitably, had a long history of poaching salmon from those waters.

It soon became clear that the six fishermen who set out in June 1925 intended to be caught poaching on the several fishery. They were fishing in broad daylight

22 See ch. 7, above. 23 *Irish Press*, 10 Aug. 1933.
24 *Dáil Debates*, vol. 49, col. 2114, 4 Oct. 1933. 25 *Irish Independent*, 9 Aug. 1933.
26 *Irish Independent*, 9 Aug. 1933. The *Irish Independent* placed similar emphasis on the Cosgrave government's contribution to the abolition of the Privy Council appeal in the aftermath of the decision in *Moore v. Attorney General*. See *Irish Independent*, 7 June 1935.

with a large audience that included several members of the local Garda Síochána. Their boat was soon intercepted and rammed by a motorboat operated by the Erne Fishery Company. As the boat sank the six would-be poachers were hauled into the motorboat and dropped off on the shore to the applause of the crowd.[27]

The entire incident had been orchestrated in order to provoke the Erne Fishery Company into taking legal action that would provide an opportunity to challenge the title to its several fishery. Members of the local community had long been collecting money to pay the anticipated legal fees through public dances and other events.[28] The incident itself was organized by local solicitor Frank Gallagher who had been preparing a legal challenge to the company's title to the fishery for several years. Gallagher had amassed a formidable array of historical evidence in order to successfully challenge a fishery that was, at the very least, three centuries old. Yet it is unlikely that Gallagher, while making his preparations for his legal campaign, could have foreseen that the Erne Fishery Case would itself make history for a number of reasons. First, the case delved into the realms of Irish history to an almost unprecedented degree with many of the most eminent historians of the day giving evidence on both sides. Historical issues concerning the Plantation of Ulster, the Anglo-Norman conquest and the nature of pre-conquest Gaelic society were argued before the courts in this case. Issues of obsolete medieval Gaelic law, also known as 'Brehon law', proved to be important in determining the outcome of the case. These ancient laws came back to life as they were interpreted by twentieth-century judges.[29] Nevertheless, the historical debates before the courts could not be interminable and final decisions had to be made. The Erne Fishery Company successfully defended its exclusive fishing rights before the High Court but the Supreme Court reversed this decision.[30] Fishing rights that had existed for over three centuries were overturned.

'Victory' declared the *Donegal Democrat*, 'the Kildoney men jubilate'.[31] The celebrations for the victory over the owners of the Erne Fishery Company in the Irish Supreme Court began on the evening of 5 August 1933 at the Mall Quay, Ballyshannon. According to a local newspaper a large crowd of people from the surrounding district gathered 'jubilant over the victory'.[32] The excited crowd considered this victory as one of local and national significance. National symbols, including large tricolor flags, dominated the celebration. Loud applause was reserved for an exultant Frank Gallagher whose crusade against the Erne Fishery Company had first provoked the dispute with the owners of the fishery back in June 1925. He told his listening supporters that 'native fishermen' would no longer

27 *Donegal Democrat*, 5 June 1925, 2 Oct. 1925 and 5 Aug. 1933.
28 For example, see *Donegal Vindicator*, 15 Nov. 1924.
29 Thomas Mohr, 'Salmon of Knowledge: Brehon Law before Twentieth-Century Courts', *Peritia, Journal of the Medieval Academy of Ireland*, 16 (2002), 352.
30 *Moore v. Attorney General for the Irish Free State* [1929] IR 191 (High Court) and [1934] IR 44 (Supreme Court).
31 *Donegal Democrat*, 12 Aug. 1933. 32 Ibid.

have to trawl the open ocean for fish in canvas boats while 'all the river mouths around the coast were in the hands of foreigners with their spurious fishing rights to which they stuck with the tenacity of brallions to a rock'.[33] Yet many of the 'foreigners' Gallagher was referring to were residents of the very same town in which the celebrations were being held. More sober voices drew attention to the many fishery employees who had all lost their jobs as a result of the Supreme Court's decision.[34] Yet the dispute was seen as more than a fishing case but as a victory for Irish nationalism. The jubilant crowd sang the national anthem while tar barrels burned into the night.[35]

The celebrations proved to be premature. The Irish government had been warned since early 1931 of the possibility that the case might eventually be appealed to the Privy Council.[36] The defeat of the Erne Fishery Company before the Supreme Court ensured that this threat became a firm reality. De Valera was anxious to avoid giving an opportunity to the Judicial Committee of the Privy Council to hear this case. The appeal in the Erne Fishery Case offered the prospect of a court based in London examining the legality of his entire programme of constitutional reforms.

OPPOSITION TO THE FINAL ABOLITION OF THE APPEAL

De Valera considered making a direct challenge to the claim that the Privy Council appeal constituted a minority safeguard for the southern Protestant community when introducing his legislation aimed at abolition. In a draft speech he was to make the surprising claim that 'this country knows nothing about religious persecution and intolerance'.[37] The draft added the oft-repeated claim that no Irish appeal had ever been made to the Privy Council concerning a religious dispute. This made the obvious assumption that all complaints from the minority community could only concern matters of religion. The application for leave to appeal in the Erne Fishery Case concerned the property rights of southern Protestants. In fact, the same paragraph in de Valera's draft speech claiming that the appeal to the Privy Council was no safeguard for the minority community was to conclude with a warning intended for the owners of the Erne Fishery Company, themselves members of that community, stating that the Irish government was prepared to take any measures to nullify or render ineffective any further appeals.[38] In the end de Valera thought better of raising questions of minority safeguards in the final version of the speech introducing the legislation abolishing the appeal.

33 Ibid. According to Bernard Share, *Slanguage – A Dictionary of Slang and Colloquial English in Ireland* (Dublin, Gill and Macmillan, 1997), a brallion or breallan means 'a good-for-nothing oaf'. This is derived from the Irish word breallán, meaning a blunderer or fool.

34 *Donegal Democrat*, 12 Aug. 1933. 35 Ibid.

36 UCDA, McGilligan Papers, P35/166, memorandum by Senator Samuel L. Brown, undated, 1931.

37 NAI, dept. of foreign affairs, 3/1, draft speech. 38 Ibid.

Nonetheless, the warning intended for the owners of the Erne Fishery Company was still delivered.[39]

There were other southern Protestants who, unlike the owners of the Erne Fishery Company, did not have any financial interest in the survival of the appeal but were, nevertheless, dismayed at the prospect of the destruction of the Privy Council appeal as a minority safeguard. The archbishops of the Church of Ireland, John Gregg and Charles D'Arcy, had raised the issue of safeguarding the minority when defending the Irish appeal in 1930:

> We would remind you that memories in Ireland are long and that the removal from the Constitution of the safeguard referred to … while it may gratify the desire of Irishmen for independence, will inevitably weaken the security enjoyed by the members of a vulnerable minority, and as time passes lead most certainly to infringements of their liberty which they would be powerless to withstand.[40]

The stand taken by the archbishops in the 1930s was also reflected in the *Church of Ireland Gazette*, which also argued that southern Protestants might need the appeal at some point in the future. Although this periodical often praised the record of the Cosgrave administration on the subject of religious liberty it was clear that this government would not hold power forever. The *Gazette* proved hostile to the policies championed by Fianna Fáil before and after it gained power. In 1930 it warned its readers of the need to maintain the safeguard of the Privy Council appeal when faced with the prospect of an uncertain future. It reminded its readers 'in this country we know only too well how some unexpected happening – even some petty matter – may suddenly stir up an outbreak of confusion and excited feeling which might compel the King's loyal subjects to invoke the protection of his Majesty's highest Court of Appeal'.[41]

De Valera had hoped that the constitutional amendment aimed at abolishing the appeal to the Privy Council would attract unanimous support in 1933, at least in Dáil Éireann.[42] This hope was dashed when professor William Edward Thrift and John Good, both independent representatives of the minority community in the Dáil, registered a strong protest at the loss of the appeal to the Privy Council. Sir John Keane also made a protest in the Seanad over what he saw as a 'thoroughly sad and discreditable' affair that was 'on a par with the whole sad and unfortunate history connected with the question of Privy Council appeals'.[43] Thrift insisted that protests had been registered on every occasion on which the constitutional provision enshrining the Irish appeal had been attacked.[44] He also argued that the

39 *Dáil Debates*, vol. 49, col. 2383, 12 Oct. 1933.
40 *Times*, 7 Nov. 1930.
41 *Church of Ireland Gazette*, 14 Nov. 1930.
42 *Dáil Debates*, vol. 49, col. 2116, 4 Oct. 1933.
43 *Seanad Debates*, vol. 17, col. 1681, 31 Oct. 1933.
44 *Dáil Debates*, vol. 49, col. 2389, 12 Oct. 1933.

Privy Council appeal had been part of a bargain concluded between the majority and minority communities in the Irish Free State and that this bargain had been one of a number of vital concessions that had won the acquiescence of the minority to the 1921 Treaty. Thrift noted that no Treaty could have emerged in 1921 without such understandings. He stressed that the minority community had honourably maintained its side of the bargain and concluded:

> When concessions are made in a bond it is not an honest way of dealing with that bond immediately to set yourself out to remove from the bargain, because you have the power, anything that you do not like in that bargain. That is not the way I understand such a bargain at any rate … Whittle away this concession and every other concession until you get the Treaty to the form in which you want it and what chance have you of making any bargain in the future with those who disagree with you.[45]

These sentiments won little sympathy from de Valera who, in the absence of concrete proof for the existence of such a bargain, flatly denied its very existence. De Valera concluded, when Thrift objected with some force to this denial of the existence of a bargain, with the words 'If there are any bargains standing in the way of the sovereignty of our people they have got to go. That is our attitude at any rate, and that is the spirit in which I move that the Bill do now pass.'[46]

The British government could not afford to dismiss protests from southern Protestants with such ease. The abolition of the Irish appeal to the Privy Council set the stage for one of the last political interventions made by Irish unionist leader Lord Edward Carson. Carson had never ceased to see the 1921 Treaty as a betrayal of Irish unionists. Nevertheless, he noted that the betrayal had been made 'under the pretext that certain safeguards were provided'.[47] Now he felt that he had lived to see every one of these safeguards 'absolutely set at naught and made useless'.[48] Carson concluded his swan song with characteristic bitterness:

> All I can say … is that every single promise we have made to the loyalists of Ireland has been broken, that every pledge of law and order has been destroyed, that everything that makes life and property safe has gone and now the last remnant is to be taken away.[49]

Abolition of the Privy Council appeal was not to prove as smooth as de Valera might have hoped. On the 10 November the owners of the Erne Fishery Company were granted special leave to appeal their case to the Privy Council. Although de Valera had indirectly warned the company that any measures necessary would be used to block the progress of their appeal, he had neglected to make the bill

45 Ibid., at 2389–90.
46 *Dáil Debates*, vol. 49, col. 2392, 12 Oct. 1933.
47 *Hansard*, House of Lords, vol. 90, col. 332, 6 Dec. 1933.
48 Ibid.
49 Ibid., at col. 335.

abolishing the Privy Council appeal retrospective in effect. Even those who supported abolition of the Privy Council appeal recognized that using retrospective legislation in order to block the progress of an individual case was 'a bad Parliamentary principle'.[50] Yet, this device had proved highly successful in blocking appeals under the Cosgrave administration. Eventually, the Fianna Fáil government heeded the warning signs and gave retrospective effect to the legislation abolishing the appeal.[51] The owners of the Erne Fishery Company were undeterred and continued to pursue leave to appeal to London.

Efforts to prevent the Privy Council from hearing the Erne Fishery Case soon attracted attention at Westminster. Edward Carson argued that this was a case that the Free State government seemed afraid of having heard. He admitted that it would be wrong for him, as a judge entitled to sit on Privy Council appeals, to comment on the facts of the case but added 'if ever there was a case that wanted investigation not merely by a judicial tribunal but by some great impartial tribunal this is one'.[52] Carson seems to have had little respect for the courts of the Irish Free State. He noted that while the case was progressing through the Free State courts five judges had found in favour of the appellants while just two judges had held against them.[53] It should be remembered that the background of the Erne Fishery Case, the removal of property rights belonging to southern Protestants that had existed since the Plantation of Ulster, was itself an emotive issue for Carson and other unionists. The use of medieval Brehon law by the Irish Supreme Court in removing valuable property rights must have seemed scarcely credible to Carson. It is hardly surprising that he went on to suggest the possibility of executive tampering with the case. He concluded that 'every possible thing that is revolting to a man who has been brought up in the administration of justice in the Courts in this country has been done'.[54]

THE POSSIBILITY OF MILITARY INTERVENTION

On 14 November 1933, the Dominions secretary, J.H. Thomas, told the House of Commons that the constitutional amendment abolishing the Privy Council appeal was a clear breach of the 1921 Treaty.[55] De Valera responded by writing a letter to Thomas in which he argued that lasting friendship was impossible under the

50 *Dáil Debates*, vol. 49, col. 2384, 12 Oct. 1933.
51 Section 2, Constitution (Amendment No. 22) Act 1933.
52 *Hansard*, House of Lords, vol. 90, col. 333, 6 Dec. 1933.
53 At the various stages of the Erne Fishery Case Johnston J, Sullivan P., Hanna and O'Byrne JJ, of the High Court, and FitzGibbon J, of the Supreme Court, had all found in favour of Moore and the other fishery owners while only Kennedy CJ and Murnaghan J, of the Supreme Court, found against them.
54 *Hansard*, House of Lords, vol. 90, col. 333, 6 Dec. 1933.
55 *Hansard*, House of Commons, vol. 281, col. 726–7, 14 Nov. 1933.
56 *Irish Times*, 6 Dec. 1933.

present relationship that bound their two countries.[56] The Irish leader raised the stakes when he told journalists that: 'The British Government has never ceased to threaten that if the Irish people exercised that fundamental right [to choose their own institutions of state] it would be regarded as a hostile act and made the excuse for aggressive action against us'.[57]

In the early 1920s senior members of the British government had been prepared to state that armed force was a real option in the event of an Irish breach of the 1921 Treaty.[58] Ernest Blythe, the Irish minister for finance, was fully convinced that an attempt at secession in the early 1920s would have resulted in military intervention.[59] Armed intervention was certainly considered in 1922 when the draft Constitution presented to the British raised serious doubts as to the commitment of the Irish government to the Treaty.[60] By the 1930s, military intervention to preserve the Treaty settlement was out of the question. It seems likely that de Valera raised the possibility of armed attack in an attempt to win domestic and international sympathy. J.H. Thomas proposed taking the wind out of de Valera's sails by making a statement that 'the question of armed intervention on our part has never been considered'.[61] Unfortunately, his colleagues in government would not agree. Lord Hailsham, secretary of state for war, agreed that the use of force was out of the question but felt that it was best to keep de Valera guessing with respect to British intentions. Hailsham's argument was supported by the attorney general, Thomas Inskip, who feared that the abolition of the Privy Council appeal was only part of an overall plan for secession that could have dangerous ramifications for the British Empire as a whole.[62] Thomas remained convinced that the absence of a clear renunciation of the use of force against the Irish Free State would hand de Valera a significant propaganda victory. When the British government's 'Irish Situation Committee' sided with Hailsham and Inskip the exasperated Dominions secretary took the matter all the way to the cabinet. Once again, Thomas found himself without significant support.[63]

The uncompromising stance of his colleagues ensured that Thomas never issued his declaration that the United Kingdom was not considering the use of armed force against the Irish Free State. It is difficult to see how the refusal to issue this statement was of any benefit to the British government. All sides were well aware that military action had long ceased to be a viable option. Lord Midleton, a leading southern unionist, recognized this reality in the House of Lords 'We all know that we are not going by force of arms to reaffirm the right of appeal to the Privy Council'.[64]

57 Ibid. 58 *Hansard*, House of Lords, vol. 52, col. 142–4, 30 Nov. 1922.

59 *Dáil Debates*, vol. 41, col. 568 and 757, 28 Apr. 1932

60 TNA, CAB 27/153 PGI 21st conclusions and Thomas Jones, *Whitehall Diary*, 3 vols (London, Oxford University Press, 1971), iii, pp 208–9.

61 Deirdre McMahon, *Republicans and Imperialists: Anglo-Irish Relations in the 1930s* (New Haven, Yale University Press, 1984), p. 132.

62 Ibid., at p. 132. 63 Ibid.

64 *Hansard*, House of Lords, vol. 83, col. 244, 1 Dec. 1931.

THE IRISH GOVERNMENT AND THE ERNE FISHERY CASE

It now seemed certain that the Erne Fishery Company would have their day in court before the Judicial Committee of the Privy Council in defiance of the Irish government. Although the Irish government had failed in its intention to block the progress of the case, it still had a number of cards to bring into play. The Irish Supreme Court refused to transmit its records of the Erne Fishery Case, as required by Privy Council procedure, and refused to release the formidable volume of evidence that had been submitted to it during the proceedings.[65] The company requested whether they could submit their own records of the Supreme Court proceedings instead. This request was granted along with the request that the Judicial Committee decide the preliminary issue concerning the legitimacy of the Irish abolition of the appeal before engaging with the complex and time-consuming issues surrounding the title to the Erne fishery.[66]

De Valera's legal advisers disagreed on what action the Irish government should take in response to this ruling. John J. Hearne, legal adviser to the department of external affairs, favoured a direct approach to the King to advise him that the Irish appeal had been validly abolished in 1933.[67] Irish attorney general Conor Maguire explored the possibility making a diplomatic protest.[68] De Valera chose neither of these options. The Irish Free State did not recognize the right of the Privy Council to act as arbiter or guardian of the Treaty. All proceedings would be officially ignored by Dublin. The Irish attorney general was instructed to boycott the proceedings and the Kildoney fishermen, who had started the entire controversy, were only too happy to follow suit. Nevertheless, the Irish government had to accept that the final decision of the Privy Council, whatever it might be, would have serious consequences for the Irish Free State.[69]

The decision that the Irish attorney general should boycott the Privy Council's proceedings in London ensured that the Irish government's position would not be represented in court. To make matters worse, the Erne Fishery Company had requested the assistance of the attorney general of England and Wales, Thomas Inskip, in the proceedings. When the Privy Council granted this request, in order that the Judicial Committee would not be entirely reliant on counsel for the Erne Fishery Company for legal advice, the odds seemed heavily stacked against the position championed by the Irish government.

65 NAI, dept. of foreign affairs, 3/1, attorney general to secretary, dept. of external affairs, 11 May 1934.
66 NAI, dept. of the Taoiseach, S6757, order in council of 25 July 1934.
67 Ibid., memorandum by John J. Hearne, 25 Sept. 1934.
68 Ibid., Conor Maguire to de Valera, 19 Sept. 1934. The Irish Free State had won the important concession of direct access to the King under the Cosgrave administration. Harkness, *Restless Dominion*, pp 229–39.
69 NAI, dept. of the Taoiseach, S6757, Conor Maguire to de Valera, 19 Sept. 1934.

THE ERNE FISHERY CASE BEFORE THE PRIVY COUNCIL

Although the application of military force was out of the question in the 1930s, the British believed that there were other, less extreme, means of challenging the abolition of the Irish appeal to the Privy Council. The attorney general, Sir Thomas Inskip, insisted that there were special legal considerations relating to the Irish Free State, notwithstanding the enactment of the Statute of Westminster, that could be used to challenge de Valera's constitutional reforms. He had the opportunity to present this argument when the Erne Fishery Case came before the Judicial Committee of the Privy Council in April 1935.

Inskip's legal argument maintained that the 1921 Anglo-Irish Treaty had created a contractual relationship between the United Kingdom and the Irish Free State. He added that this contractual agreement had not been affected in any way by the enactment of the Statute of Westminster. One of the contractual obligations that remained binding on the Irish Free State was the retention of the appeal to the Judicial Committee of the Privy Council. Consequently, any attempt to unilaterally abolish the Irish appeal would be an illegal act.[70]

Inskip was not the author of this argument that the 1921 Treaty had created a contractual relationship between the United Kingdom and the Irish Free State. The British government had used the same line of reasoning at the Imperial conference of 1930.[71] Nevertheless, the Erne Fishery Case provided the first occasion for this theory to be argued in public. Eamon de Valera had actually anticipated the same line of argument over a decade earlier. On the eve of the Civil War he rejected Michael Collins' argument that the Treaty represented a stepping stone along the path to complete independence in a newspaper interview in which he claimed:

> [I]t is not a stepping stone, but a barrier in the way of complete independence. If this Treaty be completed and the Irish Act resulting from it is accepted by Ireland, it certainly will be maintained that a solemn, binding contract has been entered into voluntarily by the Irish people and Britain will seek to hold us to that contract. It would be cited against the claims to independence by every future Irish leader.[72]

The Erne Fishery Company challenged the abolition of the Irish appeal to the Privy Council on different grounds. It based its argument on a 1934 decision of the Irish Supreme Court in a case called *State (Ryan) v. Lennon*.[73] This decision claimed an Irish origin for the Constitution of the Irish Free State but interpreted

70 [1935] AC 484 at 488–9.
71 See ch. 6, above.
72 *The World News* (Virginia), 16 Jan. 1922. See http://virginiachronicle.com/cgi-bin/virginia?a=d&d=TWN19220116.1.1# (accessed 1 Sept. 2015).
73 [1935] IR 170.

it in such a way as to limit the competence of the Oireachtas to dismantle the settlement reflected in the 1921 Treaty and 1922 Constitution.

In *State (Ryan) v. Lennon* the Irish Supreme Court decided that the Third Dáil Éireann elected in 1922 to sit as a special Constituent Assembly enjoyed a special status. The court concluded that the Constituent Assembly, whose sole task was to enact a Constitution, was a very different institution from subsequent Irish legislatures. Subsequent Irish legislatures, including the Oireachtas in the early 1930s, had no authority to amend provisions enacted by the Constituent Assembly. This meant that the 'repugnancy clause' enacted by the Constituent Assembly, that gave the 1921 Treaty primacy over all Irish law, could not have been removed by the Oireachtas in 1933. Consequently, all of de Valera's constitutional amendments that were incompatible with the terms of the 1921 Treaty were null and void under the terms of the repugnancy clause including the abolition of the appeal to the Privy Council. In fact, all three judges of the Irish Supreme Court hearing *State (Ryan) v. Lennon* in 1934 cited the repugnancy clause and treated it as if it still had legal effect.[74]

The Irish government was not represented in the pleadings before the Privy Council. This meant that the Judicial Committee never heard any defence of the Irish measures aimed at abolishing the appeal. Instead, it only heard two competing arguments as to why abolition should be deemed invalid. Yet, neither of these arguments proved acceptable to the Privy Council itself. The Privy Council could not accept the argument put forward by the representatives of the Erne Fishery Company. The judgment of the Irish Supreme Court in *State (Ryan) v. Lennon* was based on an Irish origin for the 1922 Constitution whereas the Privy Council was convinced that it had been created by the parliament at Westminster.[75] Inskip's argument concerning the contractual obligations created by the 1921 Treaty was vague and unclear and the Judicial Committee declined to express any opinion on it.[76]

The Judicial Committee of the Privy Council upheld the validity of de Valera's amendments of the Irish Constitution and so upheld the legality of its own abolition in relation to the Irish Free State. It held that the enactment of the Statute of Westminster had removed any fetters that might have been placed on the Irish Free State in amending its own law. The substance of the decision of the Privy Council could, in fact, be summarized in a single sentence delivered by the lord chancellor, Lord Sankey: 'The simplest way of stating the situation is to say

74 [1935] IR 170 at 205, 226 and 241. FitzGibbon J added that 'an amendment of Article 50 by the deletion of the words 'within the terms of the Scheduled Treaty' would be totally ineffective, as effect is given to those words by the Constituent Act itself, which the Oireachtas has no power to amend'. [1935] IR 170 at 227.

75 [1935] IR 472 at 485 and [1935] AC 484 at 497.

76 For an Irish perspective on the 1921 Treaty as a contract see Henry Harrison, *Ireland and the British Empire, 1937* (London, R. Hale, 1937), pp 196–201.

77 [1935] IR 472 at 486–7 and [1935] AC 484 at 499.

that the Statute of Westminster gave to the Irish Free State a power under which they could abrogate the Treaty, and that, as a matter of law, they have availed themselves of that power'.[77]

Scarcely a decade after the Irish delegates had signed the Treaty in London in 1921 the Irish Free State had been legally released from obeying its terms when the Statute of Westminster had been passed in 1931. In 1933 the Irish government began to dismantle the Treaty settlement and in 1935 the Privy Council itself confirmed that all this was perfectly legal.

REACTIONS TO THE ERNE FISHERY CASE

The decision of the Privy Council in the Erne Fishery Case was recognized as a victory for Irish sovereignty in 1935 but the reaction was one of vindication rather than jubilation. For example, the *Boston Herald* applauded the decision as 'a confirmation of the sovereign status of the Irish Free State'.[78] The headline in the *Irish Press'* read 'Power to Pass Act Admitted' while that in the *Irish Independent* was 'Saorstát's Policy Proved to be Right'.[79] The *Irish Independent* revealed its political orientation when it placed particular emphasis on the Cosgrave administration's contribution to the achievement of abolishing the appeal.[80]

The British press had no difficulty grasping the significance of the decision in the Erne Fishery Case. Although the Judicial Committee also upheld the validity of Canada's abolition of Privy Council appeals in criminal cases in a judgment released simultaneously to that of the Erne Fishery Case, the Irish decision received far more attention.[81] British MPs and peers who had been thwarted in their efforts to amend the 1931 Statute of Westminster in relation to the Irish Free State were particularly indignant. They focused their wrath on the attorney general, Sir Thomas Inskip. Inskip had been among those who had argued that the Irish Free State would not be released from its legal obligations under the 1921 Treaty after the enactment of the Statute of Westminster. The attorney general had had his chance to test this argument before the Privy Council and it had proved to be of little substance. Winston Churchill subjected Inskip to a deluge of criticism, blaming him, among others, for giving the government 'wrong advice both legal and political'.[82] Prime minister Stanley Baldwin, who had only taken office a month earlier, was not allowed to forget that in 1931 he had given the assurance that 'the Treaty will be just as binding, so I am advised, after the passing of this Statute [of Westminster] as before … this country has every security'.[83] Churchill condemned

78 *The Boston Herald*, 9 June 1935.
79 *Irish Press*, 7 June 1935 and *Irish Independent*, 7 June 1935.
80 *Irish Independent*, 9 Aug. 1933 and 7 June 1935.
81 *British Coal Corporation and Others v. The King*, [1935] IR 487.
82 *Hansard*, House of Commons, vol. 304, col. 441, 10 July 1935.
83 Ibid., at col. 443.

the incompetence displayed by the government and its legal advisers that had nullified his own efforts, along with those of his former colleagues, at the Treaty negotiations of 1921.[84]

The most powerful condemnation of the British government came from those who claimed to speak on behalf of the southern unionists who remained in the Irish Free State. Ulster unionist Ronald Ross was appalled at the prospect that loyalists in the Irish Free State were 'now at the mercy of the courts of that country without appeal'.[85] Colonel John Gretton demanded that the British government give some assurance to southern Protestants and guarantee their rights in the Irish Free State. Gretton was convinced that their position 'grows worse and worse under the present regime and the spirit which is being inculcated in Ireland'.[86] Unionists at Westminster were convinced that an important link between the United Kingdom and their brethren in the Irish Free State had been irrevocably severed.

CONSTITUTIONAL REFORMS 1935–7

The judgment of the Privy Council in the Erne Fishery Case resulted in the collapse of British legal arguments concerning the maintenance of the Treaty settlement. Although the British government continued to oppose de Valera's remaining constitutional reforms, it was never again in a position to seriously challenge the legality of these measures. Hardline unionists did propose that the Statute of Westminster be amended to take back some of the sovereign powers claimed by the Irish Free State but these suggestions were clearly divorced from reality.[87] In 1936 the Seanad, another purported safeguard for southern Protestants, paid the price for using its powers to delay de Valera's constitutional reforms when it too was abolished.[88] De Valera took the opportunity presented by the abdication of King Edward VIII in 1936 to pass legislation removing the King from the internal affairs of the Irish Free State.[89]

The failure of the British government to object to these unilateral amendments could be seen as representing a new spirit of pragmatism. Unlike the removal of the oath and the Privy Council appeal, there were no public declarations of a violation of the 1921 Treaty. Such objections would have lacked any legal basis in the aftermath of the decision in the Erne Fishery Case. Nevertheless, this apparent acquiescence was not without consequence as it caused the main Irish opposition

84 Ibid., at col. 439–47.
85 Ibid., at vol. 303, col. 639–40, 20 June 1935.
86 Ibid., at vol. 304, col. 408, 10 July 1935.
87 R.B. McDowell, *Crisis and Decline – The Fate of the Southern Unionists* (Dublin, Lilliput, 1997), pp 191–2.
88 Constitution (Amendment No. 24) Act 1936.
89 External Authority (External Relations) Act 1936 and Constitution (Amendment No. 27) Act 1936.

party, Fine Gael, to begin a process of withdrawal from its traditional position rooted in support for the 1921 Treaty. A Fine Gael internal memorandum concluded that if the British would not try to oppose de Valera's constitutional amendments, the opposition parties within the Irish Free State could hardly be expected to do so.[90] In 1937 de Valera introduced a new Constitution that replaced the settlement contained in the 1921 Treaty and 1922 Constitution. Fine Gael considered the failure of the British government to object to the replacement of the 1922 Constitution as releasing it from any obligation to raise opposition based on the integrity of the 1921 Treaty.[91] The final links were removed in 1949 when the remaining tenuous connections with the British monarchy were severed and a republic declared on the territory of the former Irish Free State.[92]

90 UCDA, McGilligan Papers, P35C/170, undated memorandum.
91 Ibid.
92 The Republic of Ireland Act 1948.

Conclusion

THE PRIVY COUNCIL APPEAL IN IRISH HISTORY

JUST HOW SIGNIFICANT was the Privy Council appeal in the history of the Irish Free State? The relative neglect of the appeal in historical works concerning the Irish Free State can be partly attributed to the brevity of its existence. There is also an understandable tendency to evaluate the importance of a court or tribunal in terms of the number of cases heard and it must be conceded that the number of Irish appeals was certainly low. Yet is equally important to recognize that these conclusions reflect the perspective of a twenty-first century observer and that those living in the early twentieth century saw things rather differently. Irish governments in the 1920s and 1930s had expected appeals to be extremely rare events and were deeply alarmed when the number of appeals and applications for leave to appeal was far higher than they had expected.[1] This raised serious concerns that the Judicial Committee of the Privy Council was widening the scope of the appeal in order that it might occupy the same position over the population of the Irish Free State as that enjoyed by the House of Lords before 1922.[2]

The history of the Irish appeal to the Privy Council was an integral part of the constitutional settlement begun by the 1921 Treaty and finally extinguished by the enactment of the 1937 Constitution. It was an institution imposed by stealth and, as the intended guardian of the Treaty settlement, was fundamentally based on British distrust of the infant Irish Free State. Its survival was destined to come under threat once the Irish Free State grew in maturity and confidence. A similar judgment could be passed on the Treaty settlement as a whole.

The Irish appeal to the Privy Council deserves attention because of its connection to a number of key events in the early history of the Irish state. The acceptance of the Privy Council appeal proved the most testing of all the disputes that arose during the negotiations on the draft Irish Constitution in 1922. A number of unfortunate decisions sparked some of the most acrimonious Anglo-

1 Examples include *Buggy v. Maher* [1926] IR 499; *FitzGerald v. The Commissioners of Inland Revenue* [1926] IR 585; *R. (Dillon) v. Minister for Local Government and Public Health* [1927] IR 492; *Leen v. The President of the Executive Council and Others* [1928] IR 594; *Delahunt v. Moody* [1929] IR 89; *Birmingham and Others v. Attorney General* [1932] IR 547 and *P.H. and the King (Mary Murphy) v. The Minister for Local Government and Public Health* Unreported, *Irish Independent*, 28 Oct. 1926. NAI, office of the attorney general, 243/25.

2 TNA, CAB 32/56 E(IR-26) 4th meeting, 2 Nov. 1926; *Dáil Debates*, vol. 14, col. 338, 3 Feb. 1926 and *Seanad Debates*, vol. 6, col. 409, 24 Feb. 1926.

Irish disputes of the 1920s. Attempts to abolish or at least to limit the appeal proved to be a recurrent theme at the Imperial conferences attended by the Irish Free State. The desire to secure abolition by agreement also underpinned an unsuccessful attempt to achieve a wider Anglo-Irish legal settlement in 1931. Concerns over the Irish appeal also proved to be a central theme in the parliamentary debates over the historic Statute of Westminster. British efforts to protect the appeal led them to resurrect a theory that the Irish Free State had been frozen to the constitutional position held by the other Dominions in 1921. This unfortunate legal argument brought the Cosgrave administration to the closest point it ever came to renouncing the settlement surrounding the 1921 Treaty.

The importance placed on resisting the Privy Council appeal led successive Irish governments and parliaments to take extraordinary action in the field of law. This included passing legislation with retrospective effect and refusing to enforce the decisions of the courts. The Oireachtas enacted legislation whose main purpose was to block the progress of pending litigation and defeat the object of a provision of the Irish Constitution. Although the proposed Supreme Court (Confirmation of Judgment) Bill 1931 was never enacted, the position whereby judgments of the Supreme Court could be given statutory effect must be considered one of the most extraordinary legal measures ever considered by any Irish government.

Yet, it is important not to fall into the trap of assuming that all aspects of the history of the Privy Council appeal were inevitable. Many features of the history of the appeal could not have been easily predicted in 1922. In particular, persons living in the early 1920s could not have predicted that the pace of evolution in Dominion autonomy would be so rapid as to undermine much of the Treaty settlement in less than a decade. The extent of change that occurred in such a short period of time amazed members of the Cosgrave administration and even some of its opponents. Desmond FitzGerald, minister for defence, wrote to his wife in 1930: 'Knowing the history of these last years as I do I am amazed at the way we have changed the situation'.[3] De Valera told the Seanad, soon after he came to power in 1932, 'Things were not quite the same in 1921 as they have been since the Imperial Conference of 1926'. He was willing to admit that 'There have been advances made that I did not believe possible at the time'.[4]

Another event that could not have been predicted in 1921 was the appointment of Lord Cave as lord chancellor for much of the 1920s. His personal sympathies and his term of office at this critical time ensured that the reputation of the Irish appeal sank to depths that were not foreseeable or inevitable.

For unionists in the Irish Free State, mostly found in the Protestant community, the appeal to a court in London represented a real link with a United Kingdom from which they were now excluded. Domestic resistance to the abolition of the Irish appeal reveals that many southern Protestants did feel uneasy and vulnerable in this new and untested entity. These considerations ensured that a substantial

3 UCDA, FitzGerald Papers, P80/1411, Desmond FitzGerald to Mabel FitzGerald, 21 Oct. 1930.
4 *Seanad Debates*, vol. 15, col. 938, 2 June 1932.

number, perhaps even a majority, of southern Protestants did value an appeal to an external tribunal in order to uphold their rights in the last resort. The protests that accompanied the removal of this appeal indicate that concerns over minority rights remained relevant more than a decade after the creation of the self-governing Irish state. Firmer foundations in cross-community relations were gradually established in the decades that followed. The history of the Irish appeal to the Privy Council confirms that this achievement should not be taken for granted or dismissed as being in some way inevitable.

Another important feature of the history of the Irish appeal is the revelation that the British government led by David Lloyd George intended the Judicial Committee of the Privy Council to act as arbiter and guardian of the settlement reflected in the provisions of the 1921 Treaty and later reflected in the 1922 Irish Constitution. Lloyd George and his colleagues were well aware of the argument championed by Michael Collins and others that the Treaty was a means to achieve greater autonomy that might, in time, lead to an Irish republic.[5] The British government was determined to limit these ambitions within acceptable bounds. This consideration, together with the issue of minority safeguards, underpinned efforts to prevent the Irish from restricting or abolishing the appeal in the 1920s and early 1930s. These efforts culminated at the 1930 Imperial conference when the British argued that the status of the Irish Free State was permanently frozen to the status held by the other Dominions in 1921.

No other part of the former British Empire met resistance on this level when it attempted to abolish its appeal to the Privy Council. In 1918 Lord Finlay, then lord chancellor, wrote that maintaining an Imperial appeal was a proper object of policy, but 'no attempt should be made to insist upon the maintenance of such a Court in the case of any self-governing Colony which prefers to dispense with it'.[6] It may be recalled that Lord Birkenhead told the 1926 Imperial conference that if Canada, Australia, New Zealand or South Africa wished to abolish the appeal the United Kingdom would, in the end, grant their request.[7] The Irish Free State was deliberately omitted from this list. Lord Cave spoke for many British statesmen when he said that the position of the Irish Free State was 'singular' among the self-governing Dominions.[8]

THE ABOLITION OF THE IRISH APPEAL IN IMPERIAL AND COMMONWEALTH HISTORY

The exceptional features of the Irish appeal to the Privy Council in the wider history of the British Empire are more difficult to assess. The Irish Free State was certainly the first Dominion to unilaterally abolish its appeal to the Judicial

5 Michael Collins, *The Path to Freedom* (Dublin, Mercier, 1968), p. 37.
6 TNA, LCO 2/3464, 'Privy Council appeals: memorandum by the Lord Chancellor', 1918.
7 TNA, CAB 32/56 E(IR-26) 4th meeting, 2 Nov. 1926. 8 Ibid.

Committee of the Privy Council. The abolition of criminal appeals from Canada was recognized in 1935, although this did nothing more than restore a position that the Canadians believed had existed before the fateful case of *Nadan v. The King*.[9] The complete abolition of appeals by the Irish Free State was raised during South African attempts to abolish their appeal before the outbreak of the Second World War. Opposition to the abolition of the appeal from English-speaking South Africans and fears that such abolition might impede prospects for the incorporation of Bechuanaland, Swaziland and Basutoland into the Union of South African delayed the final break here.[10] Apart from the Irish Free State, the decline in the jurisdiction of the Judicial Committee really began after the conclusion of the Second World War. The appeal survived in Canada until 1949, South Africa until 1950; India until 1950; Sri Lanka until 1971; Australia until 1986 and in New Zealand until 2003. Although the British government resisted the abolition of the Irish appeal, it quietly acquiesced to abolition elsewhere.

The unusual position of the Irish Free State as a former part of the United Kingdom created by the 1921 'Articles of Agreement for a Treaty' has often led to the marginalization of its contribution to the overall development of what would be termed the 'Commonwealth'. One history of the Privy Council appeal concludes that Canada had 'shown the way' when it finally abolished all appeals in 1949.[11] In truth, neither the Irish Free State nor Canada showed the way in abolishing the Privy Council appeal in strict legal terms. The decision of the Privy Council in the Erne Fishery Case clarified that there was no longer any impediment to the Irish Free State amending its Constitution in a manner inconsistent with the 1921 Treaty. This had little legal significance for the other Dominions who had their own internal constitutional considerations to consider. When the other Dominions decided to abolish the appeal they could not simply rely on the Irish precedent but were forced to undertake lengthy legal analyses as to how this might be achieved under their own constitutional systems.[12] The decision to abolish the appeal also raised different political considerations in every former Dominion or colony of the British Empire.

If the abolition of the Irish appeal had little impact on legal and political processes elsewhere, does the history of the Irish appeal have any real significance in the wider context of Imperial or Commonwealth history? The true value of the history of the Irish appeal is in shedding light on the primary reasons for the global decline of the Privy Council's jurisdiction. Since the late nineteenth century, many opponents of the appeal used arguments based on high costs and delay caused by vast geographic distances to justify the abolition of the appeal.[13] There are a

9 [1926] AC 482 and [1926] 2 DLR 177.

10 Bonny Ibhawoh, *Imperial Justice: Africans in Empire's Court* (Oxford, Oxford University Press, 2013), pp 25–6.

11 David Swinfen, *Imperial Appeal – The Debate on the Appeal to the Privy Council, 1833–1986* (Manchester, Manchester University Press, 1987), p. 156.

12 Ibid., at pp 156 and 164.

13 For example, NAI, dept. of foreign affairs, 3/1, draft speech on abolition of appeals to the Privy

number of observations that can be made about these arguments. First, it is worth noting that these accusations might just as easily be made about national appellate courts. Litigation has always been expensive and is seldom concluded as quickly as those involved might wish. It is worth noting that the Privy Council made determined efforts to reduce delays and costs that were not always matched by courts at national level.[14] The Judicial Committee was praised in the early twentieth century for expediency in hearing appeals.[15] On at least one occasion this feature actually worked to the disadvantage of this court. In 1927 the British government used the absence of a backlog of appeals to refuse requests for additional resources for the Judicial Committee.[16]

The Privy Council appeal was often attacked on the grounds that judges in London might not be familiar with the local conditions that existed in a particular self-governing Dominion or former colony and were therefore unsuited to serve on a court of final appeal.[17] Once again, identical arguments could be raised with respect to national appellate courts. A Canadian legal commentator noted in 1920 'Is a judge from British Columbia very much more familiar with the conditions of the Nova Scotia fishermen, or a judge from Alberta very intimate with the Civil Code of the Province of Quebec, the language of its people and its customs'?[18] An Australian commentator made a similar point in the 1920s when he asked: 'what local knowledge has the [Australian] High Court of the Northern Territory or other parts, near or remote, of this vast island continent?'[19]

Arguments in favour of abolishing the Privy Council appeal on the grounds of expense and delay that were raised throughout the Empire were repeated in the Irish Free State where the barriers of distance were far from formidable. These complaints persisted even though Irish appeals to the Privy Council never suffered unusually long delays.[20] The history the Irish appeal supports the wider argument

Council, undated 1933; TNA, LCO 2/3465, W.H. Clark, high commissioner to J.H. Thomas, 11 Mar. 1935 and Hector Hughes, *National Sovereignty and Judicial Autonomy in the British Commonwealth of Nations* (London, P.S. King, 1931), pp 92–3.

14 Howell claims that the High Court of Australia disposed of appeals more slowly and expensively in the past than the Judicial Committee of the Privy Council. Howell, *Judicial Committee*, p. 227. See also pp 209–10 and 218–19.

15 TNA, LCO 2/3464, 'Privy Council appeals: memorandum by the Lord Chancellor', 1918.

16 TNA, PC 8/1095, the supreme tribunals (additional judges) committee report, 12 May 1927. The committee did, however, approve a request for extra judicial resources for dealing with appeals on Indian law.

17 For example, see Oliver Jones, 'A Worthy Predecessor? The Privy Council on Appeal from Hong Kong, 1853–1997' in Simon M. Young and Yash Ghai (eds), *Hong Kong's Court of Final Appeal* (Cambridge, Cambridge University Press, 2013), p. 105.

18 Mr Gagnè KC, 'The Judicial Committee of the Privy Council', *Canada Law Journal*, 56:3 (1920), 89 at 94. See also Sir Charles Hibbert Tupper, 'Position of the Privy Council', *Journal of Comparative Legislation and International Law*, 3 (1921) 184 at 188–9.

19 Sir Josiah H. Symon, 'Australia and the Privy Council', *Journal of Comparative Legislation and International Law*, 4 (1922), 148.

20 For example, Hughes, *National Sovereignty*, pp 92–3.

that the global decline of the jurisdiction of the Privy Council appeal was based primarily on the growth of nationalism. Practical obstacles were, at best, secondary considerations and, at worst, nothing more than window dressing for political aims.

The history of the Irish appeal also sheds some light on the argument that the decline of the appeal to the Judicial Committee of the Privy Council was primarily caused by its failure to become a court that genuinely reflected the Empire/Commonwealth as a whole. Although judges from the colonies and Dominions did occasionally sit on appeals, the Judicial Committee has always been dominated by judges from the United Kingdom.[21] Could the decline of the appeal have been halted if greater efforts had been made to attract more judges from outside the United Kingdom to sit on the appeal?

The Irish Free State was unique among the Dominions in having a strong Irish presence on the Judicial Committee from the outset. Unfortunately, Lords Carson and Atkinson were staunch unionists and consequently the wrong sort of Irishmen as far as the Free State authorities were concerned.[22] Nevertheless, British officials made repeated efforts to encourage their Irish counterparts to send members of the new Free State judiciary to sit on the Judicial Committee but were always met with firm refusal. For example, in 1922 Winston Churchill offered a position whereby a Judicial Committee that included at least one Irish judge would hear every appeal from the Irish Free State.[23] This offer was declined. Lord Cave, despite his poor reputation in Ireland, was keen to include Irish judges on the Judicial Committee.[24] In 1927 a British offer to remove all remaining legal impediments that prevented Irish Free State judges from sitting on the Judicial Committee was declined by the Irish government.[25] In 1928, all limits on the numbers of Dominion and colonial judges that could sit on the Judicial Committee

21 Supporters and opponents of the appeal shared this impression. For the former perspective see TNA, CO 886/5B, meeting of 12 June 1911 and Robert Stokes, *New Imperial Ideas* (London, John Murray, 1930), p. 86. For the latter perspective see UCDA, McGilligan Papers, P35B/108, radio broadcast, 9 Nov. 1930; Hughes, *National Sovereignty*, pp 8 and 103–4 and Leo Kohn, *The Constitution of the Irish Free State* (Dublin, Allen and Unwin, 1932), p. 356.

22 See the fears expressed by Henry Harrison, a legal commentator and former MP, who warned the Irish government of the danger of a hypothetical 'Ulster Covenanting Judge' deciding the constitutionality of the actions of the Irish authorities. UCDA, Kennedy Papers, P4/340, memorandum by Henry Harrison on 'The Draft Constitution of the Irish Free State', 18 Sept. 1922.

23 TNA, CAB 43/1 SFB 33rd Appendix III and NAI, dept. of the Taoiseach, S4285A, Winston Churchill to W.T. Cosgrave, 11 Oct. 1922.

24 TNA, PC 8/1095, report of the supreme tribunals (additional judges) committee, 12 May 1927.

25 These legal impediments arose as a result of the position that the Irish Free State was not mentioned by name in the Judicial Committee Amendment Act 1895 or in the Appellate Jurisdiction Acts, 1908 and 1913. It was believed that no judge of the Irish Free State, even if otherwise qualified, could become a member of the Judicial Committee unless and until an Order in Council was made under Section 1(1) of the Judicial Committee Amendment Act 1895. NAI, dept. of the Taoiseach, S5090, L.S. Amery to W.T. Cosgrave, 26 May 1927.

were finally removed.[26] This reform made little or no impression in Dublin. In fact, offers to include Irish judges on the Judicial Committee often had the opposite effect intended by the British. For example, John J. Hearne noted that 'For my part, I have seen no proposal in regard to the reconstitution of the Judicial Committee that does not pave the way to Imperial Federation.'[27] The Irish government was also unimpressed when judges from outside the United Kingdom sat on Irish appeals. The Irish government was irritated at the delay in resolving the 1924 reference on the Boundary Commission that was exacerbated when the British insisted on bringing in judges from Australia and Canada to create a genuinely Imperial tribunal.[28]

The main difficulty encountered by the Judicial Committee of the Privy was not so much that it was dominated by British judges but that it was composed of foreign judges. It should be remembered that the Privy Council appeal is not analagous to the International Court of Justice, the European Court of Justice or the various international courts on human rights whose jurisdiction is limited to very specific areas of law, that is, public international law, the law of the European Union or the interpretation of human rights treaties. The Judicial Committee of the Privy Council had final jurisdiction on domestic disputes that demanded the interpretation of local law. Evidence of hostility to foreign judges fulfilling this sensitive role was certainly not limited to the Irish Free State in the early twentieth century. Canadian delegates who participated in discussions at the 1911 Imperial conference on creating a more representative Imperial court were prepared to admit in private that they did not want their cases heard by judges from the colonies or even from the other Dominions.[29] Irish governments were certainly convinced that the Privy Council appeal was 'a standing insult to the competence of their [own] judiciary'.[30] By the twentieth century, the prospect of seeing foreign judges hearing domestic disputes and interpreting domestic law became less and less acceptable to rising nationalist sentiment in all parts of the world. In 1965 the attorney general of Kenya, Charles Njonjo, acknowledged this reality when he stated 'Although the Judicial Committee of the Privy Council is a court of very high legal standing, it is not our court … it is my personal view that continuing appeals to the Judicial Committee of the Privy Council would not be in keeping with the dignity of our Republic'.[31] This rise in nationalist sentiment in all parts of

26 Section 13, Administration of Justice Act 1928.

27 NAI, dept. of the Taoiseach, S5340/2, memorandum on the abolition of the Privy Council appeal by John J. Hearne, undated.

28 Cmd. 2166, 'further correspondence relating to Article 12 of the Articles of Agreement for a Treaty', W.T Cosgrave to J. Ramsay MacDonald, 4 June 1924 and *Dáil Debates*, vol. 7, col. 2611, 18 June 1924.

29 TNA, CO 886/5B, meeting of 12 June 1911 and LCO 2/3464, memorandum by Claud Schuster, 10 July 1923.

30 A.B. Keith, *Responsible Government in the Dominions*, 2 vols (2nd ed. Oxford, Clarendon, 1928), ii, pp 1149–50.

31 Quoted in Jones, 'A Worthy Predecessor?', p. 102.

the world is the primary reason for the decline in the jurisdiction of the Judicial Committee of the Privy Council whose first manifestation was the abolition of the appeal by the Irish Free State in the 1930s.

WAS THE PRIVY COUNCIL APPEAL AN INSTRUMENT OF BRITISH GOVERNMENT POLICY?

One common feature throughout the former British Empire in hastening the decline of the jurisdiction of the Privy Council was the perception of the appeal as a 'badge of inferiority'.[32] Although this sentiment was certainly present in Irish political circles, what really set the Irish Free State apart from the other Dominions was the belief that the appeal was more than a mere symbol of colonial subservience but a very real obstacle to the further development of Irish autonomy. The Lloyd George government certainly hoped that the appeal would assist in ensuring that the Irish Free State kept to the terms of the 1921 Treaty. However, Irish observers in the 1920s and 1930s often went further and claimed that the intention behind the imposition of the appeal was to ensure that the British government would retain influence over Irish internal affairs. Patrick McGilligan, the Irish minister of external affairs, made a radio broadcast in 1930 that stressed 'Are not the British government and parliament still in a position to interfere in Irish affairs through this purely British Court, the majority of whose judges have most violently opposed the liberation of the Irish people'?[33] John A. Costello wrote, as attorney general of the Irish Free State, that the Judicial Committee had a 'political tinge'.[34]

Irish politicians and legal commentators frequently and quite openly accorded the Judicial Committee of the Privy Council the worst insult that can be given to any judicial tribunal; that of having a political agenda that overrode its duty to objectively interpret the law. The Judicial Committee was accused of acting from 'a semi-political standpoint' in the Oireachtas.[35] One commentator even went so far as to call the Judicial Committee of the Privy Council a 'pocket tribunal of the English political party in power'.[36] Darrell Figgis, one of the most prominent figures on the committee that drafted the first Irish Constitution, wrote that the expectation of impartiality from a tribunal with such political links was 'a fool's dream'.[37] These claims occasionally produced knee-jerk reactions from British

32 Swinfen, *Imperial Appeal*, p. 17.
33 UCDA, McGilligan Papers, P35/108, radio broadcast, 9 Nov. 1930.
34 UCDA, Costello Papers, P190/94, notes on the memorandum prepared for the Imperial conference of 1926 on appeals to the Privy Council, undated.
35 *Dáil Debates*, vol. 49, col. 2385, 12 Oct. 1933.
36 Donal McEgan, 'John Bull's Privy Council', *Catholic Bulletin*, 23:9 (1933), 736 at 739.
37 Darrell Figgis, *The Irish Constitution* (Dublin, Mellifont, 1922), p. 54. See also remarks of Professor Magennis at *Dáil Debates*, vol. 1, col. 1406, 10 Oct. 1922.

commentators who made similar accusations in relation to the Irish courts.[38] For the sake of balance, it is worth examining these accusations against the Irish courts before examining their equivalent with respect to the Privy Council.

The opinions of Sir Claud Schuster, who held the office of permanent secretary in the Lord Chancellor's Office for twenty-nine years and served ten successive lord chancellors, are of particular interest in examining British perceptions of the Irish courts. Schuster has been described as a Whitehall mandarin but was also a qualified barrister whose knowledge of the law, in addition to his experience and contacts, gave him unusual influence over policy decisions.[39] His biographer writes 'He was unshakeable in his friendship, but had many of the prejudices widespread among Englishmen of his class, and he often gave pungent expression to his aversions.'[40]

Schuster had a particularly low opinion of the government and institutions of the Irish Free State as a consequence of the controversies that resulted from the Privy Council appeal. He was convinced from conversations with Lord Birkenhead that the Irish had agreed to accept the appeal in the negotiations that led to the signing of the 1921 Treaty and later secured British agreement not to mention it in the text of that instrument in order to avoid domestic embarrassment.[41] This perspective reflected badly on the Irish government because it was seen as going back on its word when it attempted to resist the appeal on the grounds that it was not expressly mentioned in the text of the Treaty. Schuster accused the Irish government of lying and breaking their promises in several internal letters and memoranda concerning the Privy Council appeal.[42] He rejected any suggestion that the appeal had been placed in the Irish Constitution 'by reason of the distrust felt for the Irish people as an inferior race' and emphasized the importance of the appeal as a minority safeguard in ensuring that the creation of the Irish Free State achieved political acceptance at Westminster.[43] He was vigorous in rejecting accusations that Irish appeals to the Judicial Committee of the Privy Council could be influenced by the British government:

> To suggest that it was possible 'to square' such men as Lord Reading, Lord Phillimore, (who is dead), or Chief Justice Anglin of Canada, shows to what lengths men may be forced in controversy. I cannot imagine that anyone

38 For example, see A.B. Keith, *The Constitutional Law of the British Dominions* (London, Macmillan, 1933), pp 271–2.

39 (1869–1956) Jean Graham Hall and Douglas F. Martin, *Yes, Lord Chancellor: A Biography of Lord Schuster* (Chichester, Barry Rose, 2003).

40 Albert Napier, 'Schuster, Claud, Baron Schuster (1869–1956)', rev. Mark Pottle, *Oxford Dictionary of National Biography*, Oxford University Press, 2004. [http://www.oxforddnb.com/view/article/35976, accessed 4 Feb. 2015].

41 TNA, LCO 2/910, memorandum by Sir Claud Schuster, 6 Nov. 1930.

42 For example, TNA, LCO 2/1190, Claud Schuster to Edward Harding, 13 Nov. 1931.

43 These remarks were made in response to a suggestion by Desmond FitzGerald that the Privy Council appeal and other means of safeguarding the Treaty settlement were based on a sense of

> would be bold enough even to hint to any member of the Court what decision this (or any other) Government or person desired to obtain from them. I can well understand what would have been the fate of anyone who had undertaken such a task.[44]

Schuster's perceptions of the history of the Irish appeal combined with Irish accusations of bias resulted in his reflexively hostile view of the Irish courts:

> I have always supposed that the preservation of the right [to appeal to the Privy Council] was intended to safeguard not so much the Southern Unionists from oppression as the general body of law-abiding citizens from unjust decisions of the Irish Courts not necessarily resulting from political or religious prejudice. From what I have seen of the Irish Free State courts I should suppose that the judges are not competent and it is highly probable that they will in future become corrupt. But perhaps the proper answer to this is that the Southern Irishman has a natural liking for corruption and ought to be indulged in his tastes.[45]

Although Schuster's opinions carried influence they were not necessarily typical of British perceptions of the Irish courts. For example, a British memorandum written in 1926 acknowledged 'The new Judges appointed by the Free State Government appear to be capable men, and they have shown their entire freedom from any control by the Executive.'[46]

Irish nationalists had good cause to resent the imposition of a Privy Council appeal that they had never desired. Yet, the contention that decisions in appeals that directly or indirectly concerned the Irish Free State, in particular those associated with Lord Cave, reflected wider policy aims pursued by the British government are as difficult to sustain as Claud Schuster's equivalent claims concerning the Irish courts.[47] It has already been noted that Lord Cave saw the Irish appeal in very different terms to the Lloyd George government of the early 1920s, which had assumed that Irish appeals to the Privy Council would only be permitted in exceptional circumstances. It should also be remembered that Cave himself was a staunch defender of the autonomy of the Irish appeal to the Judicial

distrust of the Irish as a perceived inferior race. TNA, LCO 2/910, memorandum by Sir Claud Schuster, 6 Nov. 1930.

44 TNA, LCO 2/910, memorandum by Sir Claud Schuster, 6 Nov. 1930.

45 TNA, LCO 2/910, memorandum of 3 Mar. 1931 entitled 'note on Mr Walsh's conversation of 26 February'.

46 TNA, LCO 2/3465, Imperial conference 1926, Appeals to the King in Council, 1 Nov. 1926. Claud Schuster actually made a number of amendments to this memorandum but the praise levelled at the Irish courts remained largely intact. TNA, LCO 2/3465, undated draft attached to letter from C.T. Davis to Claud Schuster, 22 Oct. 1926.

47 Hector Hughes, who was unsympathetic to the institution of Privy Council appeals in the 1930s, did admit the independence of the Judicial Committee from the influence of the British government, Hughes, *National Sovereignty*, pp 42–5.

Committee of the Privy Council and firmly rejected interference in its operation by the British government. This is evident in his refusal to be bound by secret promises made by the Lloyd George government in 1922 with respect to the appeal from the Irish courts.[48] Similar considerations prompted him to veto proposals made at the Imperial conference of 1926 that the British government negotiate special limitations on the appeal that would only apply to the Irish Free State.[49]

The strongest evidence of the independence of the Judicial Committee was the frequency with which its decisions were actually in direct opposition to the interests and wishes of the British government. Many of the decisions in relation to the Irish Free State caused the British government considerable embarrassment and inconvenience. Even members of the Irish government had to admit that the decisions of the Privy Council and the policy interests of the British government did not always coincide.[50] This reality is also reflected in private comments made by officials and members of the British government in the aftermath of key decisions made by the Privy Council. Claud Schuster wrote that the cases on the transferred civil servants was 'a most unfortunate affair' and that it would have been in the interests of the British government if the decisions delivered by the Privy Council had been different.[51] L.S. Amery, secretary of state for the colonies and for Dominion affairs, wrote that the decision in *Wigg and Cochrane* was 'absurd' and was convinced that it highlighted the necessity for reform of the Judicial Committee in the very near future.[52] Amery also described the second decision on the transferred civil servants as 'alarming' and concluded that 'Only in connexion with Ireland could such a tangle ever have arisen'.[53]

Irish suspicions as to the integrity of the Judicial Committee continued right up to the decision in *Moore v. Attorney General*, or the 'Erne Fishery Case', in 1935. This can be seen in a letter from attorney general Conor Maguire to de Valera in which he expressed his suspicion that the Judicial Committee might only 'pretend to deal with the question as one of pure law'.[54] How valid were such concerns?

In fact, the Erne Fishery Case provides one of the best examples of the independence of the Judicial Committee of the Privy Council from the British government.[55] First, it is worth noting that the British cabinet declined to give the attorney general, Thomas Inskip, any instructions when he appeared before the

48 TNA, LCO 2/910, lord chancellor to Dominions secretary, 3 Feb. 1926.

49 TNA, LCO 2/3465, Imperial conference 1926, Appeals to the King in Council, 1 Nov. 1926.

50 Desmond FitzGerald, minister for external affairs, was convinced that the Privy Council had actually 'double-crossed' the British government in the case of *In re Compensation to Civil Servants under Article X of the Treaty* [1929] IR 44. UCDA, FitzGerald Papers, P80/1411, Desmond FitzGerald to Mabel FitzGerald, 6 Nov. 1930.

51 TNA, LCO 2/910, memorandum by Sir Claud Schuster, 6 Nov. 1930.

52 John Barnes and David Nicholson (eds), *The Leo Amery Diaries*, 2 vols (London, Hutchinson, 1980), i, p. 539.

53 Barnes and Nicholson (eds), *Leo Amery Diaries*, i, pp 570–1. *In re Compensation to Civil Servants under Article X of the Treaty* [1929] IR 44.

54 NAI, dept. of the Taoiseach, S6757.

55 [1935] IR 472 and [1935] AC 484.

Privy Council during the pleadings on this appeal. Inskip made it clear that his role as attorney general was to give advice on the legal issues raised by the case and not to put forward the views of the government.[56] In addition, the lord chancellor, Lord Sankey, made a point of leaving the room when the British cabinet discussed this case.[57] It is also worth noting that the final result of this case saw the Privy Council uphold its own abolition using a legal interpretation that accorded the Irish Free State a greater degree of sovereignty than many Irish legal experts were prepared to concede.[58] It was obvious that this decision went against the interests of the Judicial Committee of the Privy Council itself. It was also incompatible with the interests of the British government, which had publicly argued before the decision that the Irish attempt to unilaterally abolish the appeal was illegal.[59] The British government was forced to endure serious embarrassment and accusations of incompetence when the Privy Council went against expectations and finally upheld the legality of its own abolition with respect to the Irish Free State.[60]

THE PRIVY COUNCIL AS PROTECTOR OF MINORITY RIGHTS AND AS ARBITER AND GUARDIAN OF THE TREATY

Although the Judicial Committee of the Privy Council did maintain a position of judicial independence there can be little doubt as to the importance placed on the appeal by successive British governments. It should be recalled that the desire to establish a robust right of appeal to the Privy Council from the Irish courts was the real motivation behind establishing the constitutional link between the Irish Free State and Canada under the 1921 Anglo-Irish Treaty.[61] The determination of the British government to protect the appeal can be seen in the dogged resistance to Irish demands for abolition at successive Imperial conferences and in the extraordinary theory that Irish autonomy had been permanently frozen in 1921.[62] The importance that was attached to the Privy Council appeal was, to a great extent, based on the perception that it constituted a safeguard for the southern Protestant minority in the Irish Free State and also that it would serve as the arbiter and guardian of the entire Treaty settlement. Yet, as events transpired, these perceived safeguards were removed and the Privy Council was forced to acknowledge the legality of its own abolition in the Erne Fishery Case. Does this turn of events lead to the inevitable conclusion that the Judicial Committee of the Privy Council was a failure in these three roles as the protector of a minority community, as the arbiter of the terms of the 1921 Treaty and also as the guardian of the settlement imposed by the Treaty?

56 TNA, CAB 23/81/14, meeting of 13 Mar. 1935.
57 Ibid. 58 See *State (Ryan) v. Lennon* [1935] IR 170 as described in ch. 8.
59 *Hansard*, House of Commons, vol. 281, col. 726–7, 14 Nov. 1933.
60 For example, see *Hansard*, House of Commons, vol. 304, col. 441 and 443, 10 July 1935.
61 See ch. 2, below. 62 See ch. 6, below.

First, it is important to recognize that the Privy Council had also been intended to fulfil these three roles under successive proposals for Irish home rule. These aspects of the settlement imposed under the combined force of the 1921 Treaty and 1922 Constitution were not radical new departures. Second, there are good reasons for concluding that the Privy Council appeal did not fail in any of these three roles. Irish politicians and commentators often made use of the position that none of the cases that were appealed to the Privy Council concerned matters of religion.[63] Yet, as has already been noted, the challenges that were perceived to face southern Protestants were not confined to matters of religion; the Erne Fishery Case and the two decisions on the transferred civil servants were seen as being of particular interest to southern Protestants.[64]

It is important to stress that the Privy Council did act as the arbiter of the Treaty settlement on at least five occasions in little over a decade. It interpreted the terms of Article 12 of the Treaty in the special reference concerning the Boundary Commission,[65] it interpreted Article 10 in the two cases concerning transferred civil servants, it determined the impact of the Treaty on Imperial statutes in *Performing Right Society v. Bray Urban District Council*[66] and it decided the question as to whether certain Irish constitutional amendments could abrogate the Treaty in the Erne Fishery Case.

This leaves the question as to whether the Privy Council can be seen as a failure in its intended role as guardian of the Treaty. In fact, the Privy Council appeal worked exactly as had been intended by the British government that imposed it in 1922. When the Irish Free State passed legislation abolishing the appeal in 1933 a legal challenge that raised the issue of breaking the terms of the Treaty immediately appeared in the courts. This legal challenge was eventually placed before the Privy Council when it considered the appeal in the Erne Fishery Case. As events transpired, the guardian proved unable to protect the Treaty settlement in 1935. Yet, this failure cannot be attributed to any failing on the part of the Privy Council. Events had moved in a direction that had not been anticipated by the British government that had presided over the negotiations on the 1921 Treaty and the re-drafting of the Irish Constitution in 1922. The Empire, or Commonwealth as it was now increasingly called, had evolved at a pace that could not have been anticipated in the early 1920s. The Statute of Westminster is sometimes dismissed as doing little more than converting pre-existing practice into legislative form. Yet,

63 A petition for leave to appeal was, however, heard in a dispute concerning the construction of a specific aspect of the Canon Law of the Roman Catholic Church. This arose in the case of *Rev. James O'Callaghan v. The Right Rev. Charles O'Sullivan, Bishop of Kerry* [1926] IR 586. The Privy Council wisely refused to get mixed up in this controversy and leave to appeal was refused.

64 *Wigg and Cochrane v. The Attorney General of the Irish Free State* [1927] IR 285, 293; *In re Compensation to Civil Servants under Article X of the Treaty* [1929] IR 44 and *Moore v. Attorney General for the Irish Free State* [1935] IR 472 and [1935] AC 484.

65 *In the Matter of the Reference as to the Tribunal under Article 12 of the Schedule appended to the Irish Free State Agreement Act 1922*. Cmd. 2214.

66 [1930] IR 509.

the decision in the Erne Fishery Case illustrated the radical change that this historic legislation had made to the legal nature of the Commonwealth and also to the foundations of Anglo-Irish relations. The sentinel of the Treaty had stood to attention but found that it had been robbed of its sword. In these circumstances the Privy Council chose to take the honourable course, accept the new reality and bow out with what grace it could.

Epilogue

MEMORIES OF THE IRISH appeal to the Judicial Committee of the Privy Council were already fading when the Irish state declared itself a republic in 1949 and cut its final ties with the Commonwealth.[1] Elsewhere, the Privy Council appeal survived the move for colonial independence that rose to prominence after the conclusion of the Second World War. In the latter half of the twentieth century the Privy Council continued to hear appeals from many of the old Dominions and from the newly independent states of the British Commonwealth. Those who retained the appeal after the 1960s included Sri Lanka until 1971; Malaysia until 1985; Australia until 1986; Singapore until 1994; Gambia until 1998 and New Zealand until 2003. In June 2010 the Central American republic of Belize became the latest addition to the former parts of the British Empire to abolish the Privy Council appeal. At the time of writing Jamaica, Dominica and St Lucia appear ready to abolish the appeal. It is by no means clear that the many proposals for a new and reformed Commonwealth court would have halted this decline.[2]

Nationalistic fervour in one constituent part of the British Empire had a particularly negative impact on the position of the Judicial Committee of the Privy Council as a supranational court. One part of the British Empire proved to be exceptionally determined and successful in its refusal to submit to the jurisdiction of the Privy Council. This was not the Irish Free State or any other Dominion or colony – it was the United Kingdom, the 'mother country' of the Empire.

Appeals to the Privy Council from within the United Kingdom have long been limited to a few obscure and archaic areas of jurisdiction.[3] During the course of the twentieth century, the majority of British lawyers and statesmen remained steadfast in their opposition to accepting the Privy Council as the final court of appeal for their country.[4] The single judgment rule and the position that decisions of the Privy Council did not constitute binding precedent under British law were often used to justify this stance. Yet these drawbacks were capable of resolution if sufficient determination had existed. The real obstacle was that Dominion and colonial judges sat on the Privy Council in addition to British judges. British officials often questioned the quality of Dominion and colonial judges. For example, in 1930 a British inter-departmental committee charged with examining

1 The Republic of Ireland Act 1948.

2 For example, see David Swinfen, *Imperial Appeal – The Debate on the Appeal to the Privy Council 1833–1986* (Manchester, Manchester University Press, 1987), pp 178–220.

3 See ch. 1, above.

4 For example, see TNA, CO 886/5B, meeting of 12 June 1911.

the creation of a new Commonwealth tribunal concluded that 'though the Court might have at its disposal the best judges in the various Dominions, it is felt that they would hardly command the universal respect which is given to the highest standard of judicial talent in this country'.[5] These expressions of doubt as to the competence of colonial and Dominion judges could be seen as masking deep-seated fears and hostility to having British cases decided by foreign judges. Lord Loreburn, who served as lord chancellor between 1905 and 1912, told the Imperial conference of 1911 that the British public would perceive any proposal to amalgamate the Privy Council and the House of Lords as 'a foreign idea'.[6] British reluctance to see local cases decided by foreign judges represents the very same consideration that has spurred the decline elsewhere in the jurisdiction of the Privy Council throughout the course of the past century. There is no doubt that the reluctance of the United Kingdom, as the 'mother country' of the British Empire, to accept the jurisdiction of the Judicial Committee of the Privy Council undermined the position of that court elsewhere. This conclusion was given expression over a hundred years ago in the House of Commons by Richard B. Haldane, the future Lord Haldane, who would go on to become a judge of the Judicial Committee of the Privy Council. Haldane noted with regret that 'Though the Privy Council is considered good enough for the colonies, it is not allowed in Great Britain and Ireland to be good enough for us'.[7]

The Privy Council appeal now faces a serious threat based on considerations that could never have been predicted in the early twentieth century. A series of constitutional reforms have resulted in the creation of a new Supreme Court of the United Kingdom that began work on 1 October 2009. Members of this new court soon raised questions as to the desirability of maintaining the Judicial Committee of the Privy Council. Lord Phillips, the first president of the Supreme Court of the United Kingdom, noted 'in an ideal world' Commonwealth countries would set up their own final courts of appeal and stop using the Privy Council.[8]

It is now the turn of British lawyers to complain that the Privy Council is an anachronism that ties the court structure of their country to an uncomfortable Imperial past. Complaints of expense and delay have now re-emerged in a form that focuses on the burdens placed on the judiciary and treasury of the United Kingdom rather than on the burdens placed on litigants. It is argued that many former colonies have maintained the link with the Privy Council because it provides them with access to *pro bono* judicial expertise and saves them the expense of maintaining their own courts of final appeal.[9] Lord Phillips has complained that the Law Lords are spending a 'disproportionate' amount of time on cases coming from former colonies.[10] This could be seen as delaying the resolution of cases from the United Kingdom itself.

5 TNA, CAB 32/83 E(B)(30)2. 6 TNA, CO 886/5B, meeting of 12 June 1911.
7 *Hansard*, House of Commons, vol. 83, col. 101, 14 May 1900.
8 http://www.bbc.co.uk/caribbean/news/story/2009/09/090922_privyccjphillips.shtml (accessed 21 Oct. 2015). 9 Ibid. 10 Ibid.

The Privy Council remains the final court of appeal for the Channel Islands, the Isle of Man and the remaining overseas possessions administered by the United Kingdom such as Gibraltar, the Falkland Islands and Bermuda. It continues to hear appeals from a number of small sovereign states in the Caribbean and in the Pacific and Indian Oceans. These include, at the time of writing, the Bahamas, Grenada, Mauritius, Trinidad and Tobago, Kiribati and the Sultanate of Brunei. The Judicial Committee of the Privy Council remains in existence despite the serious reduction of its jurisdiction, beginning with the Irish Free State in the 1930s. It has survived many challenges from many different quarters over the past century. The one challenge the Judicial Committee of the Privy Council cannot survive is a determined campaign for its abolition within the United Kingdom itself. The greatest failure of the Judicial Committee over the past century concerns its inability to gain widespread attention and support within its country of origin. Unless this trend can be reversed, the future of the Judicial Committee of the Privy Council will always remain in doubt.

Yet, reports of the death of the Judicial Committee of the Privy Council remain greatly exaggerated. A unilateral severing of ties with the few former colonies that retain the appeal on the grounds of saving money would be perceived as a blow to the international prestige of the United Kingdom. It is also unlikely that all the territories that still send appeals to the Privy Council would tolerate a merger with the Supreme Court of the United Kingdom. Even the Channel Islands and Isle of Man might resist any reform that would bolster inaccurate popular perceptions that these islands are actually parts of the United Kingdom.

Lord Haldane painted a colourful picture of the litigants who might be seen entering the Privy Council chamber in the early twentieth century. He described entering the court chamber 'in company with white men, some of whom look as if they had come from the far West, and may be of American appearance; yellow men, some of whom come from Hong Kong; Burmese, who come from Burma; Hindus and Mohammedans from India; Dutch from South Africa; a mixed race from Ceylon – all sorts of people may be straying in there, and you will feel yourself in good Imperial company'.[11] Absent from this description of Imperial diversity are significant numbers of visitors from the United Kingdom itself. The barriers to actually visiting this court exacerbated the relative obscurity of the Judicial Committee of the Privy Council within the 'mother country'. The small entrance to the court on Downing Street was notoriously difficult to find.[12] In 1900 one MP gave a colourful description of his lengthy search to actually find the court

11 Lord Haldane, 'The Work for the Empire of the Judicial Committee of the Privy Council', *Cambridge Law Journal*, 1:2 (1922), 144.

12 TNA, LCO 2/3464, memorandum by Claud Schuster, 10 July 1923. Lord Haldane described the modest approach to the chamber through the back rooms of Downing Street which he saw as reflecting the belief of the Treasury that 'the more obscure a door [is] the better it will function in the Empire'. 'Work for the Empire', p. 143.

chamber, which he finally discovered by starting at the top of Parliament Street in London and knocking on every door as he worked his way down.[13]

The great increase in security in and around Downing Street in the late twentieth century almost completely isolated the court from the general public. Yet in 2009 the Judicial Committee of the Privy Council, along with the new Supreme Court of the United Kingdom, moved to the Middlesex Guildhall on Parliament Square. The Privy Council normally sits in Court No. 3, which is decorated with the flags of all the states and territories that retain the appeal.[14] The new courtroom is easy to access and is open to mass tourism on a level that far exceeds Lord Haldane's time.

Predictions of the demise of the Privy Council appeal have a long provenance. Even Arthur Berriedale Keith, one of the greatest authorities on the law of the British Empire, declared that the Privy Council appeal was 'in process of obsolescence' in 1921.[15] Lord Haldane made the most accurate prediction. He believed that the Privy Council was 'a disappearing body, but that it will be a long time before it will disappear altogether'.[16] His portrait continues to hang in the courtroom occupied by the Judicial Committee of the Privy Council almost a century after these words were uttered.

13 Swinfen, *Imperial Appeal*, p. 1.
14 http://www.jcpc.uk/about/judicial-committe.html (accessed 21 Oct. 2015).
15 A.B. Keith, *War Government in the British Dominions* (Oxford, Clarendon, 1921), pp 285–8.
16 Haldane, 'Work for the Empire', p. 154.

Bibliography

OFFICIAL PROCEEDINGS AND PUBLICATIONS

Dáil Éireann Debates
Seanad Éireann Debates
Hansard (United Kingdom)
Hansard (Canada)
Dictionary of Irish Biography, 9 vols (Cambridge, Cambridge University Press, 2009)
Oxford Dictionary of National Biography, 60 vols (Oxford, Oxford University Press, 2004)
Documents on Irish Foreign Policy, vol. I (Dublin, Royal Irish Academy, 1998)
Documents on Irish Foreign Policy, vol. II (Dublin, Royal Irish Academy, 2000)
Documents on Irish Foreign Policy, vol. III (Dublin, Royal Irish Academy, 2002)
Documents on Irish Foreign Policy, vol. IV (Dublin, Royal Irish Academy, 2004)
Saorstát Éireann Official Handbook (Dublin, Talbot, 1932)

GENERAL

Akenson, D.H. and Fallin, J.F., 'The Irish Civil War and the Drafting of the Free State Constitution', *Éire-Ireland*, 5:1 (1970), 10; 5:2 (1970), 42 and 5:4 (1970), 28

Amery, L.S., *My Political Life*, 3 vols (London, Hutchinson, 1953)

Anon., 'The Law and the Lawyers: Royal Prerogative and the Judicial Committee' *The Law Times*, 161 (1926), 183

Baker, P.J. Noel, *The Present Juridical Status of the British Dominions in International Law* (London, Longmans, Green, 1929)

Barnes, John and Nicholson, David (eds), *The Leo Amery Diaries*, 2 vols (London, Hutchinson, 1980)

Bartholomew, Paul C., *The Irish Judiciary* (Dublin, University of Notre Dame, 1971)

Bentwich, Norman, *The Practice of the Privy Council in Judicial Matters* (London, Sweet and Maxwell, 1937)

Beth, Loren P., 'The Judicial Committee of the Privy Council and the Development of Judicial Review', *American Journal of Comparative Law*, 24 (1976), 42

Biggs-Davison, John and Chowdharay-Best, George, *The Cross of Saint Patrick: The Catholic Unionist Tradition in Ireland* (Buckinghamshire, Kensal, 1984)

Bowen, Kurt, *Protestants in a Catholic State – Ireland's Privileged Minority* (Kingston and Montreal, McGill-Queen's University Press, 1983)

Cairns, Alan C., 'The Judicial Committee and its Critics' *Canadian Journal of Political Science*, 4:3 (1971), 301

Campbell, J.H., 'The Control of the Judiciary and Police' in S. Rosenbaum (ed.), *Against Home Rule* (1912), pp 153–61

Canning, Paul, *British Policy Towards Ireland, 1921–1941* (Oxford, Clarendon, 1985)

Cave, George, 'The Constitutional Question' in S. Rosenbaum (ed.), *Against Home Rule* (1912), pp 81–106

Childers, Erskine, *The Framework of Home Rule* (London, E. Arnold, 1911)

Coffey, Donal, 'British Commonwealth and Irish Responses to the Abdication of King Edward VIII', *Irish Jurist*, 44(1) (2009), 95

Collins, Michael, *The Path to Freedom* (Dublin, Talbot, 1968)

Colum, Padraic, *Arthur Griffith* (Dublin, Browne and Nolan, 1959)

Cook, Ramsay, 'A Canadian Account of the 1926 Imperial Conference', *Journal of Commonwealth Political Studies*, 3:1 (1965), 50

Cowen, Denis V., 'The Entrenched Sections of the South Africa Act', *South African Law Journal*, 70:3 (1953), 238

Crawford, Heather K., *Outside the Glow: Protestants and Irishness in Independent Ireland* (Dublin, UCD Press, 2010)

Crawford, Jon G., *A Star Chamber Court in Ireland* (Dublin, Four Courts Press, 2005)

Curran, Joseph M., *The Birth of the Irish Free State, 1921–1923* (Alabama, University of Alabama Press, 1980)

Curtis, Lionel, *The Problem of the Commonwealth* (London, Macmillan, 1915)

d'Alton, Ian, '"A Vestigial Population"? Perspectives on Southern Irish Protestants in the Twentieth Century', *Eire-Ireland*, 44:3&4 (2009), 9

Davison, J.F., 'The Irish Free State and Appeals to the Privy Council', *Canadian Bar Review*, 5 (1928), 367

Dicey, A.V., *The Privy Council*, (2nd ed. London, Macmillan, 1887)

Douglas, James G., *Memoirs of Senator James G. Douglas (1887–1954): Concerned Citizen*, ed. J. Anthony Gaughan, (Dublin, UCD Press, 1998)

Elliott, Marianne, *When God Took Sides: Religion and Identity in Ireland – Unfinished History* (Oxford, Oxford University Press, 2009)

Ewart, John S., 'Appeals to the Judicial Committee of the Privy Council – The Case for Discontinuing Appeals', *Queen's Quarterly*, 37 (1930), 456

Fanning, Tim, *The Fethard-on-Sea Boycott* (Cork, Collins Press, 2010)

Farrell, Brian, 'The Drafting of the Irish Free State Constitution: I, and II', *Irish Jurist*, 5 (1970), 115 and 343

—, 'The Drafting of the Irish Free State Constitution: III, and IV', *Irish Jurist*, 6 (1971), 111 and 345

Figgis, Darrell, *The Irish Constitution Explained* (Dublin, Mellifont, 1922)

FitzGerald, Garret, *Ireland in the World* (Dublin, Liberties Press, 2005)

Gagnè KC, Mr, 'The Judicial Committee of the Privy Council', *Canada Law Journal*, 56:3 (1920), 89

Garvin, Tom, *1922: The Birth of Irish Democracy* (Dublin, Gill and Macmillan, 1996)

Gaughan, J. Anthony, *Alfred O'Rahilly – II: Public Figure* (Dublin, Kingdom, 1989)

Griswold, Erwin N., 'The 'Coloured Vote Case' in South Africa', *Harvard Law Review*, 65:8 (1952), 1361

Gwynn, Denis, *The Irish Free State, 1922–1927* (London, Macmillan, 1928)

Haldane, Richard Burdon (Lord Haldane), 'The Work for the Empire of the Judicial Committee of the Privy Council', *Cambridge Law Journal*, 1:2 (1922), 153

—, 'The Judicial Committee of the Privy Council', *Empire Review* (1923), 716
—, *An Autobiography* (London, Hodder and Stoughton, 1929)
Hall, H. Duncan, *The British Commonwealth of Nations – A Study of its Past and Future Development* (London, Methuen, 1920)
—, *Commonwealth – A History of the British Commonwealth of Nations* (London, Van Nostrand Reinhold, 1971)
Hall, Jean Graham and Martin, Douglas F., *Yes, Lord Chancellor: A Biography of Lord Schuster* (Chichester, Barry Rose, 2003)
Hancock, W.K., *Survey of British Commonwealth Affairs*, 2 vols (Oxford, Oxford University Press, 1937–42)
Harkness, D.W., *The Restless Dominion* (New York, New York University Press, 1969)
—, 'Mr de Valera's Dominion: Irish Relations with Britain and the Commonwealth, 1932–1938', *Journal of Commonwealth Political Studies*, 8 (1970), 206
—, 'Patrick McGilligan: Man of Commonwealth', *Journal of Imperial and Commonwealth History*, 8 (1979), 117
Harrison, Henry, *Ireland and the British Empire, 1937* (London, R. Hale, 1937)
Hart, Peter, 'The Protestant Experience of Revolution in Southern Ireland' in Richard English and Graham Walker (eds), *Unionism in Modern Ireland: New Perspectives on Politics and Culture* (Basingstoke, Macmillan, 1996), pp 81–98.
Helfman, Tara, 'The Court of Vice Admiralty at Sierra Leone and the Abolition of the West African Slave Trade', *Yale Law Journal*, 115:5 (2006), 1122
Heuston, R.F.V., *Lives of the Lord Chancellors, 1885–1940* (Oxford, Clarendon, 1964)
Higgins, Pearce, *Hall's International Law* (Oxford, Clarendon, 1924)
Hogg, Peter W., 'Canada: From Privy Council to Supreme Court' in Jeffrey Goldsworthy (ed.), *Interpreting Constitutions: A Comparative Study* (Oxford, Oxford University Press, 2006), pp 55–105
Howell, P.A., *The Judicial Committee of the Privy Council, 1833–1876* (Cambridge, Cambridge University Press, 1979)
Hudson, Manley O., 'Notes on the Statute of Westminster, 1931' *Harvard Law Review*, 46:1 (1932), 261
Hughes, Hector, *National Sovereignty and Judicial Autonomy in the British Commonwealth of Nations* (London, P.S. King, 1931)
Ibhawoh, Bonny, *Imperial Justice: Africans in Empire's Court* (Oxford, Oxford University Press, 2013)
Jackson, Robert, *The Chief: The Biography of Gordon Hewart Lord Chief Justice of England 1922–40* (London, George G. Harrap, 1959)
Jones, Oliver, 'A Worthy Predecessor? The Privy Council on Appeal from Hong Kong, 1853–1997' in Simon M. Young and Yash Ghai (eds), *Hong Kong's Court of Final Appeal* (Cambridge, Cambridge University Press, 2013)
Jones, Thomas, *Whitehall Diary*, 3 vols (London, Oxford University Press, 1971)
Keith, Arthur Berriedale, *Responsible Government in the Dominions*, 3 vols (Oxford, Clarendon, 1912)
—, *Imperial Unity and the Dominions* (Oxford, Clarendon, 1916)
—, *War Government in the British Dominions* (Oxford, Clarendon, 1921)
—, 'Notes on Imperial Constitutional Law', *Journal of Comparative Legislation and International Law*, 4 (1922), 104

__, 'Notes on Imperial Constitutional Law', *Journal of Comparative Legislation and International Law*, 6 (1924), 193

__, *The Constitution, Administration and Laws of the Empire* (London, Collins, 1924)

__, *Responsible Government in the Dominions* 2 vols (2nd ed. Oxford, Clarendon, 1928)

__, *The Sovereignty of the British Dominions* (London, Macmillan, 1929)

__, *The Constitutional Law of the British Dominions* (London, Macmillan, 1933)

__, *Letters on Imperial Relations, Indian Reform, Constitutional and International Law, 1916–1935* (London, Oxford University Press, 1935)

__, *Speeches and Documents on the British Dominions, 1918–1931* (Oxford, Oxford University Press, 1961)

Keith, Kenneth, 'The Interplay with the Judicial Committee of the Privy Council' in Louis Blom-Cooper et al. (eds), *The Judicial House of Lords, 1876–2009* (Oxford, Oxford University Press, 2009), pp 315–38

Kelly, J.M., 'Hidden Treasure and the Constitution', *Dublin Univerisity Law Journal*, 10 (1988), 5

Kendle, John, *Ireland and the Federal Solution* (Kingston and Montreal, McGill-Queen's University Press, 1989)

Kennedy, Michael, *Ireland and the League of Nations, 1919–1946* (Dublin, Irish Academic Press, 1996)

Kennedy, Robert E., *The Irish: Emigration, Marriage and Fertility* (Berkeley, University of California Press, 1973)

Kennedy, W.P.M., *The Constitution of Canada* (London and Toronto, Oxford University Press, 1922)

__, 'The Imperial Conferences, 1926–1930', *Law Quarterly Review*, 48 (1932), 191

Kohn, Leo, *The Constitution of the Irish Free State* (Dublin, Allen and Unwin, 1932)

Krikorian, Jacqueline D., 'British Imperial Politics and Judicial Independence: The Judicial Committee's Decision in the Canadian Case *Nadan v. The King*', *Canadian Journal of Political Science*, 33:2 (2000), 291

Larkin, Felix M., '"A great daily organ": the *Freeman's Journal*, 1763–1924', *History Ireland*, 14:3 (May/June 2006), 44

Lauterpacht, H. (ed), *Oppenheim's International Law* (8th ed. London, Longmans, 1963)

Lavin, Deborah, *From Empire to International Commonwealth: A Biography of Lionel Curtis* (Oxford, Clarendon, 1995).

Lee, J.J., *Ireland, 1912–1985* (Cambridge, Cambridge University Press, 1989)

Lenihan, Niall, 'Royal Prerogatives and the Constitution', *Irish Jurist*, 24 (1989), 1

Lyall, Andrew, *The Irish House of Lords: A Court of Law in the Eighteenth Century* (Dublin, Clarus, 2013)

McColgan, John, 'Implementing the 1921 Treaty: Lionel Curtis and Constitutional Procedure', *Irish Historical Studies*, 20 (1977), 312

MacDonell, John, 'Constitutional Limitations upon the Powers of the Irish Legislature and the Protection of Minorities' in J.H. Morgan (ed.), *The New Irish Constitution* (1912), pp 90–111

McDowell, R.B., *Crisis and Decline – The Fate of the Southern Unionists* (Dublin, Lilliput, 1997)

McEgan, Donal, 'John Bull's Privy Council', *The Catholic Bulletin*, 23:9 (1933) 736

MacKay, Robert A., 'The Problem of a Commonwealth Tribunal', *Canadian Bar Review*, 10 (1932), 338

McMahon, Deirdre, *Republicans and Imperialists: Anglo-Irish Relations in the 1930s* (New Haven, Yale University Press, 1984)

MacNeill, J.G. Swift, 'Thoughts on the Constitution of the Irish Free State' *The Journal of Comparative Legislation and International Law*, 5 (1923), 52

—, *Studies on the Constitution of the Irish Free State* (Dublin, Talbot, 1925)

Maguire, Martin, *The Civil Service and the Revolution in Ireland, 1912–1938* (Manchester, Manchester University Press, 2008)

Mallet, Charles, *Lord Cave: A Memoir* (London, John Murray, 1931)

Mansergh, Nicholas, *The Irish Free State: Its Government and Politics* (London, Allen and Unwin, 1934)

—, *Survey of British Commonwealth Affairs: Problems of External Policy, 1931–1939* (London, Oxford University Press, 1952)

—, *The Unresolved Question: The Anglo-Irish Settlement and its Undoing, 1912–1972* (London, Yale University Press, 1991)

Marshall, H.H., 'The Binding Effect of Decisions of the Judicial Committee of the Privy Council', *International and Comparative Law Quarterly*, 17 (1968), 743

Martin, Ged, 'The Irish Free State and the Evolution of the Commonwealth, 1921–49' in Ronald Hyam and Ged Martin (eds), *Reappraisals in British Imperial History* (London, Macmillan, 1975), pp 201–25.

Mohr, Thomas, 'Law without Loyalty: The Abolition of the Irish Appeal to the Privy Council', *Irish Jurist*, 37 (2002), 187

—, 'Salmon of Knowledge: Brehon Law before Twentieth-Century Courts', *Peritia, Journal of the Medieval Academy of Ireland*, 16 (2002) 352

—, 'The Foundations of Irish Extra-Territorial Legislation', *Irish Jurist*, 40 (2005), 86

—, 'The Colonial Laws Validity Act and the Irish Free State', *Irish Jurist*, 43 (2009), 21

—, 'British Imperial Statutes and Irish Law: Statutes Passed Before the Creation of the Irish Free State', *Journal of Legal History*, 31:2 (2010), 299

—, 'A British Empire Court: An Appraisal of the History of the Judicial Committee of the Privy Council' in Anthony McElligott et al. (eds), *Power in History: Historical Studies XXVII* (Dublin, Irish Academic Press, 2011), pp 125–45

—, 'The Privy Council Appeal as a Minority Safeguard for the Protestant Community of the Irish Free State, 1922–1935', *Northern Ireland Legal Quarterly*, 63:3 (2012), 365

—, 'Lord Cave, the British Empire and Irish Independence', *Oxford University Commonwealth Law Journal*, 12:2 (2013), 229

—, 'The Statute of Westminster: An Irish Perspective', *Law and History Review*, 31:1 (2013), 749

Moore, W. Harrison, 'The Case of Pental Island', *Law Quarterly Review*, 20 (1904), 236

Morgan, J.H., 'Secession by Innuendo', *National Review* (1936), 313

— (ed.), *The New Irish Constitution* (London, Hodder and Stoughton, 1912)

Ó Briain, Barra, *The Irish Constitution* (Dublin, Talbot, 1929)

Ó Crudhlaoich, Diarmuid, *The Oath of Allegiance* (Dublin, Maunsell and Roberts, 1925)

O'Sullivan, Donal, *The Irish Free State and its Senate* (London, Faber and Faber, 1940)

Pakenham, Frank (Lord Longford), *Peace by Ordeal* (London, Sidgwick and Jackson, 1972)

Plunkett, Horace, *A Better Way: An Appeal to Ulster not to Desert Ireland* (Dublin, Hodges, Figgis, 1914)

Pollock, Frederick, 'The Judicial Committee and the Interpretation of the New Constitution' in J.H. Morgan (ed.), *The New Irish Constitution* (1912), pp 81–9

Richardson, Megan, 'The Privy Council and New Zealand', *International and Comparative Law Quarterly*, 46 (1997), 908

Roberts-Wray, Kenneth, *Commonwealth and Colonial Law* (London, Stevens, 1966)

Rosenbaum, S. (ed.), *Against Home Rule – The Case for the Union* (London, Frederick Warne, 1912)

Schneiderman, David, 'A.V. Dicey, Lord Watson, and the Law of the Canadian Constitution in the Late Nineteenth Century', *Law and History Review*, 16 (1998), 495

Sedgewick, George H., 'Appeals to the Judicial Committee of the Privy Council – The Case for Appeals', *Queen's Quarterly*, 37 (1930), 474

Share, Bernard, *Slanguage – A Dictionary of Slang and Colloquial English in Ireland* (Dublin, Gill and Macmillan, 1997)

Smith, Joseph Henry, *Appeals to the Privy Council from the American Plantations* (New York, Octagon, 1965)

Stewart, R.M., *Henry Brougham, 1778–1868: His Public Career* (London, Bodley Head, 1986)

Stokes, Robert, *New Imperial Ideas* (London, John Murray, 1930)

Swinfen, David, *Imperial Appeal: The Debate on the Appeal to the Privy Council, 1833–1986* (Manchester, Manchester University Press, 1987)

Symon, Josiah H., 'Australia and the Privy Council', *Journal of Comparative Legislation and International Law*, 4 (1922), 137

Tate, John William, 'Hohepa Wi Neera: Native Title and the Privy Council Challenge', *Victoria University of Wellington Law Review*, 35 (2004), 73

Todd, Alpheus, *Parliamentary Government in the British Colonies* (London, Longmans, Green, 1880)

Tupper, Charles Hibbert, 'Position of the Privy Council', *Journal of Comparative Legislation and International Law*, 3 (1921), 184

Ward, Paul, *Family Law in Ireland* (Leiden, Kluwer Law International, 2010)

Weeks, L., 'We Don't Like (to) Party – A Typology of Independents in Irish Political Life, 1922–2007', *Irish Political Studies* 24:1 (2009), 1

Wheare, K.C., *The Statute of Westminster and Dominion Status* (4th ed. Oxford, Oxford University, 1949)

—, *The Statute of Westminster and Dominion Status* (5th ed. Oxford, Oxford University Press, 1953)

Whyte, John Henry, *Church and State in Modern Ireland, 1923–1979* (Dublin, Gill and Macmillan, 1984)

UNPUBLISHED THESES

Mohr, Thomas, 'The Irish Free State and the Legal Implications of Dominion Status' (PhD, UCD, 2007)

NEWSPAPERS AND NEWS PERIODICALS

Boston Herald
Clare Champion
Church of Ireland Gazette
Daily Mail
Daily News
Donegal Democrat
Donegal Vindicator
The Free State
Freeman's Journal
Irish Independent
Irish Press
The Irish Statesman
Irish Times
The Law Journal: Irish Free State Section
Manitoba Free Press
Morning Post
Northern Whig
Pall Mall Gazette
Poblacht na hÉireann
Round Table
The Scotsman
The Star
Sunday Independent
Sunday Times
The Tablet
The Times (London)
United Irishman
The Watchword
The World News (Virginia)

Index to legislation

TABLE OF ARTICLES OF THE ANGLO-IRISH TREATY

TABLE OF ARTICLES OF THE CONSTITUTION

TABLE OF STATUTES

note: statutes are listed chronologically

ACTS OF THE OIREACHTAS OF THE IRISH FREE STATE (SAORSTÁT ÉIREANN) AND ACTS OF THE OIREACHTAS PASSED AFTER 1937

ACTS OF THE PARLIAMENT AT WESTMINSTER

STATUTORY INSTRUMENTS (UNITED KINGDOM)

ACTS OF THE PARLIAMENT OF CANADA

ACTS OF THE PARLIAMENT OF AUSTRALIA

ACTS OF THE PARLIAMENT OF NEW ZEALAND

Index to cases of law

SPECIAL REFERENCES TO THE JUDICIAL COMMITTEE OF THE PRIVY COUNCIL

General index

Compiled by Julitta Clancy
Note: references in *italics* denote illustration numbers

Irish Legal History Society

Established in 1988 to encourage the study and advance the knowledge of the history of Irish law, especially by the publication of original documents and of works relating to the history of Irish law, including its institutions, doctrines and personalities, and the reprinting or editing of works of sufficient rarity or importance.

www.ilhs.eu